Technical Writing for TCI

Wilson / Glazier / Smith-Worthington

Australia · Canada · Mexico · Singapore · Spain · United Kingdom · United States

Technical Writing for TCI

Wilson / Glazier / Smith-Worthington

Executive Editors:
Michele Baird, Maureen Staudt &
Michael Stranz

Project Development Manager:
Linda deStefano

Sr. Marketing Coordinators:
Lindsay Annett and Sara Mercurio

Production/Manufacturing Manager:
Donna M. Brown

Production Editorial Manager:
Dan Plofchan

Pre-Media Services Supervisor:
Becki Walker

Rights and Permissions Specialist:
Kalina Ingham Hintz

Cover Image
Getty Images*

Printed in the
United States of America
1 2 3 4 5 6 7 10 09 08 07

For more information, please contact Thomson Custom Solutions, 5191 Natorp Boulevard, Mason, OH 45040. Or you can visit our Internet site at http://www.thomsoncustom.com

The Adaptable Courseware Program consists of products and additions to existing Thomson products that are produced from camera-ready copy. Peer review, class testing, and accuracy are primarily the responsibility of the author(s).

ISBN: 978-0-324-55884-5
ISBN: 0-324-55884-8

International Divisions List

Asia (Including India):
Thomson Learning
(a division of Thomson Asia Pte Ltd)
5 Shenton Way #01-01
UIC Building
Singapore 068808
Tel: (65) 6410-1200
Fax: (65) 6410-1208

Australia/New Zealand:
Thomson Learning Australia
102 Dodds Street
Southbank, Victoria 3006
Australia

Latin America:
Thomson Learning
Seneca 53
Colonia Polano
11560 Mexico, D.F., Mexico
Tel (525) 281-2906
Fax (525) 281-2656

Canada:
Thomson Nelson
1120 Birchmount Road
Toronto, Ontario
Canada M1K 5G4
Tel (416) 752-9100
Fax (416) 752-8102

UK/Europe/Middle East/Africa:
Thomson Learning
High Holborn House
50-51 Bedford Row
London, WC1R 4LS
United Kingdom
Tel 44 (020) 7067-2500
Fax 44 (020) 7067-2600

Spain (Includes Portugal):
Thomson Paraninfo
Calle Magallanes 25
28015 Madrid
España
Tel 34 (0)91 446-3350
Fax 34 (0)91 445-6218

Contents

PROOFREADING EXERCISE

Find and correct the five fragments in the following paragraph.

Fred Astaire was one of the most popular dancers of all time. Dancing in over forty movies in his fifty-year career. Born in Omaha, Nebraska, with the real name of Frederick Austerlitz. Fred Astaire and his sister were stage stars when they were still children. Appearing as a miniature married couple dancing on top of a huge wedding cake and as a lobster and a glass of champagne. Astaire was eventually happily married to his first wife Phyllis for many years. Later in his life, Fred Astaire got married again. This time to Robyn Smith. A female jockey who was forty-five years younger than Astaire.

Source: Biography Magazine, October 2003

SENTENCE WRITING

Write ten fragments (like the ones in Exercise 5) and then revise them so that they are complete sentences. Or exchange papers with another student and turn your classmate's ten fragments into sentences. Use your own paper, and keep all of your sentence writing results in a folder.

Correcting Run-on Sentences

A word group with a subject and a verb is a clause. As we have seen, the clause may be independent (making a complete statement and able to stand alone as a sentence), or it may be dependent (beginning with a dependent word and unable to stand alone as a sentence). When two *independent* clauses are written together without proper punctuation between them, the result is called a *run-on sentence.* Here are some examples:

Classical music is soothing I listen to it in the evenings.

I love the sound of piano therefore, Chopin is one of my favorites.

Run-on sentences can be corrected in one of four ways:

1. Make the two independent clauses into two sentences.

Classical music is soothing. I listen to it in the evenings.

I love the sound of piano. Therefore, Chopin is one of my favorites.

2. Connect the two independent clauses with a semicolon.

Classical music is soothing; I listen to it in the evenings.

I love the sound of piano; therefore, Chopin is one of my favorites.

When a connecting word (transition) such as

also	however	otherwise
consequently	likewise	then
finally	moreover	therefore
furthermore	nevertheless	thus

is used to join two independent clauses, the semicolon comes before the connecting word, and a comma usually comes after it.

Earthquakes scare me; therefore, I don't live in Los Angeles.

Yasmin traveled to London; then she took the "Chunnel" to Paris.

The college recently built a large new library; thus we have more study areas.

REVIEW OF FRAGMENTS AND RUN-ON SENTENCES

If you remember that all clauses include a subject and a verb, but only independent clauses can be punctuated as sentences (since only they can stand alone), then you will avoid fragments in your writing. And if you memorize these six rules for the punctuation of clauses, you will be able to avoid most punctuation errors.

Punctuating Clauses	
I am a student. I am still learning.	(two sentences)
I am a student; I am still learning.	(two independent clauses)
I am a student; therefore, I am still learning.	(two independent clauses connected by a word such as *also, consequently, finally, furthermore, however, likewise, moreover, nevertheless, otherwise, then, therefore, thus*)
I am a student, so I am still learning.	(two independent clauses connected by *for, and, nor, but, or, yet, so*)
Because I am a student, I am still learning.	(dependent clause at beginning of sentence)
I am still learning because I am a student.	(dependent clause at end of sentence) Dependent words include *after, although, as, as if, because, before, even if, even though, ever since, how, if, since, so that, than, that, though, unless, until, what, whatever, when, whenever, where, whereas, wherever, whether, which, whichever, while, who, whom, whose,* and *why.*

It is essential that you learn the italicized words in the previous chart—which ones come between independent clauses and which ones introduce dependent clauses.

PROOFREADING EXERCISE

Rewrite the following paragraph, making the necessary changes so there will be no fragments or run-on sentences.

With all of the attention on cleanliness lately in advertising for soaps and household cleaning products. People are surprised to hear that we may be too clean for our own good. This phenomenon is called the "hygiene hypothesis" and recent studies support its validity. For instance, one study showing the benefits of living with two or more pets. Babies may grow up with healthier immune systems and be less allergic if they live with a dog and a cat or two dogs or two cats. The old thinking was that young children would become more allergic living with many pets but they don't. Somehow the exposure to pets and all their "dirty" habits gives youngsters much-needed defenses. Sometimes as much as a seventy-five percent lower allergy risk, according to this study.

Source: Los Angeles Times, September 2, 2002

SENTENCE WRITING

Write a sample sentence of your own to demonstrate each of the six ways to punctuate two clauses. You may model your sentences on the examples used in the review chart on page 95. Use your own paper, and keep all of your sentence writing results in a folder.

Maintaining Subject-Verb Agreement

As we have seen, the subject and verb in a sentence work together, so they must always agree. Different subjects need different forms of verbs. When the correct verb follows a subject, we call it subject-verb agreement.

The following sentences illustrate the rule that *s* verbs follow most singular subjects but not plural subjects:

One turtle walks.	Three turtles walk.
The baby cries.	The babies cry.
A democracy listens to the people.	Democracies listen to the people.
One child plays.	Many children play.

The following sentences show how forms of the verb *be* (*is, am, are, was, were*) and helping verbs (*be, have,* and *do*) are made to agree with their subjects. We have labeled only the verbs that must agree with the subjects.

This puzzle is difficult.	These puzzles are difficult.
I am amazed.	You are amazed.
He was sleeping.	They were sleeping.
That class has been canceled.	Those classes have been canceled.
She does not want to participate.	They do not want to participate.

The following words are always singular and take an *s* verb or the irregular equivalent (*is, was, has, does*):

one	anybody	each
anyone	everybody	
everyone	nobody	
no one	somebody	
someone		

8. But Jennifer and my other classmates (has, have) taught me something.
9. It (help, helps) to have a plan; their drawings often (turn, turns) out better than mine.
10. Either they or I (am, are) right, but I don't know which it (is, are) yet.

PROOFREADING EXERCISE

Find and correct the ten subject-verb agreement errors in the following paragraph.

I exercise in the gardens near my house several times a week. The fresh air and pretty scenery refreshes me and make me happy. There is several paths I can follow each day. One of my favorite walks go up a steep hill and down through a grove of ferns. The droplets of water on the ferns splashes on me as I brush past them. Then the path open into a grassy area that take my breath away sometimes. The late afternoon sunlight shine through the branches of a few large trees, and it create beautiful shadows on top of the grass. Another of the paths goes straight between a row of tall, narrow trees. The trunks of the trees is smooth, but their leafy tops sways in the wind because they are so high. I love my afternoon walks in the gardens.

SENTENCE WRITING

Write ten sentences in which you describe the shoes you are wearing. Use verbs in the present time. Then go back over your sentences—underline your subjects once, underline your verbs twice, and be sure they agree. Exchange papers with another student and check each other's subject-verb agreement. Keep the results in your sentence writing folder.

Avoiding Shifts in Time

People often worry about using different time frames in writing. Let common sense guide you. If you begin writing a paper in past time, don't shift back and forth to the present unnecessarily; and if you begin in the present, don't shift to the past without good reason. In the following paragraph, the writer starts in the present and then shifts to the past, then shifts again to the present:

> In the novel *To Kill a Mockingbird,* Jean Louise Finch is a little girl who lives in the South with her father, Atticus, and her brother, Jem. Everybody in town calls Jean Louise "Scout" as a nickname. When Atticus, a lawyer, chose to defend a black man against the charges of a white woman, some of their neighbors turned against him. Scout protected her father by appealing to the humanity of one member of the angry mob. In this chapter, five-year-old Scout turns out to be stronger than a group of adult men.

All the verbs should be in the present:

> In the novel *To Kill a Mockingbird,* Jean Louise Finch is a little girl who lives in the South with her father, Atticus, and her brother, Jem. Everybody in town calls Jean Louise "Scout" as a nickname. When Atticus, a lawyer, chooses to defend a black man against the charges of a white woman, some of their neighbors turn against him. Scout protects her father by appealing to the humanity of one member of the angry mob. In this chapter, five-year-old Scout turns out to be stronger than a group of adult men.

This sample paragraph discusses only the events that happen within the novel's plot, so it needs to maintain one time frame—the present, which we use to write about literature and repeated actions.

However, sometimes you will write about the present, the past, and even the future together. Then it may be necessary to use these different time frames within the same paragraph, each for its own reason. For example, if you were to give biographical information about Harper Lee, author of *To Kill a Mockingbird,* within a discussion of the novel and its influence, you might need to use all three time frames:

> Harper Lee grew up in Alabama, and she based elements in the book on experiences from her childhood. Like the character Atticus, Lee's father was a lawyer. She wrote the novel in his law offices. *To Kill a Mockingbird* is Harper Lee's most famous work, and it received the Pulitzer Prize for fiction in 1960. Lee's book turned forty years old in the year 2000. It will always remain one of the most moving and compassionate novels in American literature.

The previous paragraph uses past (*grew, based, was, wrote, received, turned*), present (*is*), and future (*will remain*) in the same paragraph without committing the error of shifting. Shifting occurs when the writer changes time frames *inconsistently* or *for no reason,* confusing the reader (as in the first example given).

PROOFREADING EXERCISES

Which of the following student paragraphs shift *unnecessarily* back and forth between time frames? In those that do, change the verbs to maintain one time frame, thus making the entire paragraph read smoothly. One of the paragraphs is correct.

1. Plastic surgery helps many people look better and feel better about themselves. Of course, there were stories of unnecessary surgeries and even heartbreaking mistakes. People could make their own decisions about whether plastic surgery was right for them. Dogs, however, can't communicate what they want. Nevertheless, some people took their dogs in for cosmetic surgeries, such as tummy tucks and face-lifts. Just like humans, dogs sometimes needed surgery to correct painful or unhealthy conditions. A dog with a low-hanging tummy could get an infection from scratches that were caused by rocks on the ground. And another dog may require a face-lift to help it stay clean when it eats. Animal lovers were worried that some canine plastic surgeries were done without good reasons.

Source: Newsweek, March 21, 2005

2. I watched a documentary on the Leaning Tower of Pisa last night. I was amazed to find out that the tower began leaning before it was even finished. Workers over several centuries adjusted their materials as they built the tower to compensate for its increasing angle. That's why the tower is actually shaped a little like a banana. I'm surprised that the famous landmark is still standing after everything people have done to it since it was finished. In the 1930s, for instance, Mussolini thought that it should be straightened. So he had workers drill holes in the foundation and pour tons of concrete beneath it. Others tried digging out the earth around the sunken part. But that just caused flooding because they went below the soil's water table. The narrator of the documentary said that every time

Correcting Misplaced or Dangling Modifiers

When we modify something, we change whatever it is by adding something to it. We might modify a car, for example, by adding special tires. In English, we call words, phrases, and clauses *modifiers* when they add information to part of a sentence. As we saw on p. 29, to do its job properly, a modifier should be in the right spot—as close to the word it describes as possible. If we put new tires on the roof of the car instead of where they belong, they would be misplaced. In the following sentence, the modifier is too far away from the word it modifies to make sense. It is a misplaced modifier:

Swinging from tree to tree, we watched the monkeys at the zoo.

Was it *we* who were swinging from tree to tree? That's what the sentence says because the modifying phrase *Swinging from tree to tree* is next to *we*. It should be next to *monkeys*.

At the zoo, we watched the monkeys swinging from tree to tree.

The next example has no word at all for the modifier to modify:

At the age of eight, my family finally bought a dog.

Obviously, the family was not eight when it bought a dog. Nor was the dog eight. The modifier *At the age of eight* is dangling there with no word to attach itself to, no word for it to modify. We can get rid of the dangling modifier by turning it into a dependent clause. (See p. 74 for a discussion of dependent clauses.)

When I was eight, my family finally bought a dog.

Here the clause has its own subject and verb—*I was*—and there's no chance of misunderstanding the sentence. Here's another dangling modifier:

After a two-hour nap, the train pulled into the station.

Did the train take a two-hour nap? Who did?

After a two-hour nap, I awoke just as the train pulled into the station.

EXERCISES

Carefully rephrase any of the following sentences that contain misplaced or dangling modifiers. Some sentences are correct.

4. Practicing for an hour a day, his tennis has improved.
5. The price of gasoline fluctuates, rising and falling several times a year.
6. Sitting on the beach all day, I made a decision.
7. They discovered a new trail hiking in the nearby mountains.
8. She felt the pressure of trying to get good grades from her parents.
9. I enjoy traveling to new places with my friends and even my family.
10. Written in green ink, the teacher's comments seemed positive even when pointing out a problem.

PROOFREADING EXERCISE

Find and correct any misplaced or dangling modifiers in the following paragraphs.

A man in Edinburgh, Scotland, has invented a device, hoping to become famous and wealthy. The device is a variation on the center-mounted brake light used in the design of many new cars, located just above the trunk and visible from behind. Instead of just a solid red brake light, however, this invention displays words to other drivers written in bold, red-lighted letters.

With simplicity in mind, the vocabulary the inventor gave the machine is limited to three words: "Sorry," "Thanks," and "Help." After making an aggressive lane change, the machine could apologize for us. Or after being allowed to go ahead of someone, the device could offer thanks to the considerate person responsible. Of course, at the sight of the "Help" display, we could summon fellow citizens for assistance.

And there is no need to worry about operating the device while driving. With three easy-to-reach buttons, the messages can be activated without taking our eyes off the road.

SENTENCE WRITING

Write five sentences that contain misplaced or dangling modifiers; then revise those sentences to put the modifiers where they belong. Use the examples in the explanations as models. Keep the results in your sentence writing folder.

Correcting for Parallel Structure

Your writing will be clearer and more memorable if you use parallel structure. That is, when you write two pieces of information or any kind of list, put the items in similar form. Look at this sentence, for example:

> My favorite movies are comic, romantic, or the ones about outer space.

The sentence lacks parallel structure. The third item in the list doesn't match the other two. Now look at this sentence:

> My favorite movies are comedies, love stories, and sci-fi fantasies.

Here the items are parallel; they are all plural nouns. Or you could write the following:

> I like movies that make me laugh, that make me cry, and that make me think.

Again the sentence has parallel structure because all three items in the list are dependent clauses. Here are some more examples. Note how much easier it is to read the sentences with parallel structure.

WITHOUT PARALLEL STRUCTURE	WITH PARALLEL STRUCTURE
I like to hike, to ski, and going sailing.	I like to hike, to ski, and to sail. (all "to ______" verbs)
The office has run out of pens, paper, ink cartridges, and we need more toner, too.	The office needs more pens, paper, ink cartridges, and toner. (all nouns)
They decided that they needed a change, that they could afford a new house, and wanted to move to Arizona.	They decided that they needed a change, that they could afford a new house, and that they wanted to move to Arizona. (all dependent clauses)

The parts of an outline should always be parallel. Following are two brief outlines about food irradiation. The parts of the outline on the *left* are not parallel. The first subtopic (I.) is a question; the other (II.) is just a noun. And the supporting points (A., B., C.) are written as nouns, verbs, and even clauses. The parts of the outline on the *right* are parallel. Both subtopics (I. and II.) are plural nouns, and all details (A., B., C.) are action verbs followed by objects.

PROOFREADING EXERCISE

Proofread the following paragraph about Shirley Temple, the famous child star of the 1930s, and revise it to correct any errors in parallel structure.

Shirley Temple was born in 1928. In 1931, when she was just three years old, someone discovered her natural talent at a dance lesson, and she was asked to be in movies. She starred in many films that are still popular today. Among them are *Heidi, Rebecca of Sunnybrook Farm,* and *Curly Top* was one of her earliest. Directors loved Shirley's acting style and the fact that she was able to do a scene in only one take, but not everyone trusted Shirley Temple. Graham Greene was sued when he claimed that Shirley was about thirty years old and in reality was a dwarf. Little Shirley's parents helped with her career, and they also earned money for their efforts. In the early days, the studios paid her mother several hundred dollars a week to put fifty-six curlers in Shirley's hair each night. That way, her famous ringlets would always be perfect, and her hair looked the same each time. Shirley's father managed her money, so much money that at one point Shirley Temple was among the ten highest paid people in America. It was 1938, and she was only ten years old.

Source: California People (Peregrine Smith, 1982)

SENTENCE WRITING

Write ten sentences that use parallel structure in a list or a pair of objects, actions, locations, or ideas. You may choose your own subject or describe a process that involves several steps to complete. Keep the results in your sentence writing folder.

Avoiding Shifts in Person

To understand what "person" means when using pronouns, imagine a conversation between two people about a third person. The first person speaks using "I, me, my . . ."; the second person would be called "you"; and when the two of them talked of a third person, they would say "he, she, they . . . ." You'll never forget the idea of "person" if you remember it as a three-part conversation.

First person—*I, me, my, we, us, our*

Second person—*you, your*

Third person—*he, him, his, she, her, hers, they, them, their, one, anyone*

You may use all three of these groups of pronouns in a paper, but don't shift from one group to another without good reason.

Wrong: Few people know how to manage *their* time. *One* need not be an efficiency expert to realize that *one* could get a lot more done if *he* budgeted *his* time. Nor do *you* need to work very hard to get more organized.

Better: *Everyone* should know how to manage *his or her* time. *One* need not be an efficiency expert to realize that *a person* could get a lot more done if *one* budgeted *one's* time. Nor does *one* need to work very hard to get more organized. (Too many *one*'s in a paragraph make it sound overly formal, and they lead to the necessity of avoiding sexism by using *s/he* or *he or she,* etc. Sentences can be revised to avoid using either *you* or *one.*)

Best: Many of *us* don't know how to manage *our* time. *We* need not be efficiency experts to realize that *we* could get a lot more done if *we* budgeted *our* time. Nor do *we* need to work very hard to get more organized.

Often students write *you* in a paper when they don't really mean *you, the reader.*

You wouldn't believe how many times I saw that movie.

Such sentences are always improved by getting rid of the *you.*

I saw that movie many times.

PROOFREADING EXERCISES

Which of the following student paragraphs shift *unnecessarily* between first-, second-, and third-person pronouns? In those that do, revise the sentences to eliminate such shifting, thus making the entire paragraph read smoothly. One of the paragraphs is correct.

REVIEW OF SENTENCE STRUCTURE ERRORS

One sentence in each pair contains an error. Read both sentences carefully before you decide. Then write the letter of the *incorrect* sentence in the blank. Try to name the error and correct it if you can. You may find any of these errors:

awk	awkward phrasing
cliché	overused expression
dm	dangling modifier
frag	fragment
mm	misplaced modifier
pro	incorrect pronoun
pro agr	pronoun agreement error
pro ref	pronoun reference error
ro	run-on sentence
shift	shift in time or person
s-v agr	subject-verb agreement error
wordy	wordiness
//	not parallel

1. _____ **A.** We had a great time on our first trip to New York City.

B. We saw a play on Broadway, walked down Fifth Avenue, and we visited the Statue of Liberty.

2. _____ **A.** There is a problem, and that is that the ATM machine sometimes runs out of cash.

B. Once, the ATM machine recorded my withdrawal but didn't dispense the money.

3. _____ **A.** I planned to go on the field trip to the museum but my car broke down.

B. The students who went said that the paintings and drawings were beautiful.

4. _____ **A.** The teacher's assistant in our biology lab is very helpful.

B. She stayed with my lab partner and I during our whole experiment.

5. _____ **A.** Everyone in the graduation ceremony received their own fake diploma.

B. The real diplomas arrived later in the mail.

6. _____ **A.** I finished my summary paragraph, printed it, and ran to class.

B. I knew that it was better late than never.

7. _____ **A.** Each of the reference books I needed were checked out.

B. The reference librarian told me that I could do some research online.

8. _____ **A.** I am planning to major in business.

B. I do well in math classes I also love to read the biographies of entrepreneurs.

9. _____ **A.** I had a conference with my fencing teacher in his office.

B. Me and him agreed that I needed to improve my footwork.

10. _____ **A.** The construction company who will build the new auditorium.

B. They came to campus for the groundbreaking ceremony.

11. _____ **A.** A person who quits smoking can recover from lung damage.

B. The tissues in your lungs slowly repair themselves.

12. _____ **A.** My car has a mind of its own.

B. I can never tell when it is going to break down.

13. _____ **A.** Last night's dinner was a disaster.

B. Cold mashed potatoes, overcooked broccoli, and tough pork chops.

14. _____ **A.** Some kind of chemical came through the vents in the classroom yesterday.

B. Everyone's eyes are watering, and they were coughing.

15. _____ **A.** At the age of four, a brick fell on his right foot.

B. He has had a scar on that foot ever since.

PROOFREADING EXERCISE

Find and correct the sentence structure errors in the following essay.

Mother Tells All

The most memorable lessons I have learned about myself have come from my own children. A mother is always on display she has nowhere to hide. And

Comma Rules 4, 5, and 6

The next three comma rules all involve using pairs of commas to enclose what we like to call "scoopable" elements. Scoopable elements are certain words, phrases, and clauses that can be taken out of the middle of a sentence without affecting its meaning. Notice that the comma **(,)** is shaped somewhat like the tip of an ice cream scoop? Let this similarity help you remember to use commas to enclose *scoopable* elements. Two commas are used**,** one before and one after**,** to show where scoopable elements begin and where they end.

4. Put commas around the name of a person spoken to.

Did you know, Danielle, that you left your backpack at the library?

We regret to inform you, Mr. Davis, that your policy has been canceled.

5. Put commas around expressions that interrupt the flow of the sentence (such as *however, moreover, therefore, of course, by the way, on the other hand, I believe, I think*).

I know, of course, that I have missed the deadline.

They will try, therefore, to use the rest of their time wisely.

Today's exam, I think, was only a practice test.

Read the previous examples *aloud,* and you'll hear how these expressions surrounded by commas interrupt the flow of the sentence. Sometimes such expressions flow smoothly into the sentence and don't need commas around them.

Of course he checked to see if there were any rooms available.

We therefore decided to stay out of it.

I think you made the right decision.

Remember that when a word like *however* comes between two independent clauses, that word needs a semicolon before it. It may also have a comma after it, especially if there seems to be a pause between the word and the rest of the sentence. (See p. 89.)

The bus was late; *however,* we still made it to the museum before it closed.

I am improving my study habits; *furthermore,* I am getting better grades.

She was interested in journalism; *therefore,* she took a job at a local newspaper.

I spent hours studying for the test; *finally,* I felt prepared.

3. The book's postcards four on each page can be pulled apart and mailed like regular ones.
4. The postcards have images of *Titanic*-related people, places, and events on one side.
5. The blank sides where messages and addresses go include brief captions of the images on the front of the cards.
6. The book's actual content the part written by Braynard offers a brief history of each image relating to the *Titanic.*
7. One of my favorite cards shows the ship's captain Edward Smith and its builder Lord Pirrie standing on the deck of the *Titanic* before it set sail.
8. Another card is a photograph of *Titanic* passengers on board the *Carpathia* the ship that rescued many survivors.
9. There is also picture of two small children survivors themselves who lost their father in the disaster but were later reunited with their mother.
10. The most interesting card a photo of the ship's gymnasium shows that one of the pieces of exercise equipment for the passengers was a rowing machine.

PROOFREADING EXERCISE

Surround any "scoopable" elements in the following paragraph with commas according to Comma Rules 4, 5, and 6.

Do you know Ryan that there is a one-unit library class that begins next week? It's called Library 1 Introduction to the Library and we have to sign up for it before Friday. The librarians who teach it will give us an orientation and a series of assignment sheets. Then as we finish the assignments at our own pace we will turn them in to the librarians for credit. Ms. Kim the librarian that I spoke with said that we will learn really valuable library skills. These skills such as finding books or articles in our library and using the Internet to access other databases are the ones universities will expect us to know. I therefore plan to take this class, and you I hope will take it with me.

SENTENCE WRITING

Combine the following sets of sentences in different ways according to Comma Rules 4, 5, and 6. Try to combine each set in a way that needs commas and in a way that doesn't need commas. In other words, try to make an element "scoopable" in one sentence and not "scoopable" in another. You may reorder the details and change the phrasing as you wish. Sample responses are provided in the Answers section.

Soup tastes best when it's hot.

Chicken noodle soup is especially good when it's hot.

I believe.

We should start a savings account.

A savings account will help us prepare for financial emergencies.

My roommate got a job in the bookstore.

Her name is Leslie.

The job allows her to get good discounts on books.

REVIEW OF THE COMMA

SIX COMMA RULES

1. Put a comma before *for, and, nor, but, or, yet, so* when they connect two independent clauses.
2. Put a comma between three or more items in a series.
3. Put a comma after an introductory expression or before a tag comment or question.
4. Put commas around the name of a person spoken to.
5. Put commas around words like *however* or *therefore* when they interrupt a sentence.
6. Put commas around unnecessary additional ("scoopable") information.

WHAT IS TECHNICAL WRITING?

GOALS

DEFINE technical writing and its importance in the workplace

IDENTIFY the characteristics of technical writing

COMPARE AND CONTRAST technical writing and other types of writing

IDENTIFY ethics in technical writing

See the Data CD for Write-to-Learn and In The Know activity worksheets.

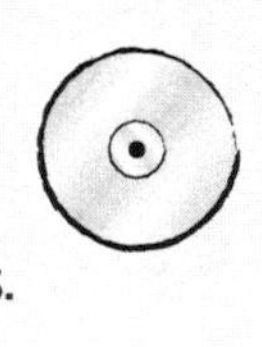

TEACHING RESOURCES

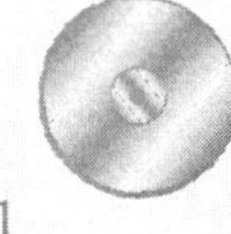

IRCD
- Lesson Plans, Ch. 1
- Chapter Activities, Ch. 1
- PowerPoint® Slides, Ch. 1
- Sample Documents, Ch. 1

techwriting.swlearning.com, Ch. 1

Exam*View*®, Ch. 1

CHAPTER OVERVIEW

Defines technical writing and points out the importance of technical writing in today's workplace.

See the IRCD for Write-To-Learn and In The Know activity worksheets.

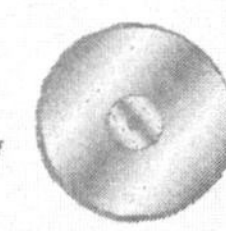

WRITE-TO-LEARN

Read the three model documents on pages 4, 5, and 6 of this chapter and think about the type of writing each model represents. In a one-page journal entry, answer these questions: Have you written similar types of documents? If so, what did you write and why? Have you read similar documents? If so, what did you read and why? Which document would you use to make a decision or to perform an action? Which type of document do you prefer to write? Why? Which do you prefer to read? Why?

In The Know

academic writing the expository and persuasive writing done in academic circles; examples include personal essays, research papers, analyses, and arguments

ambiguous more than one interpretation is possible; describes writing that means different things to different people

ethics a system of moral standards and rules that guides human behavior

expository writing writing to explain or inform

expressive writing writing to express or portray personal observation or feeling

field research research done in the field, especially through surveys and interviews

imaginative writing writing such as novels, short stories, drama, and poetry whose situations grow out of fantasy or imagination; events and people are fictional although the themes may reveal universal truths

inferences judgments about reading that the author does not make for the reader

jargon the highly specialized language of a particular discipline or technical field

persuasive writing writing to convince others

style the way an author uses words and sentences

technical communication communication done in the workplace; the subject is usually technical; the purpose and audience are specific; the approach is straightforward

technical writing writing done in the workplace; the subject is usually technical, written carefully for a specific audience; the organization is predictable and apparent; the style is concise; the tone is objective and businesslike; special features include visual elements

tone emotional overtones; the way words make readers feel

Writing@Work

Tyler Parris is a technical editor for the Windows Server Content Group at Microsoft Corporation in Redmond, Washington. As a technical editor, Tyler edits online Help for the Microsoft® Windows® Server operating systems and articles that appear on the Microsoft TechNet® web site and the Microsoft Developers' Network® web site. Specifically, he edits documentation for Microsoft® Windows Server, participates on a virtual team whose goal is to make Microsoft Help more accessible to people with disabilities, and he leads a glossary team that is responsible for coordinating the use of terms across Windows.

"Much of my time is spent communicating technical subjects to people, whether that's through print or through oral communication," Tyler says. Tyler must communicate with many employees in different locations, so he uses technology such as Microsoft Outlook® for Windows® to set up virtual team meetings. "Meetings are an important part of life here at Microsoft. It's how we share information and work together as a team."

Tyler stresses the importance of developing strong relationships with internal customers, the teams he supports, and other people he works with. "The best way to do that," he says, "is through polishing your technical communication skills." He says he is more likely to influence the documents he works on if he can diplomatically make the case for his recommended changes. "It helps to have some sort of evidence to back up recommended changes, so that writers do not think you are being arbitrary. I try to rely on usability reports, internal style guidelines, and our preferred grammar reference." Perhaps most importantly, Tyler says that flexibility is an important part of his job. "As I negotiate with writers, I try to remember that there is often more than one way to solve a problem, and my answer is not always the best one."

To help him prepare for a career in technical editing, Tyler received his bachelor of arts degree in English from Marshall University, where he took his first technical writing course. After that, he approached businesses from his hometown in Washington, DC, and wrote press releases, marketing materials, and some recruiting advertising text on a freelance basis. He also joined the Marines and received training as a network administrator, while learning some valuable leadership skills. Eventually, he completed his masters degree in technical and scientific communication from Miami University in Oxford, Ohio. After graduate school, Tyler interned at Convergys Corporation in Cincinnati, Ohio, an international telecommunications company.

About his training in computer networking, Tyler says, "Do not underestimate the importance of having communication skills to support your technical skills and knowledge. They help you gain credibility with the engineers you support, as well as other writers and editors."

APPLY

Writing @ Work
Use this feature as an introduction to the technical communication profession. The field has a wide range of jobs for people who like to write and who enjoy technology, science, and other specialties.

As an interesting activity based on Tyler's job, have students visit Microsoft's site offering improved accessibility for people with disabilities. This site, located at techwriting.swlearning.com, is filled with information about a variety of issues many students may not have considered. Can students draw any conclusions from the fact that the accessibility team is a virtual team? (Hint: Maybe some of the team members are people with disabilities.)

Tyler works on Microsoft's online Help systems. Although your students probably do not have access to a Windows® server, have them use the online help system for any software product. Is the system easy to use? Can students find answers to their questions? Do students have any advice for Tyler about improving online help?

Rebuilding Your Engine

Excessive **smoking** or **knocking** could mean it's time to rebuild your engine. When it comes time to rebuild, consider Summit's 1) Engine Kits or 2) Re-Ring Kits.

Engine Kits
Engine kits can be purchased with one of the following combinations:

- premium forged TRW pistons and moly rings,
- premium cast TRW pistons with moly rings, or
- cast TRW pistons with regular rings.

The kits also come with TRW main, cam and rod bearings; a TRW high volume oil pump; top quality Fel-Pro Blue Perma Torque gaskets; a set of oil and freeze plugs; and Clevite assembly lube. See Table 1 for a cost breakdown.

Re-Ring Kits
If your present pistons are in good shape and you don't need main and cam bearings or an oil pump, Re-Rings Kits may work. They include regular or moly rings, rod bearings, and a Fel-Prol Blue Berma Torque gasket set. See Table 2 for. . . .

Table 1 Engine Kits

Engine	Our Good Kit: Case Pistons Regular Rings	Our Better Kit: Cast Pistons Moly Rings	Our Best Kit: Forged Pistons Moly Rings
Chevy 327 '62-'66	$214.95	$219.95	$308.95
Chevy 350 '67-'80	$172.95	$184.95	$298.95
Chevy 350 '81	$181.95	$189.95	$291.95

Reprinted with permission of Summit Racing Equipment, Akron, Ohio.
Figure 1.1 Technical Writing Excerpt

The First American Automobile Race

At 8:55 a.m. on November 28, 1895, six "motorcycles" left Chicago's Jackson Park for a 54-mile race to Evanston, Illinois and back through the snow. Number 5, piloted by inventor J. Frank Duryea, won the race in just over 10 hours at an average speed of about 7.3 miles per hour! The winner earned $2,000 and the enthusiast who named the horseless vehicles "motorcycles" won $500.

Only two years earlier in Springfield, Massachusetts, brothers Charles and J. Frank Duryea had built and driven what they claimed to be the first American gasoline-powered automobile. Yet, as if by spontaneous combustion, over 70 entries were filed for the *Times-Herald* race, a response so overwhelming that President Cleveland asked the War Department to oversee the event. Following their victory in the race, the Duryeas manufactured thirteen copies of the Chicago car, and J. Frank Duryea developed the "Stevens-Duryea," an expensive limousine, which remained in production into the 1920s.

There were American antecedents to the Duryeas' winning vehicle. As early as 1826, Samuel Morey filed a patent, bearing the signatures of John Quincy Adams and Henry Clay, for an internal combustion engine. George Brayton, Stephania Reese, Henry Nadig, and Wallis Harris all produced self-propelled machines.

Charles Black developed an 18 horsepower "chug buggy" in 1891—the same year John Lambert developed a three-wheel motor buggy. After seeing the 1895 *Times-Herald* race, Lambert produced four-wheel vehicles at his Buckeye Manufacturing plant.

The Stanley twins built a steam-powered vehicle in 1897. The "Stanley Steamer" achieved fame when brother F.E. Stanley did a mile in 2:11 on a dirt track with a 30 degree incline. George Eastman bought the rights to the Stanleys' earlier photographic patents, supplying the brothers with capital to manufacture 200 standing orders for the Steamer, which eventually became the "Locomobile." By the time Henry Ford incorporated the Ford Motor Company in 1903, the Stanleys' plant already employed 140 workers.

Like its predecessor horseracing, automobile racing provided the stiff competition, which helped to "refine the breed." When the Stanleys brought their 150 horsepower "T.E. (Thoroughly Educated) Wogglebug" to the 1906 winter races at Ormond Beach, Florida, driver Fred Marriott clocked 127.66 mph, becoming the first to move faster than 2 miles per minute.

In 1911 the Indianapolis 500 was born. This famous race fostered the development of innovations such as the rear view mirror. By the time Berna Eli "Barney" Oldfield sped to the top of Pike's Peak in 1915, motorcar production was booming and automobile racing a well-established sport.

Source: The Library of Congress, *Today in History;* online at http://memory.log.gov/ammem/today/nov28.html.

Figure 1.2 Research Paper Excerpt

Owning a Car

Owning a car is not all it is cracked up to be. A year ago, I wanted to buy a car, but I could not afford one on my own. I talked to my parents about my desire to own a car, and they offered to make the down payment on a used Ford Mustang. However, I was responsible for the monthly payments, half the insurance premium, and the cost of maintenance. I thought I could handle the payments by waiting tables at Schooner's. The job promised to cover all my expenses—that is, until the restaurant closed for repairs.

I tried to find a temporary job to cover my expenses in the meantime, but no place would hire me for just a couple of months. And then my "maintenance-free" Ford sprung a leak when the radiator rusted out. One problem after another occurred: oil changes, inspection stickers, a headlight out, a fuse blown—I began to wish I lived in a big city with public transportation. Better yet, I began to wish I lived in a very small town where I could ride my bike everywhere. If I rode my bike instead of driving a car, I could save money on gas and repairs and get exercise at the same time.

After just a few months of being broke with no job and a useless car that I could not even afford to put gas in, I traded the car for a bicycle. Now I ride my bike everywhere. I do not have to put gas in the bike; I just have to put air in the tires every now and then. The best part about owning a bicycle instead of a car, besides saving money, is the exercise I am getting. I enjoy riding my bike so much that I have entered several bicycle races. I finally won my first race—the Glendale Speed Race. I won first place out of 525 entries! What could be next . . . the Tour de France?

Figure 1.3 Personal Essay Excerpt

YOU ARE A TECHNICAL WRITER!

Have you given someone written directions or drawn a map to your home? Have you written quick instructions for using a fax machine at work? Have you told someone how to change the oil in a car or how to make french toast? If you answered *yes* to any of these questions or have had similar experiences, you have already engaged in technical writing or technical communication.

© DIGITAL VISION

DEFINITION OF TECHNICAL WRITING

Candice, an award-winning saxophonist, began teaching saxophone lessons to sixth graders. For the first lesson, she drew an alto sax diagram and quickly developed a step-by-step guide explaining how to take the instrument apart and reassemble it. When she saw how easily students could follow her instructions, she was happy to know that her words were helping others learn to do something she enjoyed.

Candice might have been surprised to learn that she was using technical communication. She was giving practical information to a specific audience, information that would enable her audience to take action. When she referred to the diagram and explained the procedure aloud to her students, she was using **technical communication.** When she wrote the instructions to accompany her diagram, she was using **technical writing.**

Technical documents can range from a half-page memo announcing the winner of a DVD raffle to a research grant proposal requesting money to build an animal shelter. The term *technical writing* describes documents produced in areas such as business, science, social science, engineering, and education. Sales catalogs, business letters, financial reports, standard operating procedures, medical research studies, lab reports—all of these and more are examples of technical writing.

WARM UP

Think about a profession you are interested in. What kinds of documents will you write in that profession?

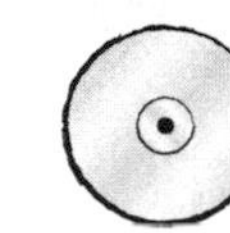

See the Writing Model worksheet on the Data CD for activities for Figures 1.1 to 1.3.

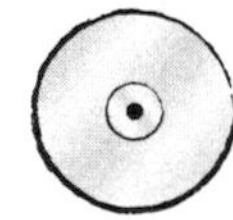

Brainstorm the types of technical writing you already know. Use the You are a Technical Writer worksheet on the Data CD to guide you.

FOCUS

Warm Up

Use the Warm Up to help students picture themselves as writers on the job, to show how relevant technical writing is in their future, and to create enthusiasm for technical writing.

See the Writing Model

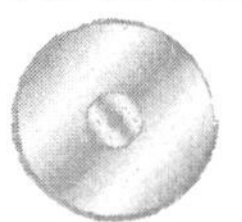

worksheet on the IRCD for activities for Figures 1.1 to 1.3.

TEACH

Use this section to reduce the apprehension some students may feel about technical writing. Technical writing can be fun and challenging because it covers a variety of subjects.

APPLY

Have students brainstorm the

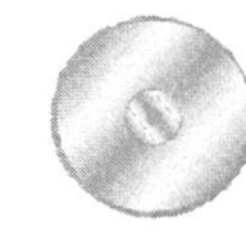

types of technical writing they already know. Use the You are a Technical Writer worksheet on the IRCD.

TEACH

Demonstrate the importance of technical writing in the workplace by having students think of professions that may *not* use writing. Make a list of these professions. Then, have students break into groups and brainstorm ways these professions *do* use technical writing. Use this activity to show that nearly all professions require communication skills, even if most of the writing involves filling out forms.

ENRICH

To identify how people use technical writing on the job, invite several people from industry or business to visit the classroom and describe the writing they do. Invite representatives from a variety of professions. Before your guests arrive, tell students to prepare questions specifically about technical writing to ask the representatives.

TECHNICAL WRITING IS ESSENTIAL IN THE WORKPLACE

Written communication is essential in the workplace for many reasons. Written communication allows readers to read and study at their own convenience, pass along information easily to others, and keep a permanent record for future reference.

An executive reserves the afternoon hours between meetings to review employment resumes. A financial report becomes part of an organization's financial history, which can be read by stockholders and against which later financial reports can be compared. Written communication allows writers to craft their message until it is complete and accurate and communicate the same information efficiently to readers in different locations.

A computer programmer rewrites the specifications for new software until they are accurate and complete. A news release announcing a merger of two publishing firms or the firing of a football coach is read by readers in different locations. A memo written to prepare employees for a plantwide shutdown is introduced one way to administrative assistants anticipating a few days off, another way to plant supervisors who must work through the shutdown, and yet another way to vendors who will be told to hold all shipping for a week. The basic information remains the same, but the implications for each of these readers are different.

Everywhere you look, information from every direction competes for your attention: television, radio, newspapers, magazines, books, e-mail, the Internet, CD-ROMs, DVDs. Because of information overload, you need to be able to read documents quickly and efficiently, you need to understand them the first time, and you need to know that the information is accurate. Up-to-date information provides companies with a competitive edge, speeding critical decision making and allowing job specialization.

Technical writers who help companies manage the information overload are vital resources. They understand that their readers must be able to skim text, skip text, and find important information quickly. Good writers understand that they will not always know who is reading their writing (especially with e-mail) or how it is used. As a professional in great demand, the technical writer faces a challenging, exciting, and rewarding future.

ALL PROFESSIONS REQUIRE TECHNICAL WRITING

Regardless of the career you choose, you will write in the workplace. Conservative estimates suggest that you will spend at least 20 percent of your time writing in a technical or business occupation. Professionals in engineering and technology careers spend as much as 40 percent of their time writing. In a series of interviews with business and technical managers at six major employers in the southeastern United States, these managers all agreed that clear and effective writing is a crucial skill needed to advance in the corporate world.

Different careers generate different kinds of reports: Nurses chart a patient's medical condition so that the nurses on the next shift can continue patient care. Police accident reports record facts for later use in court. Chemists and engineers document procedures to comply with government regulations; accountants prepare annual client reports. Sales representatives write sales proposals; professors write grant proposals; park rangers write safety precautions; insurance claims adjusters write incident reports; travel agents design brochures; and public relations officers write news releases, letters, and speeches.

When you write, you demonstrate your ability to analyze, solve problems, and understand technical processes. For example, Johann Buchner, personnel director for Osgood Textile Industries, impresses his supervisor and earns his colleagues' respect when his tax-deferred retirement plan proposal is approved. On the other hand, the drafting crew at Stillman Manufacturing is frustrated with Tetrianna Danielli's instructions for

TEACH

Bring writing that students may not consider to be technical writing, such as a marketing brochure you have received in the mail or a note written to a family member telling that person what to buy at the grocery store. Explain why these types of writing can be technical writing.

To demonstrate that technical writing will be required in their careers, have students search for job listings in professions they are interested in. (This can be an online search, a newspaper search, and so on.) Students can share their job descriptions with the class (they should find at least five descriptions). Have students point out the jobs that require good writing and communication skills. For this activity, have students

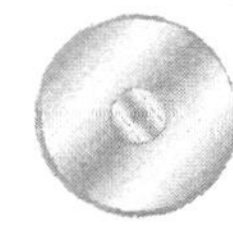

use the Technical Writing on the Job worksheet on the IRCD.

installing wireless computing at the industrial site. The crew must redraft plans because Tetrianna's instructions are vague and incomplete. When writing is not clear, the thinking behind the writing may not be clear either.

All careers rely on technical communication to get the job done. Technical writing is the great connector—the written link—connecting technology to user, professional to client, colleague to colleague, supervisor to employee, and individual to community. No matter what career you choose, you can expect to read and compose e-mail, send accompanying attachments, give and receive phone messages, and explain procedures.

In addition to work-related writing, the responsibilities of being a community and family member require technical communication. Figure 1.4 shows how Sergeant Thomas Hardy of the Palmer City Police Department, father of two and concerned citizen, uses technical communication on the job and at home.

Colleagues: e-mail, collaborative incident reports

Boy Scout Den Parents: fund-raiser announcements, directions to jamboree, invitations to join troop

Victims: incident reports, investigative reports

Legislators: letter and e-mail in favor of clean-air regulations

Lawyers, Court Officials: depositions, testimonies, statements (may be televised)

State FBI Office: letter of application and resume for a position that would advance his career

Greenpeace Volunteers: journal of nature hike

Community Members: safety presentation at the high school

Supervisees: employee regulations, letters of reference, training procedures

Local Newspaper Editor: letter thanking community for help with jamboree; press release announcing purchase of state-of-the-art police car

Suspects: incident reports, interrogation results, procedures, recommendations for sentencing or early release

Children: letter while they are at summer camp

Figure 1.4 Sergeant Hardy's Technical Communication at Home and on the Job

ONGOING ASSESSMENT

Stop and Think

Bring examples of poor writing other students have written in a past class (delete names) or that you find on the Internet. Ask students whether they would hire the person who wrote the documents and ask whether they would like to work on a project with that person. Discuss students' reasons.

Tell students that writing affects their chances for advancement because when they write, they demonstrate their ability to analyze, solve problems, and understand technical processes.

Discuss the importance of technical writing in the workplace. Why do you think writing affects your chances for advancement?

CHARACTERISTICS OF TECHNICAL WRITING

Technical writing shares many characteristics with other kinds of writing, but it is also significantly different. From the factual treatment of the subject to audience considerations, technical writing is unique. Subject, audience, organization, special features, style, and tone all contribute to the description of writing appropriate for the workplace.

SUBJECT

The subject of each model at the beginning of this chapter is cars, but the approach to this subject is different for each document. The personal essay expresses a young driver's frustration at the cost of owning an automobile, an experience with which you can probably identify. **Expressive writing** is created to convey personal observations and relies on personal experience for research.

The research paper's purpose is not to relate personal experience, but to explain facts gained from library research. Writing to explain or inform is **expository writing.** While most academic research papers are factual papers written on topics interesting to the reader, the technical document (even a technical research document) is written to fulfill a need.

Often the need is to get information or to perform an action. Here someone with a vintage car may need to rebuild an engine; the technical document fulfills the special needs of a specific reader. The writer of this technical document also hopes to persuade the reader to buy the kits from the Summit catalog instead of somewhere else. Persuasive writing may require library research, scientific observation, or field research (use of surveys and interviews). Whether to inform or persuade, technical writing relies on data presented with precision and accuracy.

AUDIENCE

The writer of the personal essay expects some understanding from his or her readers as they share experiences; the writer also expresses his or her point of view. The writer of the research paper may be interested in the subject and hopes a reader will read the research paper for facts.

The technical writer, however, expects more from a very specific reader—one needing information about engine kits and possessing knowledge of the topic and its specialized vocabulary. The technical writer not only expects the reader to understand the writing, but also wants the reader to do something after reading—order an engine kit. When you want something specific from a reader, you must work hard as a writer to meet the reader's needs.

WARM UP

Review the three models on pages 4, 5, and 6 of this chapter. Describe the research required for each document. Why might someone read each document? What does each writer want from his or her audience? What has the writer done to consider the reader's needs? Use the Comparing Writing Environments worksheet on the Data CD.

FOCUS

Warm Up

Use Warm Up as a discovery learning activity to help students analyze the differences in various writing environments and to build on what they learned in the introduction section of this chapter. Use the

Comparing Writing Environments worksheet on the IRCD.

TEACH

Have students bring examples of their favorite type of writing to share with the class. Ask them to share how they use that type of writing and why the author chose to write it in a particular way.

Ask students to compare examples of technical writing to their examples, specifically focusing on subject and audience.

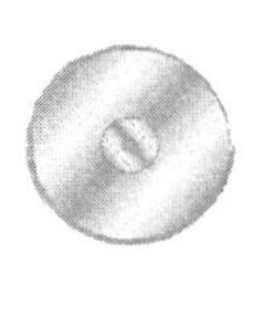

See the sample documents on the IRCD for an example of a poem for comparison.

In technical writing, the needs of the reader dictate every decision the writer makes. In the technical writing model, the writer worked hard to present the information the reader needs in a format that is easy to read. The headings, boldface type, special table, and no-frills language show that the writer is conscious of the reader.

Communication Update

Technical writers must be familiar with desktop publishing software to do their jobs. Using programs such as Microsoft® Word, Adobe® PageMaker®, or QuarkXPress™, they can apply special features to their documents, such as boldfacing, underlining, bulleted lists, tables, graphs, and diagrams. Most desktop publishing software even allows writers to make professional-looking newsletters, brochures, and books.

Use the Communication Update worksheet on the Data CD to practice applying special features.

COMMUNICATION UPDATE

See the IRCD for the Communication Update worksheet that allows students to practice using software programs to apply special features.

ENRICH

Bring several copies of *Intercom,* the magazine of the Society for Technical Communication. You may also bring other technical journals from specific fields.

Ask students to examine at least two articles. Then, have them list all the special features they find.

ORGANIZATION

The personal essay and research paper make standard use of a topic sentence and transitional expressions, but you still need to read far into each document before the main point and the organization become apparent.

The technical writing model, however, uses headings to help you perceive the organization at a single glance before you read. The use of *1)* and *2)* in the first sentence helps draw your eye to the subject of this document before you read. Also, headings give readers an opportunity to read only what they want or need to read. When a customer who is interested in rebuilding an engine wants to price only the re-ring kits, the heading "Re-Ring Kits" allows his or her eye to travel quickly to the information needed.

SPECIAL FEATURES

The technical document is the only document of the three examples at the beginning of this chapter to use special features. Technical writers use special features such as bold, italics, capital letters, columns, underlining, and bulleted lists to draw attention to certain words and help important information stand out. Also, the use of graphics, such as tables, graphs, pictures, and diagrams, helps relay complex information quickly for the audience.

More than the research paper or personal essay, the technical document relies on special features. Technical documents require more visual effort to grab and hold the readers' attention. Writers use some of the following special features to make their documents more effective for the audience:

1. Columns—one, two or three?
2. Color—which ones and how much?
3. Letterhead and logo—how large? where to place? middle, upper left or right, or side?
4. Graphs—one-, two-, or three-dimensional? horizontal or vertical? with color?
5. Tables—how many columns? with or without color?
6. Photos—what subject? what style? black and white or color photos?
7. Sidebars—what information to highlight? where to place?
8. Clip art—to add humor, set a tone, or celebrate a season?
9. Font size and style—how many are appropriate? What size is readable for the audience?

Technical writers face a double challenge: not only must they write with clear, accurate, and specific words, but they also must design the document to look inviting and attractive. Technical writers, therefore, are production artists: writing with precision to locate the best word and sentence structure for the message *and* designing pages that combine a professional image with a user-friendly approach. To do so, technical writers use a tool of their trade: desktop publishing software that allows them to craft documents that meet their readers' needs.

STYLE

The **style** of a document usually gives an audience an idea of the type of document they are reading. For example, the personal essay is casual, almost conversational, and predictable for an essay. You are probably comfortable with this style, having written personal essays in school. The writer uses examples and some description. The style of the research paper is also predictable for a research paper.

The technical document uses a simple, concise, straightforward style that is easily understood. The long sentences are simply lists. The other sentences are short, and the sentence order is predictable. There are no surprises for the reader. The vocabulary is highly specialized, the **jargon** of the automotive technician.

TEACH

Have students attend a poetry reading or literary discussion. Ask them to write a report analyzing the differences between types of writing at the events and technical writing, focusing on audience, organization, special features, style, and tone.

COMMUNICATION DILEMMA

Point out that Isabel's dilemma is common in the workplace. Discuss Isabel's options and the pros and cons of each. Students should look at the dilemma from different perspectives: loyal corporate citizen, technical writer, marketing writer, manager, and so on.

Isabel was recently assigned as the lead Technical Communicator on a team that is developing a high-profile sofware package known as SpeedQuest. She is responsible for coordinating communication between the programming team and the marketing team. For Isabel, this position means a likely promotion and career advancement. She knows a promotion would help her support her family, so she is eager to do a good job.

One evening Isabel overhears the lead computer programmer tell the project manager that SpeedQuest is not as advanced as advertised in the company's marketing materials. The programmer recommends delaying the launch date, but the project manager ignores the suggestion, deciding to issue a second release after the product is complete.

The next day in the meeting to discuss the marketing materials, Isabel struggles to decide whether she should list in the brochures SpeedQuest features that do not work yet. She knows the features would help sales of SpeedQuest. On the other hand, she knows that if she tells the truth and decides not to publish information about the features, she may not get the promotion she is counting on. What should Isabel do?

TONE

Tone describes the emotional flavor (the way the words make you feel) of a document. The tone of a document also gives the audience an idea of the kind of document they are reading.

The tone of the personal essay is casual. The tone of the research paper is objective. The tone in technical writing is best described as objective or businesslike.

The expressive nature of a personal essay can run a range of emotions—sadness, excitement, irony, humor. The aim of research papers or technical documents is not to convey emotion. In fact, emotion can get in the way of a technical document.

Readers of technical documents read for information, not for entertainment. They read to learn something or to take action. Some say technical writing is boring because of its lack of emotion. For the person needing or wanting that information, the topic is not boring.

FOCUS ON ETHICS
Use Focus on Ethics to relate ethics to workplace writing. Have students visit the web site of a company at which they may be interested in working some day. Have them read that company's code of ethics and note anything that relates to technical communication. Make sure students focus not only on technical writing but also on oral presentations and graphics. Use this feature as an introduction to the ethics section at the end of this chapter.

ONGOING ASSESSMENT
Stop and Think
Encourage students to incorporate the concepts about technical writing from this chapter in their definition: subject, organization, audience, style, tone, and special features. Have them compare and contrast their definition with other students' definitions.

Focus on Ethics

When you enter the workplace, you may be asked to sign a code of ethics, no matter what profession you pursue or where you work. Just as different careers generate different kinds of documents, different documents must follow a strict set of guidelines, laws, or principles outlined in the company's code of ethics.

Many companies have their code of ethics posted on the Internet for anyone to see. For example, large companies such as General Electric, Merrill Lynch, Kroger, and Eli Lilly post codes about a variety of concerns–from animal drug testing to diversity. Most likely, your school has a code of ethics that you follow.

Sometimes an individual's ethical code may conflict with others' behavior. If your personal ethics conflict with workplace practices, you can define yourself by how well you stand up for your own ethics. Doing so is not easy, however. If you discover that the company paying your salary is falsely advertising, you may find it can be difficult to criticize. If you believe that making fun of a person with a physical challenge is wrong, but you find yourself in a work group who is laughing at such a person, then your personal code conflicts with the group's. You need to be courageous to behave ethically, and such courage, although not always initially rewarded in the workplace, will help to establish yourself as an ethical employee, eventually.

Anderson, Paul V. *Technical Communication: A Reader-Centered Approach* Harcourt Brace and Company, 1999.

Drawing from the activities in this section's Warm Up, write your own definition of technical writing. Make sure you incorporate concepts from this section, such as subject, organization, audience, style, tone, and special features.

HOW TECHNICAL WRITING COMPARES TO OTHER WRITING

Technical writing has much in common with the academic writing you have experienced in school. Technical writing also shares aspects of the literature you have read. The differences, however, set technical writing apart from other writing that is familiar to you.

WARM UP

From your experience with writing, what characteristics does good writing share? In other words, how would you describe good writing?

FOCUS

Warm Up

Use Warm Up to think about the characteristics of all good writing, such as unity, coherence, effective organization, use of standard English, and appropriate style. State that technical writing also requires good writing.

TEACH

Use this section to point out that technical writing is not new for students. It shares characteristics with all good academic writing, and students can build on many of the writing skills they already use.

REVIEW

Make sure students understand the differences between technical writing and the writing they already know: differences in presentation, subject matter, and audience considerations.

TECHNICAL WRITING AND ACADEMIC WRITING

Academic writing, such as a personal essay or research paper, must be unified, coherent, and well organized. Technical writing must be unified, coherent, and well organized. Style and standard usage (the spoken and written English expected in business communication) are important in academic and technical writing. Both types rely on a process of thinking and writing that takes place over a few hours, a few days, or several weeks. The purpose is often the same: to inform or persuade.

The difference between the two is in the presentation, audience, and approach. Academic writing includes paragraphs—usually an introductory paragraph, paragraphs that develop a thesis (a statement of purpose), and a concluding paragraph. Academic writing is written for an academic audience—an instructor, your classmates, or a group of interested scholars. Its purpose is to expand on an idea or make observations about human experience. For example, Francis Bacon's essay entitled "On Reading" elaborates on the benefits of reading. Mark Twain in "Two Views of the Mississippi" observes that while a close study of the river is necessary to reveal its dangers, the study also takes away its mystery. Human experience is vast, open to interpretation according to the beliefs of the writer. As a result, the subject matter, style, and tone in academic writing are more varied than the subject matter, style, and tone in technical writing.

SEE THE SITES

Check out the College View web site for information about the technical communication career, salaries, the job outlook, and more. Learn about a typical day in the life of a technical communicator.

Discover the technical communication field by going to the Society for Technical Communication web site. This site provides articles about the profession, ethical choices, employment news, resume tips, information about loans, and networking opportunities.

You can find the url for both sites in the web links on techwriting.swlearning.com. You will also find a worksheet for activities.

SEE THE SITES
Refer to the See the Sites worksheet on techwriting.swlearning.com for activities.

ONGOING ASSESSMENT
Stop and Think
Use answers to show students similarities and differences between technical writing and other types of writing.

Technical writing also includes paragraphs. It, too, often begins with an introduction and closes with a conclusion. But technical writing (with its headings, itemized lists, boldface type, and graphics) looks different from academic writing. Technical writing is written for a specific audience. The subject is generally technical, business-related, or scientifically oriented. Generally, there is less flexibility in the subject matter, style, and tone.

TECHNICAL WRITING AND IMAGINATIVE WRITING

Imaginative writing also holds principles of unity, coherence, and standard usage. Imaginative writers also let their ideas emerge and develop over time. However, such writing is less academic and more artistic and creative than technical and academic writing.

Imaginative writing can be **ambiguous,** meaning different things to different people. Imaginative writing also requires the reader to draw inferences, to make judgments that the writer does not state.

Technical writing should be unambiguous and direct. A work of literature may be rich because it means different things to different readers. A reader might ponder the different meanings of the old man's voyage in Hemingway's *The Old Man and the Sea,* but W. Earl Britton says "that the primary, though not the sole, characteristic of technical and scientific writing lies in the effort of the author to convey one and only one meaning in what he says" (114).

The meaning of a sentence in technical writing must be clear. "Turn there," the man said, and the woman turned left when he meant for her to turn right. The word *there* can have different meanings for different people. However, "Turn right at the next paved road, called Nottingham Road" has only one meaning.

Imaginative writing requires you to make inferences. When Emily Dickinson writes: "Because I could not stop for Death—He kindly stopped for me— The Carriage held but just Ourselves—and Immortality," at first, you may have more questions than answers. Why is death being personified? Why does Dickinson capitalize *Death, Carriage, Ourselves,* and *Immortality?*

You expect to make inferences about poetry. You do not expect to make inferences about technical writing. If the poet's doctor gave the following instructions to a nurse, what would happen? *Because I could not remember the name of Ms. Dickinson's medication, would you kindly call the pharmacy and ask for the bottle that holds the blue and red pills?* Poor Ms. Dickinson. She'd find more comfort in the words of her poem than in the advice of her doctor.

Write a paragraph comparing technical writing to academic and imaginative writing.

ETHICS AND TECHNICAL WRITING

Ethics is a system of moral standards and rules that guide human behavior. Ethical systems vary from one culture to another and from one individual to another, but their common intent is to work toward a fair and just treatment of human beings. Ethics (from the Greek word *ethos,* which means "character") determine what treatment is right or good. Ethics include a person's character, the inner strength and personal sense of integrity that allow him or her to behave in an acceptable and ethical manner. Ethical conduct is found wherever there is a spirit of mutual respect and the desire for responsible behavior.

WARM UP

As a member of your school's web site design team, you find a current story about two students to be misleading. What is the right thing to do in this situation?

FOCUS

Warm Up

Use the Warm Up to get students thinking about the consequences of misleading statements that appear in print.

ENRICH

Have students share situations in which they have witnessed unethical practices. Have them share the consequences of those practices. Remind students to review the Focus on Ethics feature in this chapter.

ETHICS IN THE WORKPLACE

Ethical conduct is important in the workplace—so important that ethical standards are protected by the legal system. Companies can be sued for such ethical misconduct as endangering the environment, selling a product that hurts customers, or failing to hire workers fairly. Tobacco companies have been sued for endangering an individual's health. Accident victims claim neglect on the part of car manufacturers. At any time, you can find examples such as these in news reports of companies whose ethics are questionable. Behind each ethical infraction is writing—memos, letters, advertising, meeting minutes—that helped to hide or expose the misconduct.

People have a choice. They can choose to act ethically or unethically. Even a choice not to act carries ethical implications. When top officials at Enron chose to misrepresent financial data, some employees remained silent. As a result, thousands of employees lost their retirement funds. Enron crashed, its stock plummeted, officials were indicted, and court trials began. When people lack the character to stand up for the ethical codes that define them, the consequences are far-reaching.

Use the Code of Ethics worksheet on the Data CD to see how Jeoffrey follows STC's code of ethics on his job.

ENRICH

Have students create a bulletin board using the STC code of ethics. Or, have them create their own "life" code. Let students decide whether to share their "life" code with classmates. Students also can list consequences if their "life" code is violated.

Use the Code of Ethics worksheet on the IRCD to help students see specifically how Jeoffrey follows STC's code of ethics on his job.

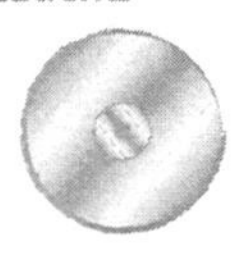

ETHICS FOR TECHNICAL COMMUNICATORS

The Society for Technical Communicators (STC), an organization dedicated to advancing the technical communication profession, has adopted a code of ethics for its members. Read the code in Figure 1.5, written specifically for technical communicators. In the example that follows the figure, see how Jeoffrey Bolushi follows this code on the job.

Legality We observe the laws and regulations governing our profession. We meet the terms of contracts we undertake. We ensure that all terms are consistent with laws and regulations locally and globally, as applicable, and with STC ethical principles.

Honesty We seek to promote the public good in our activities. To the best of our ability, we provide truthful and accurate communications. We also dedicate ourselves to conciseness, clarity, coherence, and creativity, striving to meet the needs of those who use our products and services. We alert our clients and employers when we believe that material is ambiguous. Before using another person's work, we obtain permission. We attribute authorship of material and ideas only to those who make an original and substantive contribution. We do not perform work outside our job scope during hours compensated by clients or employers, except with their permission; nor do we use their facilities, equipment, or supplies without their approval. When we advertise our services, we do so truthfully.

Confidentiality We respect the confidentiality of our clients, employers, and professional organizations. We disclose business-sensitive information only with their consent or when legally required to do so. We obtain releases from clients and employers before including any business-sensitive materials in our portfolios or commercial demonstrations or before using such materials for another client or employer.

Quality We endeavor to produce excellence in our communication products. We negotiate realistic agreements with clients and employers on schedules, budgets, and deliverables during project planning. Then we strive to fulfill our obligations in a timely, responsible manner.

Fairness We respect cultural variety and other aspects of diversity in our clients, employers, development teams, and audiences. We serve the business interests of our clients and employers as long as they are consistent with the public good. Whenever possible, we avoid conflicts of interest in fulfilling our professional responsibilities and activities. If we discern a conflict of interest, we disclose it to those concerned and obtain their approval before proceeding.

Professionalism We evaluate communication products and services constructively and tactfully, and seek definitive assessments of our own professional performance. We advance technical communication through our integrity and excellence in performing each task we undertake. Additionally, we assist other persons in our profession through mentoring, networking, and instruction. We also pursue professional self-improvement, especially through courses and conferences.

Adopted by the STC Board of Directors, September 1998

Used with permission from the Society for Technical Communication, Arlington, Virginia.

Figure 1.5 Ethical Principles for Technical Communicators

Jeoffrey Bolushi is an English instructor with credentials in technical communication. He is a freelance writer for Fontaine Powerboat Company's sales catalog. Jeoffrey often faces ethical dilemmas, but if he follows the principles of the STC code, he will meet his legal obligations.

On the news, he hears that the fire extinguisher he described in last week's draft has been recalled. He calls the executives at Fontaine to make sure they know about the product recall and then honors suggestions not to include the extinguishers in the catalog until Fontaine resolves the matter. He will meet his deadlines and will make sure the products he describes, such as floatation devices, meet safety standards.

Jeoffrey describes products honestly. He writes and rewrites—even simple catalog descriptions—to be concise and accurate, double-checking measurements for marine batteries so the company does not misrepresent their size and strength. When a Fontaine yacht wins second place at a national boat show, Jeoffrey is careful to quote the exact wording of the award and does not attempt to cover up the second-place rating. He obtains written permission from the customer who agreed to be quoted in the catalog. He works on the catalog only at night or on weekends, careful not to spend time at school on this project. He uses his own computer and e-mail service for the catalog. After the catalog has gone to print, Jeoffrey discovers a pricing error and calls the printer to stop production until he can send the correction.

Jeoffrey keeps Fontaine's business practices confidential. He does not disclose the prices of products to his friends, even though he knows what the markup is for every item. As an incentive to get customers to look through the catalog, the company inserts trivia quizzes whose answers are found throughout the catalog. Correct answers carry discounts on products, but Jeoffrey does not tell his brother, a boating enthusiast, where the answers are. When Wan Lee Shirt Factory wants to hire Jeoffrey to write a similar catalog, Jeoffrey asks permission from Fontaine to show Wan Lee the catalog he wrote for Fontaine.

Because Jeoffrey helps the company produce a catalog with concise and accurate descriptions, the company exceeds sales quotas for the year. With the increase in sales comes a bonus for Jeoffrey and the satisfaction of knowing that folks are enjoying the waterways. When IRS auditors ask to see pricing records, the catalog is submitted as evidence of fair sales.

As you can see, Jeoffrey does more than simply describe boats, motors, lights, and flotation devices. He creates the link between customers and sales representatives, IRS auditors and company owners, corporate returns and public safety. In short, he is the guardian of a company's reputation: his catalog is the face the company wears for its mail-ordering public.

ONGOING ASSESSMENT
Stop and Think
Principles may include the following: technical communicators are the bridge between those who create ideas and those who use them; technical information must be communicated truthfully, clearly, and economically; all laws and terms should be consistent with STC principles; technical communicators are fair, professional, and honest at all times.

What specific responsibilities do the "Ethical Principles" assign to a technical communicator?

TEACHING RESOURCES
IRCD
Chapter Activities, Ch. 1
Work Is A Zoo!, Ch. 1
PowerPoint® slides, Ch. 1
Exam*View*®, Ch. 1
techwriting.swlearning.com, Ch. 1

CLOSE
Summary
Use the summary to highlight the important points in the chapter. Ask students to write a brief document summarizing the points they thought were the most important. Have them use headings, special features, bullets, and so on.

Chapter 1 Review

SUMMARY

1. You have probably already used technical writing if you've given someone directions, written a recipe, or explained closing procedures at work.
2. Readers use technical writing to get information, make a decision, or complete a task. Not every piece of technical communication is a written document; technical communication also can be an oral presentation.
3. Technical writing is critical in the workplace. Writing effectively improves your chances of being hired and promoted.
4. Technical writing is required in all professions.
5. Technical writing exhibits the following characteristics: subject—technical, factual; audience—carefully considered; organization—predictable, apparent; special features—visual elements; style—concise, direct, specialized vocabulary; tone—objective, businesslike.
6. Technical writing differs from traditional academic writing in its presentation, approach to subject matter, and audience. Technical writing differs from imaginative writing in its "one-meaning-and-one-meaning-only" presentation.
7. Ethics is a system of moral standards and rules that guide human behavior. Ethical conduct is important in the workplace—so important that ethical standards are protected by the legal system.
8. The Society for Technical Communication has adopted the Ethical Principles for Technical Communicators, a code of ethics to guide the behavior of its members. The principles address the communicator's responsibility to respect the law, promote public good, protect the confidentiality of clients, produce top-quality writing, keep business dealings fair, and improve skills.

CLOSE
Checklist
Use the checklist as a review tool for students. Divide the class into two groups. Ask each group to work together to answer the questions in the checklist. Give each group five minutes. When the time is up, designate two students from each group to write the answers on the board. See the Chapter 1 Review on the IRCD for suggested answers to the checklist.

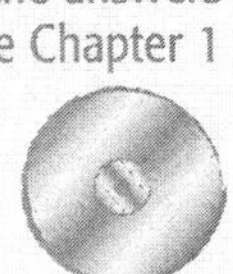

Checklist

- Can I define technical writing?
- Can I list the characteristics of technical writing?
- Can I give examples of technical writing in the workplace?
- Can I list ways technical writing differs from academic and imaginative writing?
- Can I list ways technical writing is similar to academic writing?
- Can I define ethics?
- Can I explain why ethics is important in the workplace?
- Can I give an example of how ethics is used in the workplace?
- Can I explain the Ethical Principles for Technical Communicators adopted by the Society for Technical Communication?

Build On What You Know

1. What characteristics does technical writing share with other writing?
2. Which of these subjects would most likely be written about in a technical style? Which of these subjects would most likely be written about in an academic style?

a sunset	homelessness	a first car
electric circuits	graduation	a wedding
a computer screen	a close friend	flowers

3. Which of the statements below would you expect to come from a technical writing document? Which would come from imaginative literature? How can you tell? What are your clues?
   a. My memory of her will never fade; she brought music into my life.
   b. There are two types of computer RAM (random access memory): static RAM and dynamic RAM.
   c. Most intriguing is the adaption of Corvette Z52 calipers to the car.
   d. The mist peeked over the marshland.
   e. Once upon a time, there was a princess who ruled a great country.
   f. The video output stage simply provides the voltage amplication and driving power for the cathode-ray tube and accepts the vertical and horizontal blanking signals.
4. Find a piece of technical writing (or any kind of writing) that you think is ineffective. Write a brief analysis of the writing, focusing on the characteristics that make it ineffective. Then analyze a piece of writing that you believe is effective. Compare the two pieces of writing for subject, audience, organization, style, tone, and special features.
5. In groups, discuss the ethical dilemma in the following situations.
   a. You are the owner of Fresh Air, an air-conditioner repair company. You have recently learned that your most requested air conditioner repairperson lets Freon® escape into the air (an illegal activity).
   b. You are making $60,000 a year at Weller Pharmaceuticals. You have just heard a rumor that an expensive anticancer drug produced by the company is ineffective; in fact, the drug weakened the immune system of patients who have used it. Your company has invested $2 million in developing the drug and must continue sales for another year just to recover the costs.
6. Juan is hoping to get a promotion and a raise next month. His manager asks him to report on Mark's efforts. Mark is Juan's coworker, who happened to apply for the same promotion as Juan. Even though Mark has handled projects well, Juan does not want him to look too good in the eyes of his manager. Juan tells his manager that Mark missed some deadlines and disappointed some clients. Did Juan act ethically? List possible consequences of Juan's behavior.

ASSESS

Build On What You Know

1. All writing follows principles of unity, coherence, standard usage, and correct grammar and mechanics.
2. **Technical:** electric circuits and a computer screen; **academic:** a sunset, homelessness, graduation, a close friend, first car, a wedding, and flowers.

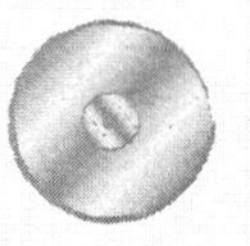

See the Build On What You Know worksheet on the IRCD for an additional activity.

3. **Technical:** b. (RAM); c. (Corvette, Z52); f. (output stage, voltage amplication, cathode-ray tube) **Imaginative:** a. (memory, music); d. (mist peeked); e. (Once upon a time, princess)
4. Use this activity to point out characteristics of effective and ineffective writing.
5. **a.** Releasing Freon® directly into the air is a violation of ethics because it is not consistent with regulations, and it does not promote the public good. **b.** The company also is violating ethics because its actions are not consistent with regulations, and the company does not promote the public good.
6. Juan did not act ethically because he was dishonest. Possible consequences: Mark and Juan's manager would learn the truth, which could hurt Juan's career; Juan could get passed over for future promotions, fired, or prevented from finding another job.

ASSESS

Apply What You Learned

7. Use this question to personalize a discussion about technical writing careers.
8. Students can view the additional web sites in the web links directory on techwriting.swlearning.com.
9. Answers include headings, concise diction, graphics, lists, boldface type, white space, and so on.
10. Reinforce to students that all careers use some type of writing.
11. Use this activity to illustrate that all professions rely on technical writing in some way.
12. Use this question to point out the significance of technical communication at work.

13–14. Use the Apply What You Learned worksheet on the IRCD to guide students through questions. Students can share their findings and their samples of writing.

13–14. Use the Apply What You Learned worksheet on the Data CD for examples of sample questions.

Apply What You Learned

7. Do you think you will make a good technical writer? Why or why not? What skills do you think you need to improve your technical writing? How do you think you can acquire those skills?
8. Conduct an Internet search for the keywords *technical writing, technical editing,* and *technical communication.* Write a summary of your findings and share your summary with the class.
9. Read an article in your favorite magazine or textbook. Choose three technical writing features. How do those features make the writing easy to read?
10. Write a short report describing the writing skills that are required in three of the following careers. You may need to research some of the job titles to learn the kinds of writing the jobs require. Or choose three careers that interest you and write a short report describing the writing skills those careers require.

Computer Software Engineer	Desktop Publisher	Physical Therapist
Database Administrator	Medical Assistant	Audiologist
Personal and Home Care Aide	Research Scientist	Veterinary Technologist
Reference Librarian	Accountant	Real Estate Agent
Acquisitions Editor	Electrical Technician	Interior Designer
Food Service Aide	Project Manager	Purchasing Agent

11. Find an example of technical writing written by someone who holds a job you might like to have someday. Ask a family member, friend, or employer for an example or search the Internet. Explain the purpose of the example and the way the author used technical writing characteristics to achieve the purpose.
12. Watch the local news and read your local newspaper to find a news story that reports a breach of ethics by a company, an employee, a sports figure, or a politician. Bring the story to class. In small groups, discuss the consequences to the company or the consequences to the individual under scrutiny.
13. Interview a businessperson about his or her technical writing on the job. What types of documents does this person write most often? Ask if you may bring a sample of the writing to class.
14. Ask a technician or scientist about his or her technical writing on the job. Ask whether a mistake has ever been made as a result of imprecise reporting.

Work Is A Zoo!

Several months ago you were hired as a marketing and public relations assistant at the regional zoo. You enjoy the work, especially because it combines two of your life interests—wildlife conservation and marketing.

Your newest project is ZiPS (Zoo in Partnership with Science), an outreach program that targets science instructors. Soon ZiPS will kick off with a children's contest in which contestants draw and submit a logo for the petting zoo. Other parts of the program are still in the planning stages.

Anya Erhard heads the public relations division in the marketing department. Anya has helped orient you to working at the zoo. You also work with Tyrone Johnston, the other full-time public relations person.

When Anya was explaining her work, she said, "You'll never believe how much writing I do here!" She went on to tell you that she communicates with coworkers through e-mail, phone calls, and even informal conversations at lunch. Anya also writes letters, reports, and proposals to the zoo board and to local instructors.

She offered some advice: "A few weeks ago I wrote to some science instructors and told them that we use learning technologies in our programs. I was talking about computers and multimedia tools, but some of them thought I meant coming to the zoo to watch TV! Make sure you think out your message ahead of time—it is a big part of being a success here!"

It is now June, a busy time at the zoo. To keep track of all that is going on, you create a checklist of upcoming assignments for your new job.

Use the Work Is A Zoo! activity checklist on the Data CD to help you start planning your assignments.

WORK IS A ZOO

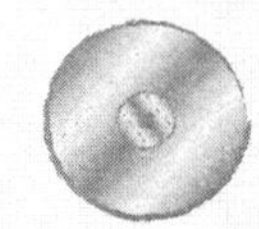

Each chapter in *Technical Writing for Success* uses the ZiPS case study. Each installment of the case study involves a writing assignment related to the current chapter. The assignments and worksheets are on the IRCD.

For the first assignment, students become familiar with the Work Is A Zoo! activity checklist on the IRCD. Explain to students that they will be keeping track of their Work Is A Zoo! activities on this checklist. At the end of the semester, they will submit all of their Work Is A Zoo! activities to you in a portfolio.

TECHNICAL RESEARCH

GOALS

DISTINGUISH the differences between researching at school and at work

IDENTIFY and locate secondary sources

DOCUMENT secondary sources

EVALUATE and TAKE notes from sources

COLLECT primary data

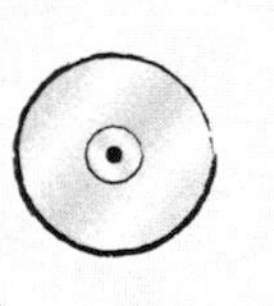

See the Data CD for Write-to-Learn and In The Know activity worksheets.

TEACHING RESOURCES

IRCD
- Lesson Plans, Ch. 3
- Chapter Activities, Ch. 3
- PowerPoint® Slides, Ch. 3
- Sample Documents, Ch. 3

techwriting.swlearning.com, Ch. 3
ExamView®, Ch. 3

CHAPTER OVERVIEW

Explains the need for research in the workplace and shows how to locate, document, evaluate, and take notes from secondary sources as well as how to collect primary data.

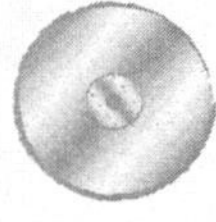

See the IRCD for Write-to-Learn and In The Know activity worksheets.

WRITE-TO-LEARN

Think about a time when you researched a topic. What was the reason for your research? What did researching the topic involve? In other words, how did you conduct the research? Did your research include a survey, an experiment, or an interview? What did you learn from your research activities?

In The Know

archives collections or repositories of documents

citations written indications of the sources for borrowed materials

close-ended questions questions that restrict the number of possible answers

direct quotation the use of borrowed ideas, words, phrases, and sentences exactly as they appear in the original source

documentation a system of giving credit for borrowed ideas and words

open-ended questions questions that encourage the respondent to provide any answer he or she likes; the questions give no suggested answers

paraphrase presenting someone else's ideas in your own words, phrases, and sentence structure

periodicals materials published at specified intervals of time, such as magazines, journals, newsletters, and newspapers

plagiarism the act of using another person's words and/or ideas without properly documenting or giving credit

population the group from whom you want to gather data

primary sources direct or firsthand reports of facts or observations, such as an eyewitness account or a diary

reliable data provides results that can be duplicated under similar circumstances

respondents people chosen to answer questions

sample a subgroup with the same characteristics as the entire population

secondary sources indirect or secondhand reports of information, such as the description of an event the writer or speaker did not witness

summarize to condense longer material, keeping essential or main ideas and omitting unnecessary parts, such as examples and illustrations

valid data provides an accurate measurement of what you intend to measure

Writing@Work

Selam Daniel is a product research engineer at Procter & Gamble in Cincinnati, Ohio. In her position as product research engineer, she acts as the link between the consumer and the technology.

Selam's research is focused on understanding more about what consumers want, need, and believe. Her job is to link what she learns about consumers to Procter & Gamble's technical capabilities so that P&G can better meet the needs of its consumers. As a result of Selam's research, Procter & Gamble should be better able to understand its consumers and therefore develop products to meet consumers' needs, resulting in more sales than the competition.

In her position, Selam must write many documents for claims support. In its marketing communications, P&G makes claims to consumers about product benefits. All claims must be backed by consumer and technical data. Consumer data determines whether the claim is meaningful to the consumer. Technical data must prove that products can technically deliver what they claim to deliver. These documents must be able to answer any challenges raised by competitors.

Selam's documents must be well written and contain solid information. At times, a competitor's challenge may be taken to court. In these instances, it is imperative that Selam's research be thorough and her reports be well written and understandable. If Selam's reports are not solid and her information not properly documented, Procter & Gamble may lose the challenge. A lot rides on the depth of her research, but also on her ability to accurately communicate that research in her reports. P&G relies on Selam to be able to communicate effectively through her writing and to appropriately report the sources of her information.

Selam has a bachelor's degree in chemical engineering and a bachelor's degree in marketing, both from Massachusetts Institute of Technology. "In my engineering degree I learned the science, but my marketing degree was where I learned to make the data meaningful to the consumer and other nontechnical audiences," Selam explains.

APPLY

Writing@Work

Use the Writing@Work feature to point out the importance of thorough, accurate research on the job. Have students think of results that might occur if Selam's writing is not accurate and thoroughly researched, or if it does not keep the consumer/audience in mind. Some results might include lawsuits being filed over inaccurate information, competition winning over consumers because of inaccurate consumer descriptions, and products failing to deliver as promised in the claims support documents.

Working Bibliography

Alika, Rachel, and Andrew M. Dalton. "Bacteria: The Good, the Bad, and the Uncertain." *Raleigh News and Observer* 23 Oct. 1980, east. ed.: A1 +

Berlin, Robert E., and Catherine C. Stanton. *Radioactive Waste Management.* New York: Wiley, 1989.

Kapsner, Jake. "Researchers Develop Munching Bacteria." *The Minnesota Daily Online* 21 Oct. 1998. 26 June 2003 <http://www.mndaily.com/daily/1998/10/21/news/>

Schrempf, Rosalind. "World's Toughest Bacterium Has a Taste for Waste." *Energy Research News* Aug. 1998. 12 June 2003 <http://www.pln.gov/08_98?art2.htm>

"Witches' Brew of Weird Bugs." *Frontiers: The Electronic Newsletter of the National Science Foundation* Oct. 1996: 7 June 2003 <http://www.nsf.gov/od/lpa/news/publicat/frontier/>

Yarrow, Houston. "Re: Questions on Medical Waste Management, Radiation." E-mail to the author. 24 May 2003 <http://www.nsf.gov/od/lpa/news/publicat/frontier/>

Figure 3.1 Working Bibliography Model

RESEARCHING AT WORK

Employees rely on information they collect to solve problems, make decisions, answer questions, and perform many other work functions. On the job, research is usually involved in all of these situations (and more):

- Developing a new product
- Handling a production problem
- Purchasing equipment or services
- Establishing safety procedures
- Selecting employee benefits
- Planning an advertising campaign
- Expanding a market area

Unlike writing for school, writing on the job provides information to help the business operate effectively, not to show the writer's knowledge of the topic.

For example, if a nurse writes a fact sheet explaining how patients should manage their diabetes, the nurse is not writing to show how much he knows about the subject, but to teach patients how to stay healthy. If a chef creates standard operating procedures, the chef does not write the document to impress readers with how much she learned in school, but rather to ensure food safety. All of the information writers and researchers gather and present is used for effective job performance.

Before you can write at work, you often need to conduct research. In fact, many decisions and actions at work require more information than you have at hand. You probably begin by determining what you already know. Then, considering your audience, purpose, and scope, you gather and evaluate new information and probably form conclusions about the material you read. Before you conduct the research, you must make sure you know who,

WARM UP

Recall research tasks you may have done in a work setting. For each task, what was the purpose of the research? How was the workplace research different from research you have done for pleasure or at school? For example, how is researching the best solution for a Japanese beetle infestation in a lawn you are managing for a client different from finding more information about your favorite entertainer?

FOCUS

Warm Up

Use Warm Up to help students realize that they have a great deal of experience with research, even if it is as simple as finding tips on how to win favorite video games or learning the latest exploits of a rap star.

After finding comfort in their experiences, students can compare situations in which they were self-motivated to conduct research to the more highly pressured situations of work, such as choosing the most nutritious snack food for children or finding a reasonably priced herbicide for treating poison ivy that will not harm the family dog.

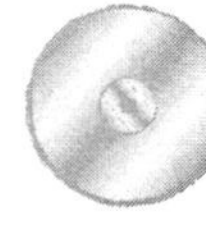

Show the Works Cited Transparency on the IRCD.

what, where, when, why, and how. For example, who is involved and who will use your research? What do they need to know? Where will you search for information, within or outside your organization? Why are you researching this topic? How will you collect information, and how will it be used? You also need a strategy for:

- Finding and evaluating the right material and the best sources.
- Conducting the research and reading efficiently.
- Carefully and accurately recording the information you find so you do not accidentally violate the owner's copyright.
- Documenting where you found the information so you or someone else can find it again.

Researchers may find some data easily, as in production figures that are readily available on the corporate network. Sometimes, though, they must search extensively for information.

Employees have two basic sources of information: secondary sources and primary sources. **Secondary sources** are reports or accounts of what someone else sees, hears, or thinks. When a newspaper reporter describes what executives of a closing textile plant said, that description is a secondary source. **Primary sources,** on the other hand, are direct or firsthand presentations of facts or observations. The writer or speaker is the one who witnessed the event or developed the idea.

© DIGITAL VISION

For example, a diary is a firsthand account of the writer's experiences and is, therefore, a primary source. However, if you use ideas from another person's diary in a report on healthy lifestyles, the borrowed ideas become secondary data in your report because you did not experience or observe them yourself.

Likewise, hearing the company president, rather than the reporter, give reasons for the plant's closing is primary information.

Researchers generally start with secondary sources because they often give general overviews and offer good background information. Secondary sources are usually easier and less expensive to consult than primary sources. The overviews these sources can give help researchers understand what is already known about the topic. A problem solver may even learn that someone has already discovered a solution.

How is researching at work different from researching at school? Why do professionals conduct research?

ENRICH

Ask professionals involved in research to share their experiences and insights with your students. Examples include people in research and development departments, public relations workers, grant writers, and personnel officers.

Take students to the library and demonstrate the almost limitless possibilities of electronic data collection.

ONGOING ASSESSMENT

Stop and Think

Use Stop and Think questions to review differences between academic and work-related research and reasons professionals search for information.

FINDING SECONDARY DATA

To solve most problems, your first step is to explore the available secondary data. After all, you do not want to reinvent the wheel. If the answer already exists, you do not need to spend time, effort, and money to rediscover it.

For work-related research, you will probably use one or more of the following sources of secondary data: your organization's correspondence and report **archives,** a library catalog, periodicals, and general reference materials. While these secondary data sources may be available in print or hard copy, most will be available in print and electronically.

CORRESPONDENCE AND REPORT ARCHIVES

A logical place to begin looking for an answer to a problem is in the organization where the problem occurs. Most organizations keep archives of all correspondence and reports. Especially in large organizations, archives are generally maintained in an electronic format, such as on computer disks or CDs.

On the other hand, some highly regulated organizations, such as pharmaceutical companies, may be required to keep print as well as electronic copies of essential information. Employees may use archived documents to learn about the history of the problem or topic. They may find letters, memos, or reports explaining when problems were first noted; what kind of investigation was conducted; and whether the solution was successful.

When the research topic does not have a history, relevant facts and statistics may be found in a variety of sources within the organization's records.

WARM UP

As a new sales representative, you are going to Japan to meet your first prospective customer. If you know little about Japanese people and customs, where can you go to find out whether you should take the customer a gift and what is a good choice if you do take a gift? List several things you need to know and where you think you can find the information.

FOCUS

Warm Up

Use the Warm Up to explore what students already know about research.

Students will probably begin by saying that they would ask a Japanese friend or a person who is well traveled to explain customs, etiquette, and business practices. Beyond asking someone, students should be aware that what they are seeking is general background knowledge that they can find online or in library sources.

ENRICH

To convince students that libraries can be fun and exciting places to spend time, develop a scavenger hunt for specific information. Select facts, statistics, quotations, and graphics relating to the students' potential career fields.

TEACH

As students explore potential sources, remind them that no resource for research is more helpful than their own ability to think critically.

If an employee at a boat manufacturer is asked to find out why one component of the boat is reported to be defective more than any other, the employee might search company records first to see if any problems were identified in the production process or with parts purchased from certain vendors. If no answer is found within the company records, the employee might search electronic databases, the Internet, and external libraries.

LIBRARY CATALOG

The researcher's next stop is either the company's library or a public or school library. Some large businesses have an in-house library that contains specialized materials relating to the business it serves. In addition to company-produced reports such as production figures, accident reports, and personnel information, these internal libraries typically hold materials employees need to stay current in the field in which they work. A software company's library probably contains books and journals specializing in software development and marketing. Since these company libraries focus specifically on the needs of employees, they do not compete with public or other libraries by carrying all types of reading and research materials. They often contain more electronic than paper resources. If no in-house library is available to the problem solvers, they must go to a school, municipal, or regional library.

Whether in an internal or public library, employees looking for secondary data find materials through the library catalog. The library catalog will help you find books, pamphlets, periodicals, audiovisual materials, and other holdings. Most libraries have computerized catalogs that are searchable by subject, title, author, and sometimes other categories, such as date or keyword.

After the user types the author's name, a title, or a subject, the online catalog displays a list of sources and their locations. Since materials are usually cataloged using authorized subject headings from *The Library of Congress Subject Headings*, using keywords found in this reference can make a search more effective. If a search yields one book with useful information, a new search using the keywords found in that book's entry will likely produce other useful sources. Most catalog systems also print requested entries. Generally, libraries have integrated systems so the online catalog can tell where a book is located and whether it is checked out.

If a researcher finds that a particular book is not in the library, the researcher may request that the book be ordered from another library through interlibrary loan. The book also may be found online through a service such as NetLibrary, which offers scanned electronic books.

Most online catalogs are user-friendly, but you should not hesitate to ask a librarian for help. Librarians can explain how to use the equipment, what the standard subject headings are, and how to search so you find what you need quickly and efficiently. Remember that the catalog will lead you to sources for background and in-depth information. For more recent data, use periodicals or Internet sources.

PERIODICALS

Magazines, journals, newsletters, and newspapers are called **periodicals** because they are published at specified intervals of time. (Journals are magazines that are published for a scholarly or academic audience.) When you need current information, periodicals, whether online or in print, are one type of source you should seek. All periodicals are more current than books, but newspapers, especially daily papers, provide even more current information than periodicals. In addition, many periodicals, such as *Newsweek* and *The New York Times,* are now published on the Internet and in print.

The next question is how to find the articles you need in the periodicals. Library catalogs will tell you what print periodicals the library holds in different subject areas, but to find specific articles, you need to search an index or a database.

In the past, indexes, printed on paper and bound as books or magazines, were time-consuming to use. Today most periodical searches are conducted electronically. Many web-based databases, available to libraries by subscription, index periodicals. SIRS, Gale, EbscoHost, ProQuest, and Elsevier are some of the best-known database providers. Some of the databases, such as Lexis-Nexis and Academic Universe (the academic version of Lexis-Nexis), are general; others are type-specific, such as SIRS, which includes publications dealing with the social sciences. In addition, some databases, such as Wall Street Journal Index and New York Times Index, specialize in newspapers.

You can access other indexes through a service provider such as OCLC (Online Computer Library Center, Inc.). For example, World Cat is an OCLC index of physical holdings (recordings, tapes, books, papers, and dissertations).

GENERAL REFERENCE MATERIALS

General reference materials such as encyclopedias, dictionaries, handbooks, almanacs, and fact books are quick ways to get information. Many users rely on easy access to general reference sources for background information. They may first check those available online, such as Grolier Online Encyclopedia or Merriam-Webster Online.

Some web sites even offer access to reference tools. For example, the Encyclopedia Britannica web site provides an encyclopedia, a dictionary, and an atlas. Also, the Bartleby Books site gives users access to several reference tools, including dictionaries, thesauruses, fact books, and books of quotations. Some materials are available on CD-ROM, such as Encarta, another encyclopedia.

Reference materials come in general interest versions. Some examples include *World Book Encyclopedia, Encyclopedia Britannica,* and *Webster's Dictionary.* Others are special interest versions, such as *Encyclopedia of Space Science and Technology (2003)* and *The American Heritage Stedman's Medical Dictionary (2002).* In addition, *The Encyclopedia of Educational Technology,* a web site created and maintained by San Diego State University, covers performance, training, and instructional design and technology.

ELECTRONIC RESOURCES

In addition to periodical databases, indexes, and online general reference materials such as encyclopedias and dictionaries, computers provide a wealth of information on countless topics. Because the Internet (also known as the World Wide Web, or simply the Web) is a worldwide collection of computer networks, it is an information highway connecting

When you go to the library, you may have access not only to that physical library, but also to thousands of other libraries throughout the world. World Cat, an Online Computer Library Center, Inc. (OCLC) service provider, links you through your library to the collections of more than 24,000 member libraries of OCLC. With this service you have access to more than 36 million records for books, manuscript collections, audiovisual materials, and countless computer files in a variety of languages.

COMMUNICATION UPDATE

Give students a current topic, something that happened within the last two weeks. Ask them to find at least two sources on the topic. They should read the two sources and develop notes to use in an informal oral report to the class. The sources will most likely be newspapers or other periodicals.

ENRICH
If your school has technology experts (a computer club, librarians who specialize in electronic services, computer teachers, or a resident Internet wizard), invite one of them to speak to your class about the wonders of electronic information.

government, military, educational, and commercial organizations and private citizens to a range of services and resources. Therefore, you can get information from a huge variety of sources over the Internet.

Users with access to local area networks (LAN) or to the Web may participate in bulletin boards, e-mail, listservs, and other means of exchanging information. If, for example, someone had problems with a particular car and was not able to resolve the issue with the car dealer, the car owner could retrieve consumer information from the manufacturer, advocacy groups, legal professionals, and other consumers online.

Finding Electronic Information How does a researcher get to the tremendous amount of information on the Internet? You can search the Web using a search engine such as Yahoo, Google, AltaVista, HotBot, Excite, and MetaCrawler in much the same way you search a database, using keywords and topics.

However, search engines do not look through all of the information on the Web. Each engine searches through only a portion of all of the sites. Even the metasearch engines, such as Momma and Metacrawler, do not cover the entire Web.

Even though search engines cover only a portion of the Web, the concern often is how to filter through so much information to find what is useful. Search engines use "spiders" to go out periodically and view web pages and links within sites; an "index" that catalogs words, Internet addresses, and other information about the pages the spider finds; and software to filter through all of the pages in the index to find matches when a search is requested. Since the "spider" goes out every few days or weeks, it detects changes made in web pages. However, until the information has been indexed, it is not available for researchers.

Because each search engine visits and indexes different sites and is updated at different times, you should routinely use at least three search engines. Then compare the results of your searches to determine which search engines are most effective.

Searching with Keywords Choose specific, precise keywords; then consider using the advanced or custom (terms may vary with search engines) search procedures to refine your search. The guidelines within the custom search or the Help section of the search engine should explain how to use logic or keyword connectors to limit or expand your search. The connectors listed below are typical.

TO LIMIT A SEARCH:

When you connect keywords with ...	the search yields sites containing ...
AND or +	both keywords
Example: juvenile AND diabetes	Sites that deal with juvenile diabetes
NOT or –	the first keyword, not the second
Example: diabetes-juvenile diabetes except juvenile	sites that deal with any type of
"keyword keyword" beside each other	the same keywords in the same order
Example: "capital punishment"	the same phrase

TO EXPAND A SEARCH:

OR	either keyword
Example: diabetes OR juvenile	diabetes and/or juvenile as the topic
Key* (wildcard)	the base or root within a word
Example: biblio* bibliophile, bibliotheca	bibliography, bibliographer,

Remember that you can get the same data in many different ways. One researcher may find an article by skimming a journal from the library shelf. Another researcher may do an online search in the library or on a home or office computer. Another may find a link to an online journal in a discussion group. Explore the many tools available to you for research.

Using the list you drafted in the Warm Up, underline the information that would come from secondary sources. For those underlined items, add any other sources or methods you can think of for accessing information.

ONGOING ASSESSMENT
Stop and Think
Use Stop and Think to check comprehension. If students understand the definition of secondary sources, they should be able to identify the secondary sources in their own list.

WARM UP

Has someone else, intentionally or accidentally, received credit for your ideas or work? If so, how did you feel? If not, imagine how you might feel.

FOCUS

Warm Up

Assign a brief journal-writing exercise based on the Warm Up. Through the writing, students who may have seen documentation as unnecessary busywork will be open to the role of ethics. Ethics is a critical issue in documentation. Being responsible and careful is important not only to English instructors, but also to coworkers.

Another way to use the Warm Up is to assign small groups to explore the questions relating to the cost of poor documentation. You may ask the groups to share their work orally, or you may require written notes.

Answers may include lawsuits for copyright violations, job dismissal, lost time in repeating work and research already performed, lost confidence in researchers who are sloppy or dishonest, lost knowledge, ruined relationships between colleagues in a field, and bad decisions based on inaccurate reporting.

DOCUMENTING SECONDARY SOURCES

Documentation is a way of giving credit to another person (writer or speaker) for his or her work; it is using a citation system to note whose ideas or words the writer is using and where he or she found them. Responsible writers document ideas and materials they borrow or use.

Plagiarism is the term used at school for the act of using another person's words and ideas without giving credit. While plagiarism is a serious academic offense, sometimes causing students to fail a course or to be expelled from school, it is even more serious in the workplace. Theft of another's work often results in lost jobs, lawsuits, and ruined reputations.

In the musical version of plagiarism, members of the singing group Milli Vanilli actually were lip-syncing, rather than singing, their songs. When the public discovered the singers' deception, their careers were over.

Likewise, Doris Kearns Goodwin, a respected historian who won the Pulitzer Prize for History in 1995, taught and served on the Board of Overseers at Harvard, assisted President Lyndon Johnson with his memoirs, and won many awards, admitted to plagiarism in a book she wrote in 1987.

Despite a long career with many achievements and honors, this admission caused Goodwin to be ridiculed in public, scorned by her peers, and subjected to significant financial loss. The University of Delaware withdrew its invitation to her to make a graduation speech; PBS placed her on indefinite leave from the Jim Lehrer news show; she had to defend the credibility of all of her other books; and her publisher had to pay Lynn McTaggert, the author of the book from which Goodwin had extensively plagiarized. As you can see, plagiarism, intentional or accidental, can be damaging.

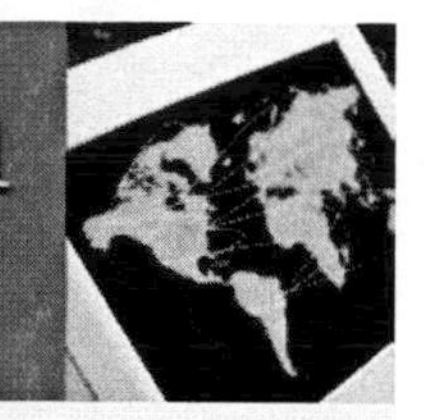

Communication Dilemma

You and your good friend Armando work for a desktop publishing company that creates marketing materials for bands giving concerts in your area. Your job is to contact the bands, design the posters and other marketing materials, and publish and distribute the materials. You have recently learned that you and Armando know the band members who are coming to your town to give a concert. In fact, you know the band members so well that you have copies of some of their unpublished songs they have written that they shared with you before they became famous.

Armando is in charge of creating the marketing materials for the band. When you look over the finished products, you notice he included parts of the unpublished songs as a way to lure fans to the concert. You feel uneasy about publishing these, but you know that you cannot reach the band members to ask permission because they are in Europe touring for a month before coming to town.

1. If you and Armando publish the songs, are you breaking copyright laws?
2. How can you find out?

COMMUNICATION DILEMMA

Explain to students that all writing is copyrighted as soon as it is drafted, even if the writer has not gone through the legal process of copyrighting or whether the document does not include copyright notation or the copyright symbol.

Note that copyright owners may charge fees or restrict use when giving permission for materials to be used.

Explain *public domain:* Works created by or for the U.S. government and works with expired copyrights are examples of materials in the public domain. Furthermore, writers may choose to make their works available by placing them in public domain.

You may ask, "What exactly do I document?" You document anything you use from another person's work. Remember, if you do not document, you are no longer borrowing; you are stealing and will be treated as an intellectual property thief. Therefore, to keep your credibility, reputation, or job, document borrowed phrases, sentences, or ideas in the form of summaries, paraphrases, and direct quotations. For instance, if you reported on the environmental impact of a new soy ink for your company's publications division, you would document researched facts, contradictory statements, and unique ideas.

On the other hand, you do not need to document common knowledge or information your audience typically knows. Yet common knowledge may differ for each audience, particularly expert audiences. For instance, the fact that Bill Gates is chief executive officer of Microsoft Corporation is common knowledge for an audience of computer engineers. Gates's management philosophy might be common knowledge for business school graduates. If information is common knowledge for your target audience, you do not need to document it. The same information directed to a different audience may not be common knowledge and, therefore, would need to be documented.

The writer's field determines the documentation format. For example, Modern Language Association (MLA) format, most likely taught in your English class, is the documentation system used in the humanities. Other documentation systems include the American Psychological Association (APA) system for social sciences and the Council of Biology Editors (CBE) system for biological sciences.

TEACH

Tell students that they may see names other than *Bibliography,* such as *References, Citations,* or *Works Cited.*

SEE THE SITES

Give students keywords such as *quotations, documentation, proper names,* and *URLs.* Have each student look up a word on the Chicago Manual of Style web site and report what they find.

Have students browse and listen to the radio programs on the MLA site. Have them pick a topic and give a report on what they hear.

© DIGITAL VISION

Although the University of Chicago Press online edition does not replace the book edition of the *Chicago Manual of Style,* you can still get information on how to cite books, electronic resources, journals, and newspapers.

The Modern Language Association (MLA) web site gives the history of MLA along with many book titles about the English language. You also can listen to archives of MLA radio programs.

You can find the url for both sites in the web links on techwriting.swlearning.com.

In addition, most fields have a style manual. A style manual is a book of rules for developing a document, including formatting and documentation. *The Chicago Manual of Style*, the stylebook of The University of Chicago Press, is the preferred style manual for many technical fields.

Since each documentation system has a particular format, consult your instructor (or employer) for the appropriate style manual. For example, if, as a human resources officer, you investigate the effectiveness of a test used to screen job applicants (a psychology-related topic), you will probably use American Psychological Association (APA) style. However, a report outlining the water quality of a prospective site for a trout farm (a biology-related topic) may require that you use Council of Biology Editors (CBE) style guidelines.

All documentation systems explain how to identify each source. However, the emphasis, order, and punctuation may be different. The APA and CBE, for instance, emphasize publication dates in citations because dates are critical in the sciences. The MLA emphasizes the author and location in the text. This book uses the MLA system.

Documentation comes in two parts: 1) the Works Cited (or Bibliography), or list of sources at the end of the document and 2) the internal citations. The documentation process begins with a working bibliography.

BIBLIOGRAPHY AND WORKS CITED

A bibliography (also called Works Cited in MLA) is a list of sources that you used. While collecting data, researchers develop a working bibliography. They continue to locate and add new sources to the list during the research process. Sometimes they delete a source from the list when they find a more recent or reliable one.

When the research is finished, writers use the list's final form to prepare a bibliography. A bibliography accomplishes three purposes: 1) it establishes credibility by showing readers what sources you consulted; 2) it allows others to find your information path so they can continue or evaluate the study; and 3) it gives credit to other people's thoughts, words, and sentences that you used.

As you look at secondary sources, you develop a paper or an electronic working bibliography. You can enter publication information for each source on a 3″3 5″ index card. Cards allow you to arrange entries easily for the final source list. However, many writers prefer to maintain bibliographic data electronically. Like the cards, computers allow you to easily add, delete, or move sources. In addition, software that automatically puts source information into MLA form is available. Hypertext programs show images of cards where users key bibliographic information.

After you complete the research and draft the document, you remove the sources you did not use. You place sources you did use in order. For MLA, use alphabetical order by the first author's last name or by the word that appears at the beginning of the entry, often a title if the author is not given. Other systems arrange sources differently. You will use the arranged cards to compose the Works Cited page, as shown in Figure 3.1. This page goes at the end of the document or report.

TEACH

Students may complain about the precise, detailed information required for bibliographic entries. The process of finding and correctly placing and punctuating all of the necessary information may bother them. If so, remind them that the style manual was developed to allow writers and researchers all over the world to communicate effectively, not to frustrate and annoy students. In other words, learning to create bibliographic entries is not busywork.

For each type of publication, such as newspapers, pamphlets, government documents, edited or translated books, e-mail, and listserv postings, MLA requires a unique bibliographic entry. For these variations, tell students to refer to the required style manual.

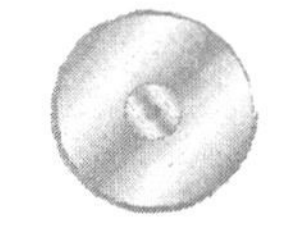

Show the Model Bibliography Cards Transparency on the IRCD.

Focus on Ethics

Another aspect of borrowing or using others' words and ideas involves copyright. Copyright legally protects the rights of writers and gives them a way to control how their work is used. Copyright applies only to tangible and original expression, not to oral presentations.

Using copyrighted work requires special considerations. If the way you plan to use someone's words or ideas fits the definition of fair use, then you may use the work without payment or permission. Yet you still must give credit to the creator. Fair use guidelines are special exceptions that allow others to use a portion of a writer's work in a limited way. Fair use evaluates the purpose and nature of the new use, the character of the copyrighted work, the percentage of the work being used, and the effect of the use on the original's marketability. Ultimately, fair use requires that the new user not damage the original or profit from its use.

When you are uncertain about whether to request copyright permission or to document a source, consult other writers, your supervisor or mentor at work, or others with experience in the field. If you are still in doubt, it is better to request permission and to document. No writer or professional has ruined a reputation or career for overdocumenting, but many have for lack of documentation.

FOCUS ON ETHICS

When discussing Focus on Ethics, generate a list of people in various work and academic situations students might consult.

INTERNAL CITATIONS

People will assume ideas are yours unless they see a citation in the text. **Citations** are written indications of the source of borrowed materials. Enter internal documentation immediately after each summary, paraphrase, and direct quotation to tell your reader where you found the information. Internal citations in MLA consist of the author's last name (or a shortened form of the title if no author is named) and the page number. If the author's name is mentioned in the introductory sentence, only the page numbers appear in the citation. Readers then use the author's name or the title to find the full bibliographic entry in the alphabetical listings of works cited. At the end of the sentence (or group of sentences) containing the source material in your document, place the citation. Enclose the citation in parentheses and place the period after the ending parenthesis, as shown in Figure 3.2.

TEACH

Use Figure 3.2 to show the connection between in-text documentation and bibliographic entries in the Works Cited at the end of the document. Point out, for example, that the parenthetical documentation for Amanda Spake's article in *U.S. News & World Report* tells readers the particular page on which the borrowed idea appears in the source.

For additional examples, refer to the Internal Citation and Works Cited Transparency and the Numbered Reference System Transparency on the IRCD.

ONGOING ASSESSMENT

Stop and Think

Use Stop and Think to encourage students to consider the consequences of incorrect and incomplete documentation. Ask students to interview a professional for case information, to research cases, or to write a journal entry from their own knowledge and experience. Possible responses include businesses and professionals wasting time and money repeating tasks when they cannot find records, as well as making poor decisions. Legal disputes and other serious problems may result. Writers who do not receive credit for their work and ideas may lose career opportunities, esteem and reputation, and financial gain.

Excerpt from Research Document

A bacterium that can break down toxic waste and survive heavy doses of radiation, suggests one report, could help the United States speedily and inexpensively deal with its estimated 3,000 dump sites (Kapsner). This bacterium, according to an article in a National Science Foundation newsletter, is named *Deinococcus radiodurans*, which means "strange berry that withstands radiation," for its red color and its ability to live through 3,000 times more radiation than it would take to kill a person ("Witches Brew"). Not only can this bacterium survive, it even grows when constantly exposed to normally lethal doses of radiation. Perhaps the key is in the structure of the DNA repair systems, says one recent report (Spake 67).

Excerpt from Works Cited

Works Cited

Kapsner, Jake. "Researchers Develop Munching Bacteria." *The Minnesota Daily On-line* 21 Oct. 1998. 26 June 2003 <http://www.mndaily.com/daily/1998/10/21/news/>

Spake, Amanda. "Conan's Little Secret." *U.S. News & World Report* 20 Jan. 2003: 67.

"Witches' Brew of Weird Bugs." *Frontiers: The Electronic Newsletter of the National Science Foundation* Oct. 1996: 7 June 2003 <http://www.nsf.gov/od/lpa/news/publicat/frontier/>

Figure 3.2 Internal Citation and Works Cited

What happens when writers incorrectly or incompletely cite sources? What are the costs to businesses? to professionals?

EVALUATING SOURCES

As you have discovered, not everything that appears in print (or on your computer, radio, or TV) is true. In fact, many mistakes, untruths, and half-truths that you would not want to repeat are published. A financial planner who uses an unreliable source's information to make faulty investments for clients, for instance, will not stay in business. So, when you research, choose your data sources critically and carefully.

© GETTY IMAGES/PHOTODISC

These guidelines for evaluating sources will help you get started.

PUBLICATION DATE

When you want to know the most recent discoveries and happenings in a particular area, you need up-to-date information. Therefore, you must check publication dates. Data in a book may be even older than the copyright date indicates, since some books take two or more years to be published. Likewise, web sites without dates may not have been checked or revised in years.

AUTHOR'S CREDENTIALS

Often the preface or introduction in a book outlines the education and experience of the writers or editors. Likewise, magazine and journal articles sometimes include brief biographies. Check web sites, particularly the beginning and ending pages, for an author's biography and credentials. If the publication gives no information about the author or editor, consider factors such as the reputation of the journal, publisher, or associated business or organization.

WARM UP

Have you ever repeated something someone else said only to have others say it is untrue? If so, how did you feel about the person who told you the story in the first place? Did you continue to share information he or she told you? How do you decide whose information to repeat and whose not to repeat?

FOCUS

Warm Up

Use Warm Up to begin a class discussion exploring what students already know about evaluating sources. The sources are probably peers and other acquaintances. Some possible conclusions include experience the speaker has on that particular subject and history—whether that speaker has been trustworthy in the past.

ENRICH

Bring several sources to class—some reliable, such as reputable scholarly journals, and some not as reliable, such as tabloids. Allow students to examine the sources and discuss their ability or inability to justify using the sources in a research paper or project.

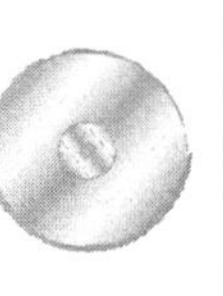

Use the Guidelines for Evaluating Sources Transparency on the IRCD.

APPLY

Help students use the discussion on evaluating sources to develop their own checklist. It might include questions such as the following for each source:

- Is it up to date?
- Is it authoritative?
- Is it accurate?
- Is it reliable?
- Is it complete?
- Is the evidence compelling?
- Is it unbiased?

You also can check an author's reputation in reference sources such as *Who's Who in America, Contemporary Authors, Who's Who in Science,* and *Who's Who in Small Business and Entrepreneurship Worldwide.* Some of these references, such as *Contemporary Authors,* are found online.

Based on what you learn about the author's credentials, determine whether he or she qualifies as an expert in the field. If you have two sources on the same topic, you might find one author to be more credible than the other.

Check the author's methods and resources Usually, in the introduction of a book or in the opening paragraphs of an article, the author or editor will explain the methods used to reach the conclusions. If you believe those methods are flawed, the book or article loses credibility as a potential source. Likewise, you may evaluate a potential source by the resources its author uses. Resources may be mentioned in the text and listed in a works cited section or bibliography.

These guidelines will help with many sources, but the increasing availability of electronic materials means that researchers are spending more time and effort searching online. Therefore, you should give special consideration to evaluating electronic sources. Since its materials are not screened in any way, the Internet contains more trash than treasure. Remember that anyone, from the bored 10-year-old next door to the busy physics professor, can post a web site.

The following guidelines are especially useful in evaluating electronic information:

Is an author or sponsoring group listed? Are credentials or experiences noted to show that the author is an expert on the subject covered? Is the author or sponsor mentioned in other sources? If no author or sponsor were given, a critical reader would wonder why. For instance, an animal rights supporter could maintain an anonymous site emphasizing abusive aspects of corporate farming methods.

Electronic address The abbreviation in the web address should show that the source originates from:

Educational institution	.edu
Government organization	.gov
Military	.mil
Nonprofit organization	.org
For-profit or commercial organization	.com

Sites sponsored by schools are usually academic and objective, providing reliable information. Government-sponsored sites—whether local, state, national, or international—typically present reliable information, such as U.S. census data. However, these sites may be biased. For example, the President controls the press secretary's message and focus of a given story.

Likewise, many nonprofit organizations, such as the American Lung Association, maintain trustworthy sites, but some will be biased by the organization's agenda. For example, the National Rifle Association site is unlikely to provide statistics on the number of children killed by guns in their homes, but is more likely to show how many burglaries are stopped by homeowners with guns. However, commercial sites will almost always be biased. After all, readers cannot expect a web page sponsored by Gerber to tell parents why they should not feed Gerber baby food to their children.

References and/or links Does the web site include a list of sources used in preparing the page that readers can check? Are links to other reputable, reliable sites included? Are the links to scholarly sites or to commercial or obviously biased sites?

Balance and purpose Does the site present the subject fairly? Does it include opposing viewpoints? Is the design clear and careful to aid the reader's understanding, or does the design encourage strong reactions or confusion? Offensive images and cluttered, irrelevant information may be intended to create a particular response from users. For instance, viewers are more likely to have an emotional reaction than a logical response to an image of caged animals in a medical research facility. Understanding a site's purpose—to sell ideas, products, or services; to share knowledge; or to incite strong reactions—can help determine how reliable the information is.

Read this case and consider possible outcomes: Colleen received time and money to study the effects of a particular veterinary medicine on humans. Her report requesting permission for this project was based primarily on one study published in an animal science journal. Over the last year, this study was largely discredited in animal and human medical journals.

ONGOING ASSESSMENT

Stop and Think

Form small groups to discuss Stop and Think. Answers will vary for each group, but at the end of the discussion, point out that if Colleen's entire research project is based on one discredited or invalid study, her study is likely to suffer the same criticism. As an extension of this activity, discuss a responsible and ethical response for Colleen to take.

WARM UP

Examine the notes you take during class. Approximately what percentage of the notes are written exactly in the instructor's or speaker's words? Approximately what percentage are written in your own words, your interpretation of the instructor's or speaker's comments? How many notes are your ideas or perhaps conclusions you came to as a result of something someone else said?

FOCUS

Warm Up

Use Warm Up to remind students that note taking is a skill they already practice. Then they can see that they are building on what they already know when they learn about taking notes from sources. Students will probably say that most of their notes are written in their own words while only a small portion are written exactly as the instructor or textbook stated them. In addition, most students will say that they add their own insights and conclusions to the notes they summarize, paraphrase, and quote.

TAKING NOTES FROM SOURCES

Employees doing research note information they collect, just as you do when writing a paper in school. When you discover data you believe will be helpful, write complete and careful notes. Some researchers prefer to use 4″ × 6″ note cards because they are easy to arrange and carry. At the same time, laptop and handheld computers encourage most researchers to take notes electronically. The computer user can then transfer notes into the first draft of the report without having to retype them. Researchers reading a document online can copy and paste material they want to quote directly into the draft document.

Before making notes, read the source material carefully. Understanding your sources thoroughly is an important part of being a successful researcher.

Read the excerpt in Figure 3.3 below from an article describing potential uses of the bacterium *Deinococcus radiodurans*. Jake Kapsner wrote the article, "Researchers Develop Munching Bacteria," for the *The Minnesota Daily Online*. You will find the complete bibliographic entry at the beginning of this chapter. This passage will be used to discuss note taking.

> Although the Cold War ended years ago, genetic researchers at the University are still fighting a $200 billion legacy of contaminated nuclear waste sites.
>
> A toxic-waste-munching bacterium that stands up to even the toughest radioactive environments could make cleaning up the approximate 3,000 nuclear waste sites in the United States quicker and cheaper. "The bug survives radiation . . . while diminishing liquid organic toxic waste," said Cleston Lange, a research co-author who finished his doctoral work in microbial biochemistry at the University. "Millions of gallons of toxic waste were amassed during the past 50 years of nuclear proliferation, primarily at U.S. Department of Energy sites where solvents were used to purify uranium," Lange said.

Figure 3.3 Excerpt from a Research Article

On each card or with the note-taking software you use, include 1) the information you want to use—only one idea per card, 2) the topic, and 3) the source and page number(s) from which you took the data. Figure 3.4 illustrates the way some researchers use note cards.

Use for Deinococcus rad. Kapsner

According to a researcher at the University of Minnesota, the bacterium Deinococcus radiodurans could help the United States clean up around 3,000 nuclear waste dumps left over from the Cold War.

Figure 3.4 Model Note Card (Paraphrase)

You can use borrowed information in your notes in these three ways: 1) summary, 2) paraphrase, and 3) direct quotation.

SUMMARY

To **summarize** is to condense longer material, keeping the essential or main ideas and omitting nonessentials, such as the examples and illustrations. Be consistent with the source's idea, but use your words. When doing job-related research, you might summarize a journal article or chapter of a book that is helpful supporting evidence in a report. The original material you summarize might be an entire book, but your summary might be a few paragraphs or one sentence. The note in Figure 3.5 summarizes the original material you read in the article about bacterium.

Bacterium to clean up nuclear waste dumps Kapsner

During the Cold War's 50 years of increasing nuclear arsenals, the United States developed a $200 billion problem in approximately 3,000 locations where toxic waste remained after liquids were used to purify uranium. A bacterium able to survive extreme radiation and to "eat" or break down pollutants may be a solution, reports an expert in microbial biochemistry at the University of Minnesota.

Figure 3.5 Summary Note Card

PARAPHRASE

To **paraphrase** is to borrow or use someone else's idea and to present it in your own words, phrases, and sentence structure. While a summary should be shorter than the original material, a paraphrase generally is about the same length or even a bit longer than the original. A writer paraphrases when the material supports a point but is not unique or dramatic enough to be quoted. Most of the materials writers use from other sources are paraphrased. Paraphrasing allows writers to include the thinking of many others while putting the borrowed ideas into the writer's own words and sentences. As you practice paraphrasing, you may find this process helpful:

1. Read the original carefully.
2. Put it aside.
3. Write the idea in your own way.

TEACH

Ask students to note the following in Figure 3.4: The source tag in the upper right corner has no page number because the electronic source had no page numbers. The topic tag in the upper left corner summarizes as specifically as possible the note's one idea.

For an additional example of notes taken from a research article, show the Article

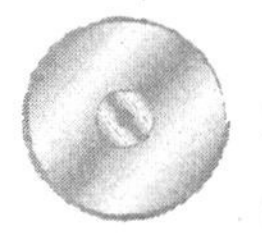

Excerpt and Model Note Card Transparencies on the IRCD.

RETEACH

Remind students to work carefully when taking notes. They are responsible for others' words and ideas.

Since the notes they take may be their own ideas, ideas borrowed from other sources, or a combination of the two, tell them to distinguish their own ideas by writing them in a different color, highlighting them, or putting them in brackets.

TEACH

Tell students that summaries may vary greatly. A writer may summarize a 500-page book in one sentence or two paragraphs in two or three sentences.

Ask students to compare the summary with the original material from Kapsner's article. Does the summary accurately reflect Kapsner's intended meaning? Does the summary include only the most important areas? Are the wording and sentence structure dramatically different from Kapsner's?

TEACH

Students should understand that one of the most important elements of note taking is reading. Students cannot effectively paraphrase or summarize (or even quote) unless they first understand the material.

ENRICH

If you have access to note-taking software or if it is available in your library or computer labs, give students a demonstration. Compare the software to the use of index cards. Explain that the software was developed using the same principles researchers used with index cards.

4. Compare your version with the original.
5. Be certain you have used your own words and sentence structure and have accurately conveyed the author's idea.

Figure 3.6 contains a paraphrase of the first sentence from the excerpt on bacterium. Notice that the wording and sentence structure is significantly different. Changing or moving a word or two is not effective paraphrasing. Avoid plagiarism by stating the borrowed idea in your own way, choosing words and sentence structure you would normally use, and properly crediting the author of the source.

Benefits of Deinococcus rad. Kapsner

Bacteria that can break down toxic waste and survive heavy doses of radiation, suggests one report, could help the United States speedily and inexpensively deal with its estimated 3,000 nuclear waste sites.

Figure 3.6 Paraphrase Note Card

DIRECT QUOTATION

Direct quotation is the third way writers incorporate borrowed material into their documents. When quoting, a writer uses ideas, words, phrases, and sentences exactly as they appear in the original. However, be careful not to overuse quotations; avoid a cut-and-paste patchwork style by making less than 20 percent of your document direct quotations. Copy phrases and sentences directly only when you cannot present the idea as well in your own words. For instance, if the original writer or speaker chose unusual words or composed unique or dramatic sentences, you may want your reader to get the flavor of the original by quoting directly. Another reason for using direct quotation is to enhance your credibility by using the words of a well-known authority. Figure 3.7 is a model of a notecard using direct quotation.

Damage Remaining after Cold War Kapsner

While the age of nuclear proliferation has ended, according to one source, the United States is "still fighting a $200 billion legacy of contaminated nuclear waste sites."

Figure 3.7 Direct Quotation Note Card

Introduce quotations Writers introduce quotations to make the writing smooth. Do not let quoted sentences stand alone. You can integrate quotations into your text with words such as "according to one expert" and "Greg Markham claims" or with complete sentences such as:

Benjamin Franklin gave this advice in *Poor Richard's Almanac:* "Early to bed, early to rise, makes a man healthy, wealthy, and wise."

Indicate added or omitted material When you need to add to or edit a direct quotation for clarity or conciseness, use brackets to set your changes apart from the quoted words, as in the sentences below.

© GETTY IMAGES/PHOTODISC

Original: "After the board meeting in which a 2 percent fine was approved, she signed her resignation letter."

Addition for clarity: "After the board meeting in which a 2 percent fine was approved, [Margaret Fletcher] signed her resignation letter."

You may need to quote only part of a sentence. In this case, use an ellipsis, three spaced dots, to show where you omitted words from the original. However, if you include a paraphrase of the idea (rather than omit it), you will not need an ellipsis. If the reason for Fletcher's resignation is not important to your work, you might quote the source this way:

Omission: "After the board meeting [..., Margaret Fletcher] signed her resignation letter."

The ellipsis shows that the clause "in which a 2 percent fine was approved" was left out of the quotation.

When should a writer use direct quotation? Would you use an ellipsis or brackets to indicate that you left out part of a quoted sentence?

TEACH

Explain that ellipses and brackets are used only in direct quotations.

For additional examples, show the Summary, Paraphrase, and Direct Quotation Notecards Transparency on the IRCD.

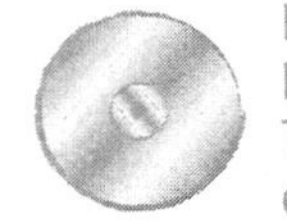

ONGOING ASSESSMENT

Stop and Think

Assign Stop and Think to check reading comprehension.

Use a direct quotation when an idea is worded in such a unique way that you cannot express it as well in your own words or when you want to enhance your credibility.

Use an ellipsis to indicate that you left out part of a quoted sentence.

WARM UP

What could you do in the following situation?

You stained your new sweater with a chemical from the chemistry lab. You do not know the name of the chemical, but you remember the experiment and probably would recognize the bottle containing the chemical. You want to have the sweater cleaned, but you are afraid to do so without knowing which chemical caused the spot.

FOCUS

Warm Up

Use Warm Up as a discovery exercise. The lists should give students an inventory of the types of research, especially primary research, someone might do to solve a problem or answer a question. Entries may include questioning the chemistry instructor, reading the sweater care instructions, asking a professional cleaner, reading the chemical container label, and testing water or a cleaning solution on the stain. Each answer represents a research type. For example, questioning the instructor or the professional is surveying, and testing a cleaning agent is experimentation.

COLLECTING PRIMARY DATA

Many job-related problems or questions are too unique or too current for secondary sources to answer. A commercial fisher may learn more about a new net's effectiveness by asking other users and by experimenting than by reading the literature on nets. To solve work-related concerns, primary data may be more help. Primary data is gathered through field research: surveys, interviews, observation, and experimentation. Some field research is conducted in person, some by telephone, and some online.

SURVEYS

Surveys gather facts, beliefs, attitudes, and opinions from people. Many businesses rely on surveys to collect information for decision making. One example is a questionnaire accompanying a product registration form for small appliances such as hair dryers. The manufacturer uses the data to determine who is buying the product, how the buyer learned of the product (what advertising method worked), and how satisfied the buyer is.

A survey works only when you know what you want to learn before you begin. Once you decide what you want to learn, you should 1) carefully select your audience or **respondents**, 2) decide how you will administer your survey, and 3) carefully plan your questions.

When you choose an audience, you must select a sample broad enough to represent that audience. **Population** is the target group from which you want to gather data. A garden center owner who wants to know whether customers will use a repotting service would have a population of all of the business's customers. If the owner cannot question all customers due to expense, time, or distance, she may choose a sample to provide representative answers. A **sample** is a subgroup that represents (has the same characteristics as) the entire group. Keep in mind that the sample must be small enough for you to be able to tabulate and analyze the results but large enough to provide meaningful results. In some situations, companies hire specially trained people to design and conduct surveys.

Once you know your audience, the next step is to decide how to administer the survey. You can administer questionnaires in person, by mail, by telephone, or by e-mail; many businesses survey by e-mail now. This decision is based on the kind of data you seek, how much time you have, and your budget. If you are asking personal or controversial questions, use a confidential mailed survey to ensure a higher return rate. And although many people believe their e-mail is private, it is far from secure. In fact, in the workplace, employers have the right to access information on company computers, so your e-mail there is subject to scrutiny. If time is a concern, telephone, e-mail, and in-person surveys offer faster responses than mail surveys. Also, remember that all survey methods can be costly.

Consider these suggestions as you prepare surveys:

Explain why you need the information and how it will be used Because you are asking respondents to share data, they have the right to know what you plan to do with the information. In a cover letter or an opening paragraph, explain what prompted the survey. Then describe the benefits. Estimate the time required to complete the survey. Many surveys also offer to send respondents results of the study.

Convince your audience to participate After all, you are asking for their time and thoughts. They may wonder what you are giving them in return. You might consider offering an incentive, such as coupons, free merchandise or services, improved or additional services, or discounts.

Logically order questions, beginning with easy-to-answer items If respondents have difficulty with the first questions, they are not likely to continue. The initial questions should ask for information that is easy to recall and not too personal. Also, arrange questions in logical groupings to aid respondents' memory.

Ask only necessary questions If you do not need the answer, do not ask the question. For example, do not ask about income if income is not relevant to the data you seek. People will not respond if they believe you are wasting their time.

Write clear and nonleading questions For responses to be useful, questions must be clear and precise. Compare the following two questions:

- Do you shop by mail often?
- Do you shop by mail once a month?

With the first question, the respondent will answer based on his or her definition of *often*. Such an answer may not be useful. Likewise, questions should not lead respondents to particular answers. Consider the following questions as an illustration:

- Don't you believe that the cost of class rings is outrageous?
- Why don't you buy your lunch in the school cafeteria?

ENRICH

When you teach surveying, give students more information concerning methods researchers use to guarantee representative responses. Many sources, probably available in your library, cover statistical analysis and probability (random, systematic random, and stratified random) and nonprobability sampling.

Collect and share surveys you receive in the mail. Help students critique one of them. Be aware of the critical role of audience analysis in effective surveying.

RETEACH

Show the Tips for Preparing Surveys Transparency on the IRCD.

TEACH

Some people believe that you can make statistics say anything you want them to say. Have the class discuss the ethical use of collected data, even when the data are not favorable or not what they expected.

ENRICH

Invite an expert on data analysis to share insights with your class. For example, many colleges, universities, and government agencies have institutional researchers who can describe their jobs and how their organizations collect and use information.

The wording suggests a particular answer. Consider changing to:

- Do you believe the cost of class rings is reasonable or unreasonable?
- Is cost a factor in your decision to purchase lunch in the school cafeteria?

Make the question's purpose clear If the survey is to learn about consumers' reaction to your newspaper's new type style, do not ask such general questions as "Why did you purchase this newspaper?" Answers to this general question may vary tremendously, from "It was the cheapest one on the newsstand" to "This is the one my father reads." Such responses will not help you find what you want to know—whether people like the new type style.

Prefer facts to opinions When designing questions, seek facts whenever possible. Facts provide stronger, more credible evidence. For example, ask "Do you purchase from a mail-order catalog once a month or more?" rather than "Do you like mail-order shopping?"

Stick to one topic per question While you might be tempted to include several issues in one question, the answers will be useless if you do not know to which topic the person is responding. Suppose respondents say yes to the question "Are you ever concerned for your safety as you walk through the parking deck and up the stairs into the Whitley Building at night?" You do not know what concerns them—the deck, the stairs, the building, or the darkness.

Plan for tabulation Remember that once responses come in, you need to evaluate and interpret them. Your job will be easier if you design questions whose answers are stated as numbers. When you already know the range of possible answers, **close-ended questions**, such as these two, allow for a limited number of responses and are easy to tabulate.

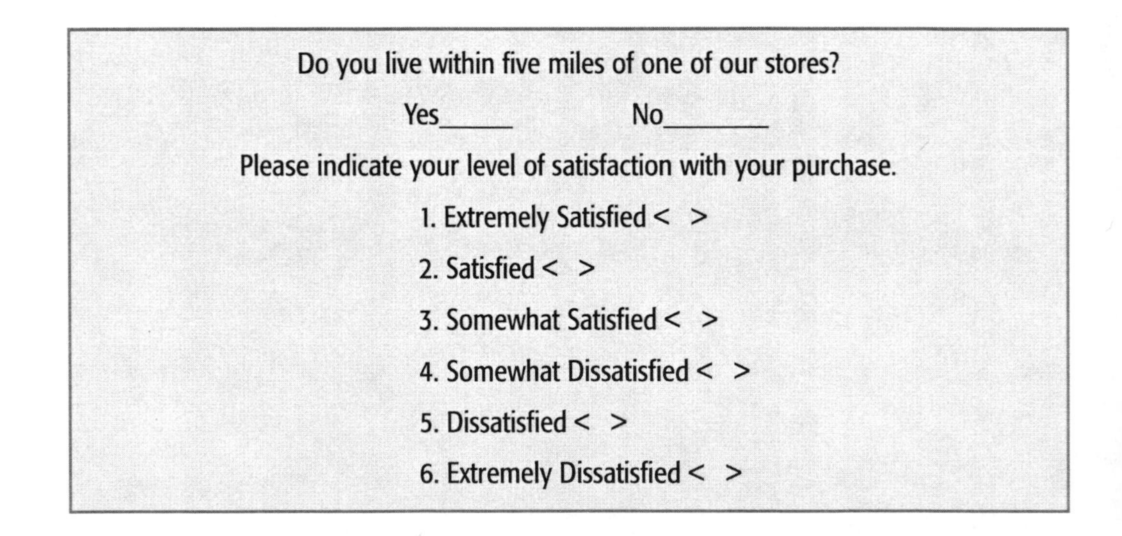
Do you live within five miles of one of our stores?

Yes_____ No_______

Please indicate your level of satisfaction with your purchase.

1. Extremely Satisfied < >
2. Satisfied < >
3. Somewhat Satisfied < >
4. Somewhat Dissatisfied < >
5. Dissatisfied < >
6. Extremely Dissatisfied < >

Although more difficult to tabulate, **open-ended questions** are sometimes necessary to discover respondents' thoughts and feelings; unexpected attitudes or information may be uncovered this way.

Open-ended questions ask respondents to supply words, sentences, or short essays, as shown in the example on the next page:

How do you think RFG's board should respond to the new regulations?
What could Apgard Limited do to improve service to you and your organization?

Leave adequate space for answers when asking open-ended questions. Figure 3.8 gives examples of different types of questions.

Phi Rho

"Working Together to Serve"

Residents of Glenhaven:

We are considering your Glenhaven Retirement Community for our annual service project. With your help, we would like to learn more about your interests. We would like to contribute something worthwhile and lasting to your neighborhood.

States the reason for the survey and how the results will be used.

Please take about five minutes now to answer these questions and then place the completed form in the box marked "PHI RHO" in the Recreation Center by August 25. In case you'd like to know the outcome, we will post a copy of the results in the same location in August 30.

Tells how much time the survey will take to complete; explains how to return the survey.

1. Your age is __45 or younger __46-55 __56-65 __66-75 __76-85 __86 or older

Single answer/ multiple choice

2. Do you live alone? __yes __no

Dual Alternative

3. Indicate your preferences for our service project by ranking the items below from 1 to 7, 1 being most important and 7 being least important.
   __nature trail __picnic area __flagpole __shuffleboard game
   __square-foot garden sites __exercise path __croquet lawn

Rank order question

4. Check the item which best reflects your opinion for completing the following sentences. If a new outdoor area is installed in the community, I am. . .
   __willing to spend two hours per month on maintenance. __willing to pay $5 or less a year to hire a maintenance service. __not willing to maintain the area.

Single answer/ multiple choice question

5. Mark your level of satisfaction with the outdoor facilities now available at Glenhaven.
   Very Satisfied < > Somewhat Satisfied < > Satisfied < > Somewhat Dissatisfied < > Dissatisfied < > Very Dissatisfied < >

Close-ended question

6. What outdoor activity (or activities) do you most enjoy?
   ____
   ____

Open-ended question

Thank you for your participation!

Figure 3.8 A Mailed Survey

ENRICH

Role playing is one way to prepare students for conducting interviews. This experience will give them confidence to handle the difficult moments in real interviews, such as when an interviewee gives a one-word answer or says nothing at all.

Another activity is to assign students to view and critique an interview on a television news show or on an educational video. In doing so, they can review the strategies for successful interviewing and identify elements that the interviewer can improve.

If your school or district has a public information officer, invite him or her to advise students about interviewing.

INTERVIEWS

Interviews, like surveys, are an excellent source of primary data. Interviews give you access to experts' facts, opinions, and attitudes that you might not find any other way. However, interviewing can be time-consuming and costly. To make the process as successful as possible, use the following guidelines:

Define your purpose Know exactly what information you want from each interviewee. Write down the purpose and review it before talking to the interviewee.

Make an appointment Telephone, write, or e-mail the respondent to describe the topic and to request an interview. Whether you will be interviewing someone by telephone, by mail, via e-mail, or in person, ask the respondent in advance for a convenient time to conduct the interview. If the interview will be in person, offer to visit the respondent or to arrange a suitable place to conduct the interview. If the interview will be via mail or e-mail, agree on a time frame for sending questions and receiving answers. For interviews by instant messaging, set an appointed time. Make certain that the respondent understands the topic and that you have allowed reasonable preparation time. Moreover, be professional in your appearance, writing, and speaking.

Do your homework Do not expect the respondent to make all of the effort. Know as much as possible about the topic before you conduct the interview.

Plan and write your questions Prepare questions to bring out specific, detailed information. Avoid vague questions such as "How do you feel about responding to emergency calls involving hazardous materials?" Instead, ask clear, specific ones, such as "What training experiences have you had to prepare you for emergency situations involving toxic gases?" Also, avoid questions that require a yes or no response; they do not encourage the speaker to elaborate. In addition, avoid questions that reflect an opinion or bias, such as "Isn't it true that management overemphasizes shop safety?" Instead, ask for the respondent's views: "In regard to shop safety, does management underemphasize, overemphasize, or adequately emphasize?"

Many interviewers develop questions on a laptop or handheld computer. This lets them read the questions from the machine and record answers on it as the interview takes place. Some interviewers write questions on one sheet of paper and record answers on another. Others prefer to write each question along with its answer on a note card. A tape recorder may be helpful, but ask permission to record the interview before you begin. Choose the system that works best for you.

Conduct the interview in a competent and courteous manner Remember, you are in control and the success of the session depends on you, not the respondent. Make sure you do the following:

Be on time.	Dress appropriately.
Introduce yourself.	Speak in a clear, distinct voice.
Explain the purpose of the interview.	Be assertive, but not arrogant.
Keep on track; stick to the topic.	Avoid small talk.
Take notes, but not excessively.	Thank the respondent for his or her time.
Listen attentively.	Offer a handshake as you leave.
Ask for clarification or more details, if needed.	Add to your notes with a more complete summary as soon as you leave.

OBSERVATION

In addition to surveying and interviewing, observing is another method of collecting primary data. Professionals frequently rely on observation to solve problems in their jobs. Medical professionals observe patients to diagnose illnesses. Crop scientists observe the numbers and types of weeds and insects in a field to decide whether the crop should be sprayed. Highway departments count vehicles to decide where to place traffic signals. However, be careful when gathering data by observation; observers may be biased, or subjects may act differently if they know they are being studied. To collect credible data by observation, use these guidelines:

Train observers in what to look for, what to record, and how to record If you wanted to know about traffic at a certain intersection, you would train people to count vehicles; in addition, you would need to tell the observers the rules. For example, how would they count mopeds? If one observer counted mopeds with passenger vehicles, another observer counted mopeds with commercial vehicles, and the third did not count them at all, the data would be flawed. Also, be sure all observers are using terms the same way. For example, what is a peak period? If you tell observers that peak period is

RETEACH

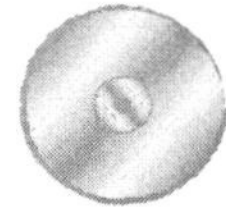

Show the Tips for Interviewing Transparency on the IRCD.

ENRICH

One of the most difficult factors in observing people is recording external actions, rather than motivations. Have teams of students practice recording observations somewhere on campus, perhaps in the cafeteria or student commons. For example, assign an observation of student eating habits—eating food from the school food service, bringing lunch from home, purchasing from vending machines, or skipping lunch. Then discuss and review students' recorded observations.

ENRICH

Many classroom experiments can be carried out easily and inexpensively. Some examples are testing to see whether people really can tell the difference between two brands of soft drinks (Coke® and Pepsi™), a regular and a fat-free food product, or a brand name and a store brand product. Ask students to use the guidelines in this chapter to devise and conduct the experiment.

from 11 A.M. until 2:30 P.M., their traffic counts for peak period will be useful data because each observer counted during the same period.

Make systematic observations For instance, if the observers counting vehicles work only from 7–9 A.M. and 4–6 P.M., will you get an accurate picture? Since people are commuting to work and school during these times, you are likely to get inflated numbers.

Observe only external actions You cannot project internal actions or reasoning. For example, you may observe that 24 percent more people displayed flags this Independence Day than last, but you cannot say that more people are flying flags because they feel more patriotic. Report only actions you can see.

Quantify findings whenever possible Being able to assign statistics adds credibility, showing that an action or event was consistent.

Support your observations If you cannot quantify, support generalizations with details, examples, and illustrations. You might even make drawings or take photographs.

While observation can be a valuable source of primary data, consider the time, equipment, and cost. For instance, hiring and training people to count vehicles can be time-consuming and expensive. Even if you decide to place a mechanical device across the highway to count vehicles, it must be paid for and it will not describe the vehicles.

EXPERIMENTATION

Experimentation is causing an event so that an observer can test an assumption or a hypothesis (a statement of what the tester believes will happen). Experiments test whether a change in one factor will cause

another factor to change. For example, if the owner of a car-cleaning business wants to know whether his current car wax or a new product gives the longest-lasting shine, the owner might polish half a car with the current wax and the other half with the new wax. He then would check the car periodically for shine.

Employees frequently use experiments in the workplace. Manufacturers often test new products in limited markets to see whether they will be successful. Managers may compare a current operating plan in one plant with a new one in another plant. Researchers may gather samples of air, water, soil, food, medicines, body tissues, or even construction materials for testing.

As with observation, experimenters must be careful to avoid elements that will make the experiment and its results invalid. Sometimes other factors or variables can affect the results of an experiment. For instance, using different cleaners on the two halves of the car would affect the results of the wax study. Using adults for conducting clinical trials of a drug meant for children would not provide meaningful information about how the drug will work on pediatric patients. Therefore, when you design an experiment, try to eliminate as many outside factors as you can.

Surveys, interviews, observation, and experimentation all serve as useful tools for getting information, and many researchers use a combination of these methods. Remember the stain on the wool sweater in the Warm Up? Even such an everyday problem as how best to clean a favorite garment may require you to interview, observe, and experiment to find a solution.

VALIDITY AND RELIABILITY

To maintain credibility, primary researchers look for valid and reliable data. You have **valid data** when you have accurately measured what you intended to measure.

For example, a clothing store owner wanted to know whether his business would attract as many customers if it were open on Sunday as it did on weekdays. He devised a test to collect data. The Sunday he chose was during a weekend when two big football games were being played in town and visitors filled the area hotels. Comparing the number of customers on that Sunday with the number of weekday customers would not generate valid data. The large number of visitors in town on that particular Sunday would influence the results.

Reliable data means that, under similar circumstances, the results can be duplicated. If you explain that mixing two liquid chemicals will create a solid, then others could try the same test. If they follow your procedures, the mixed liquids should solidify. Being able to repeat the test with the same results represents reliable data.

What are three methods of collecting primary data? Why should you plan observations?

ONGOING ASSESSMENT

Stop and Think

Assign Stop and Think to check reading comprehension.

The methods of collecting primary data are surveying, interviewing, observing, and experimenting. (Students must name three.)

Observations must be planned so that observers can be trained as to what to look for and when to look, what terminology to use, and how to avoid projecting internal actions or reasoning.

TEACHING RESOURCES

IRCD
- Chapter Activities, Ch. 3
- Work Is A Zoo!, Ch. 3
- PowerPoint® Slides, Ch. 3

Exam*View*®, Ch. 3
techwriting.swlearning.com, Ch. 3

CLOSE

Summary

1. Researchers usually start their research with easy-to-access information found in secondary sources.
2. Writers may search, in print or electronically, correspondence and report archives, library catalogs, periodicals, reference materials, and other electronic sources.
3. Documentation includes in-text citations and a Works Cited or Bibliography at the end of the document or report.
4. Additional guidelines for evaluating electronic sources include reviewing the author or sponsoring organization, the electronic address, and the references or links, as well as checking for balance and the purpose of the site.
5. Such data is often necessary to solve problems in business.
6. Such data often supplies more current and relevant information than data gathered using secondary sources.

CLOSE

Checklist

Have students use the checklist as a reference guide when doing research.

Chapter 3 Review

SUMMARY

1. Researching at work involves finding information to help people solve problems, make informed decisions, answer questions, and perform many other functions.
2. Secondary data, reports of information from someone other than the witness or the person directly involved, are usually found in a business, school, or public library through print or electronic means.
3. Writers must give credit for borrowed material by documenting the source. Failure to credit others for their words and ideas means risking reputation, employment, legal action, and financial reward.
4. Writers should evaluate sources by checking publication dates, the author's credentials, and the author's methods and resources.
5. As researchers find useful material, they take notes using one method or a combination of three methods—summary, paraphrase, and direct quotation—on note cards or a computer disk.
6. Primary data, information direct from the person involved, may be collected by surveys, interviews, observation, and experimentation.

Checklist

- Have I defined the problem or need for information?
- Have I considered what information I already have?
- Have I reviewed information available in my organization's archives relating to my problem or need?
- Have I viewed the library catalog, online when accessible or in the library when not accessible online?
- Have I searched periodical indexes and databases for more recent secondary sources?
- Have I relied on general reference materials, electronic or in print, for quick background information and for references to other sources?
- Have I searched the Web using strategies to filter for useful information, and have I found the most up-to-the-minute information?
- Have I given credit, using an appropriate style system, for borrowed words and ideas, unless the information is considered common knowledge or material in the public domain?
- Have I critically evaluated all sources of information before using the data?
- Have I developed notes using summary, paraphrase, and direct quotation?
- Have I considered collecting primary data using surveys, interviews, observations, and/or experimentation to find information not available through other sources? Have I planned for validity and reliability?

Build On What You Know

1. Compose a note card for each item below.

   a. On page 14 of *Farm Review*, Edwin F. Roberson's and Julius Schwartz' article, "Hog Farmers and Homeowners: Zoning Solutions," notes that municipal and regional governments are "legislating distance" between the farms' waste lagoons and residential areas. The article appears in the November 2003 issue of the magazine.

   b. In her 2004 book *Swine Herd Disease Management*, Dr. April P. Nuez writes, "Careful record keeping and close observation are the key to disease management." The book is 463 pages long, and this statement appears on page 259. The book was published by Delmar, a publisher located in New York.

2. Paraphrase each of the items below.

   a. The Center for Marine Conservation reported that volunteers scouring ocean beaches and inland shorelines cleaned up more than 7 million pieces of trash, including cigarette butts, bottles, cans, lightbulbs, syringes, and plastic bags.

   b. Yesterday, the Highway Department reported approval of a plan to open an 8.5-mile corridor between Henderson and Mount Clemmons. However, the new road may be a little bumpy because two sections of experimental asphalt, one designed to combat hydroplaning and the other made of crumbled tire rubber, are being used.

3. Choose a technical or scientific topic (for example, taxation of Internet sales, irradiation of food supply, or cosmetic use of botox). Find five sources, print and electronic, about the topic. Develop a working bibliography with each source listed in correct MLA bibliographic form.

4. You are calling Sanford Weiss to set up an interview about a new type of home security system he invented. What arrangements should you discuss with him? List at least three things you should cover in the phone call to set up the interview.

5. In small groups, locate and evaluate a web site. Consider purpose, types of information and graphics, evidence and references, factual or emotional information, design, completeness, and balance. Write several paragraphs describing the effectiveness (or lack of effectiveness) of the site based on your evaluation.

6. Identify a company where you might like to work and gather information that would help you apply for a job there. For instance, learn about products, services, or activities. Find out about the way the company is organized, the business philosophy it uses, and its niche in the marketplace. Write a report that would be helpful to other students who also might be interested in seeking employment with the company.

ASSESS

Build On What You Know

1. **a.** left corner: Distance Legislation; right corner: Roberson and Schwartz 14; body: "Hog Farmers and Homeowners: Zoning Solutions" states that governments, both municipal and regional, are legislating distance between farms' waste lagoons and residential areas. **b.** left corner: Key to Disease Management; right corner: Nuez 259; body: The key to disease management is careful recordkeeping and close observation.
2. **a.** According to a report from the Center of Marine Conservation, volunteers on the beaches and inland waterways picked up over 7 million pieces of trash, everything from cigarette butts to syringes. **b.** The Highway Department approved a plan for an 8.5 mile stretch of road between Henderson and Mt. Clemmons yesterday. One part of the new road will be used to test new asphalt created to combat hydroplaning, and another section will test asphalt created from crumbled tire rubber.
3. Have students work in editing teams to check bibliographic entries.
4. Discuss the purpose of the interview; if it will be tape recorded; and when, where, and how long to meet.
5. This activity will remind students they must evaluate all sources.
6. Use this assignment to practice research skills and to point out the need for information before job interviews.

ASSESS

Apply What You Learned

7. Students will recognize that they used many methods, including reading, experimenting, observing, interviewing, and surveying.
8. Students should gain insight into the wealth of information handily available in reference sources.
9. Most of the professionally created questionnaires will be effective.
10. Use this assignment to discuss what not to do during an interview.
11. Use this activity to demonstrate how different search engines produce different results; thus, students should use more than one when conducting research.
12. Use this activity to heighten understanding of advanced search techniques as well as to compare how various search engines work.
13. Use this activity to familiarize students with library databases.
14. Use this assignment to show students how relevant research is to their experience.
15. Students should learn how important gathering information is to solving problems in business.
16. Use this activity to practice survey techniques.
17. Use this activity to practice research skills.
18. Allow students to practice experiment design and analysis with this activity.

Apply What You Learned

7. Think of a subject or hobby that you know a lot about. In a brief essay, describe how you acquired your knowledge.
8. Find three specialized reference sources, such as a medical dictionary or an aerospace encyclopedia, relating to your future career field or a topic of interest. At least one of these reference sources should be online. List the reference sources and a description of what each one offers.
9. Collect questionnaires for class analysis. Determine effective techniques as well as weaknesses in the surveys' strategies.
10. Watch a televised or videotaped interview. Note the strategies the interviewer uses to make the interview effective.
11. Using the same keyword, use three different Internet search engines. Bring to class the first ten listings shown by each search and compare the results.
12. Go to the help section of any Internet search engine. Learn how this particular system works. Share what you learn with your classmates.
13. Using a full-text database available in your school or community library, find and print an article relating to your career field or term project. Write a summary of the article and bring the summary and the article to class.
14. Choose a topic relating to your career field. Search for secondary information to provide basic background information. Write an essay summarizing your findings and prepare a bibliography.
15. Prepare questions and interview someone in your field of interest. From that person, collect information about a particular research project he or she undertook. Ask about methods, difficulties, and the outcome of the research. Record your findings on your sheet of prepared questions.
16. In a small group, identify an issue at your school.
    a. Develop a survey to collect facts and opinions about the issue.
    b. Establish your audience and administer the survey in person.
    c. Tabulate the survey results.
17. Identify a problem at school, in your community, or at work.
    a. Decide what information you need to solve the problem.
    b. Determine how and where to find the information.
    c. Conduct the necessary research.
18. Choose a product to compare with a similar product or a product whose effectiveness for a particular use might be questioned. With that product in mind, design an experiment to test the question. Write a report on the experiment design, the findings of the experiment, or both. Be sure you collect valid and reliable data.

Work Is A Zoo!

ZiPS will only succeed if science instructors and their students use it! And to find out how to make it successful, you need to go to the instructors themselves.

You and Anya are developing a survey for instructors to find out how often they come to the zoo, what they like and dislike about coming, how the zoo can help them meet their classroom goals, what obstacles they foresee, and what suggestions they have.

You also are interested in learning the best age of students to target. Who is more likely to come? Is there a way to target all ages? Would it be good to talk to some students directly?

Develop a survey form for science instructors, keeping in mind your overall purpose. Think about some of these questions as you design your survey:

- How often do the instructors come to the zoo with their classes?
- What do they like about the zoo?
- What do they dislike?
- How can the zoo help them meet their classroom goals?
- What obstacles are there in a program like ZiPS?
- What other suggestions do they have?

Instructors do not have a lot of extra time, so be sure that the survey:

- Is easy to read and fill out.
- Asks only for necessary information.
- Is customized for the audience and purpose.

Remember to leave enough room for the user to fill out the form. Provide instructions for returning the survey.

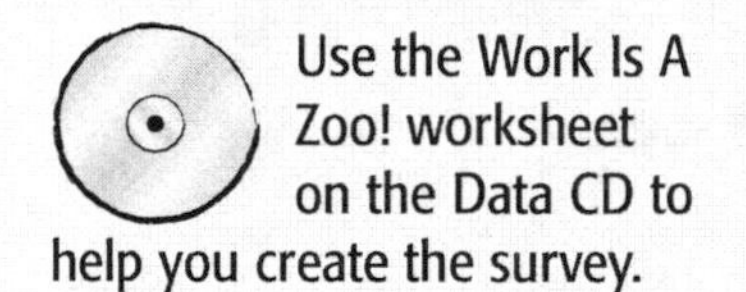

Use the Work Is A Zoo! worksheet on the Data CD to help you create the survey.

WORK IS A ZOO

Use Work Is A Zoo to help students see a real-world application for surveys. Students need to think about the overall purpose of the survey before creating it.

Use the Work Is A Zoo! worksheet on the IRCD to assist students in creating the survey.

CHAPTER

5 BRIEF CORRESPONDENCE

GOALS

IDENTIFY brief correspondence

ANALYZE the audience for brief correspondence

PREPARE for and DETERMINE how to format e-mails, memorandums, and letters

UNDERSTAND and USE strategies for composing good news, bad news, and persuasive messages

See the Data CD for Write-to-Learn and In The Know activity worksheets.

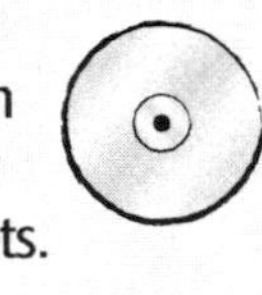

TEACHING RESOURCES

IRCD
- Lesson Plans, Ch. 5
- Chapter Activities, Ch. 5
- PowerPoint® Slides, Ch. 5
- Sample Documents, Ch. 5

techwriting.swlearning.com, Ch. 5
Exam*View*®, Ch. 5

CHAPTER OVERVIEW

Presents e-mails, memorandums, and letters and explains their function in the workplace.

See the IRCD for Write-to-Learn and In The Know activity worksheets.

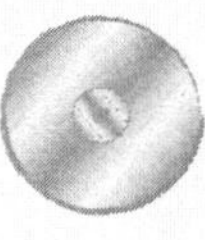

WRITE-TO-LEARN

Consider the information you need to share with others in any work situation, whether it is a collaborative paper or a project for class, a task you manage at home, or a job you do for a wage. With one task or job in mind, write a few paragraphs about the information you need to give or receive from others and how you communicate. For example, if you are doing a team project, you might need to schedule a meeting or set a deadline. Is time a factor in the method of communication? Is a record of your communication an important factor? Is your communication usually face-to-face, over the telephone, in notes or letters, by e-mail, or through other means? What advantages and disadvantages have you found with the types of communication you use? In addition to the paragraphs, list in two columns advantages and disadvantages of each form of communication you use.

In The Know

block style the letter style that aligns the return address, dateline, and closing flush with the left margin

buffer something positive written to soften bad news to come

external audience a receiver outside the sender's organization

format the layout of a publication; standard elements of a document's presentation

goodwill the feeling of friendship; the value of doing things that create mutual admiration and respect

hooks attention-getters; words or sentences designed to engage the reader or to create interest in an idea

internal audience a receiver inside the sender's organization

Maslow's Hierarchy of Needs the division of human needs into basic needs (physiological, safety, and belonging) and higher-order needs (esteem and self-actualization)

memos/memorandums brief written internal communication

modified block style the letter style that begins the return address, dateline, and closing at the center of the page

sociological influences social factors such as culture, family, and class that cause buyers to purchase certain goods and services

testimonials personal stories or people's statements (often famous people) endorsing a product or service

Writing@Work

Brian Minick serves as senior technology lead for General Electric Aircraft Engines. He is responsible for coordinating technology efforts between different areas of the business.

As senior technology lead, Brian must correspond with people in other countries. The majority of his communication is through e-mail. In situations where Brian is communicating with people of different nationalities, he may have a question about the gender of the person he is corresponding with. Luckily, GEAE has a system in place to handle potentially embarrassing situations. For every project, Brian participates in team-building exercises to help him get to know the people he will be working with. One exercise consists of filling out a questionnaire. Some questions are personal, while others focus on what each team member will be able to bring to the project. When the questionnaires are complete, each team member is responsible for introducing someone else to the rest of the colleagues. This thorough communication ensures that team members will know something about each other and that they will feel more comfortable working together.

With a company like GEAE, much information sent via e-mail will be proprietary. GEAE addresses this sensitive issue with a standard footer that must be included at the end of each e-mail. This footer labels the information in the e-mail as proprietary and instructs the addressee not to distribute, copy, or publish the information. When Brian sends proprietary information to another company, he must ensure that the company agrees not to duplicate it.

As most companies do, GEAE has a policy regarding employees using e-mail for personal correspondence. GEAE's policy is reasonable–if the e-mail is helpful, such as employees' verifying doctors' appointments or arranging for child care, then it is OK. As long as employees are not abusing their e-mail privileges, then everything is fine. However, employees can be terminated on the spot for sending e-mails with inappropriate content.

Brian has a bachelor's of applied science degree in systems analysis from Miami University in Oxford, Ohio. He has worked at GEAE for four years.

APPLY

Writing@Work
This feature focuses on e-mail communication in the workplace and describes an exercise employees use to get to know team members they have never met. Although your students probably know each other, have them complete a questionnaire with some personal questions and some questions pertaining to skills they possess. Then have each student introduce another student to the rest of the class. Refer to the Personal Questionnaire worksheet on the IRCD.

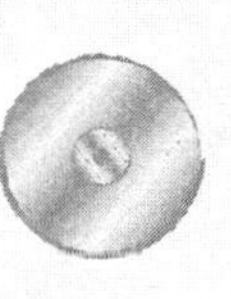

It is just as important to be professional with e-mail correspondence as it is with a written letter. Assign students to a company (either real or imagined) and have them write two business letters to be sent by e-mail. One might be to another person working at the same company, and one might be to someone at an outside company. Stress the importance of professionalism and the need for sensitivity when relaying proprietary information.

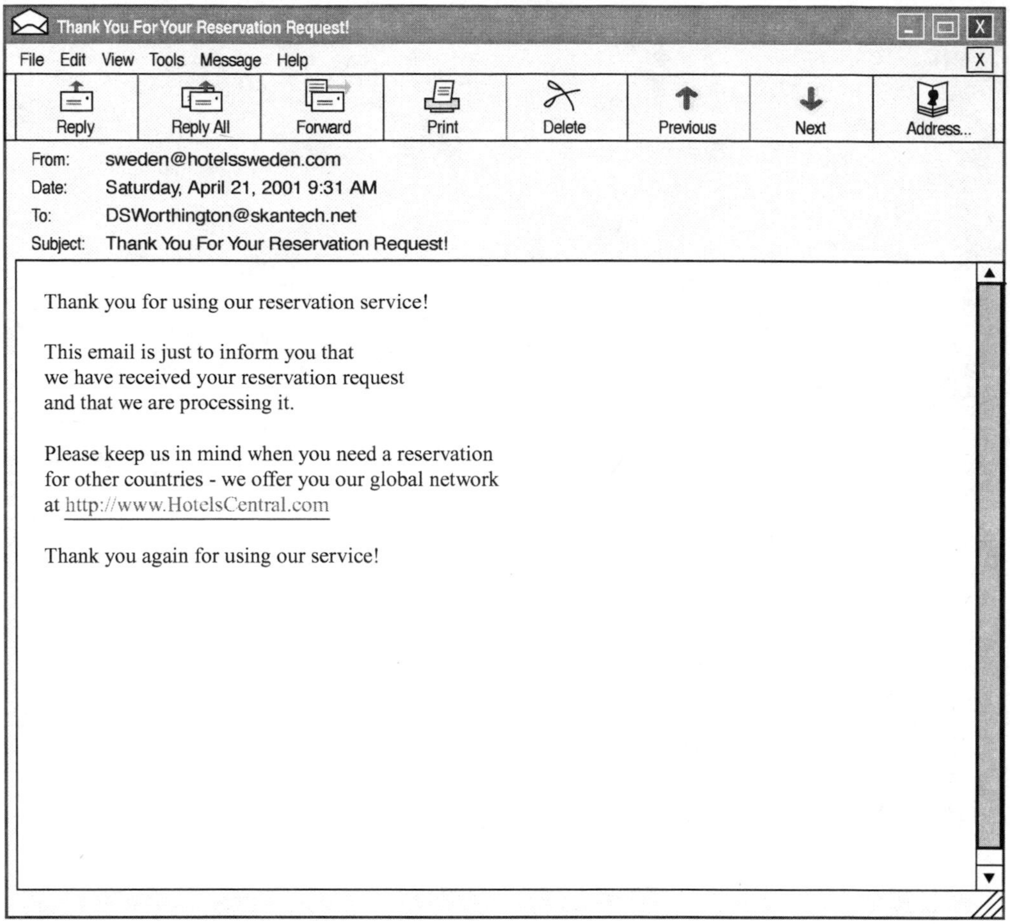

Thank You For Your Reservation Request!

File Edit View Tools Message Help

Reply | Reply All | Forward | Print | Delete | Previous | Next | Address...

From: sweden@hotelssweden.com
Date: Saturday, April 21, 2001 9:31 AM
To: DSWorthington@skantech.net
Subject: Thank You For Your Reservation Request!

Thank you for using our reservation service!

This email is just to inform you that
we have received your reservation request
and that we are processing it.

Please keep us in mind when you need a reservation
for other countries - we offer you our global network
at http://www.HotelsCentral.com

Thank you again for using our service!

Figure 5.1 Sample E-mail

Ayden-Grifton High School

Route 3, Box 172
AYDEN, NORTH CAROLINA 28513
Telephone:
252-555-0183

MEMORANDUM

To: Mrs. Lopez, Ms. Parham, and Members of FHA/HERO

From: Mr. James D. Gray, Principal

Date: February 6, 20—

Subject: CONGRATULATIONS ON HOMELESS SHELTER PROJECT SUCCESS

Congratulations, students, on the outstanding contributions made to the Pitt County Homeless Shelter by the members of FHA/HERO and compliments, Mrs. Lopez and Ms. Parham, for the leadership you provided.

This project involving the entire school and community helped make us all more aware of the difficult conditions faced by many members of our community. I was especially pleased that so many of our students and parents participated in donating food, money, and consumable items for this worthwhile program.

I thank you for organizing and seeing this project to completion. This effort is a great example of teaching and learning.

Member of Southern Association of Colleges and Schools

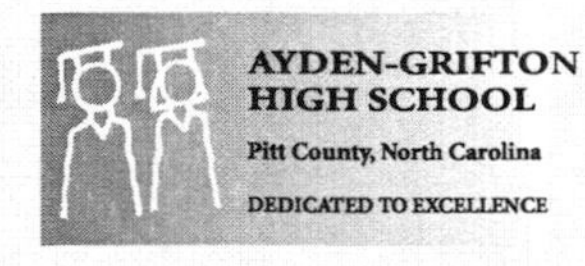

AYDEN-GRIFTON
HIGH SCHOOL
Pitt County, North Carolina
DEDICATED TO EXCELLENCE

It is the Purpose of Pitt County Schools to Provide
Equal Opportunity Regardless of Race, Color,
National Origin, Sex, or Handicap

Figure 5.2 Sample Memorandum

Ayden-Grifton High School
Route 3, Box 172
AYDEN, NORTH CAROLINA 28513
Telephone: 252-555-0183

6 February 20—

Ms. Janine Wooten, Director
Pitt County Homeless Shelter
2003 Jordan Way
Greenville, NC 27835

Ladies and Gentlemen:

Students, faculty, staff, and friends of Ayden-Grifton High School thank you for the certificate of appreciation in the attractive gold frame you sent us. We have placed it in our library in an area with other honors and awards where everyone can see and enjoy it.

However, we also should thank you for this opportunity. Collecting items and assembling emergency kits for your agency taught all of us valuable lessons. The students not only used skills they are building in the classroom, such as writing letters to the business community requesting donations of products, but also learned that effective teamwork makes even a big task possible. Yet the most important lesson that the students as well as the adults who assisted learned is that one person, no matter what age, can make a difference in the lives of others.

Ayden-Grifton High School looks forward to working with the Pitt County Homeless Shelter on a similar project next year.

Sincerely,

Mr. James Gray

Mr. James Gray
Principal
Ayden-Grifton High School

pts

Figure 5.3 Sample Letter

INTRODUCTION TO E-MAILS, MEMORANDUMS, AND LETTERS

Communication is essential for being able to act and make decisions in the business world. People must be able to share information. Some communication can take place face-to-face, but a great deal is conducted through e-mails, **memorandums,** and letters. All three may be used for brief correspondence; however, each one has its own distinguishing characteristics. For instance, e-mail is the fastest, most efficient means of written communication. A writer can compose a message, send it electronically around the world, and receive an answer immediately.

Unlike electronic correspondence, memorandums and letters take more time. Of the two, memorandums are more efficient than letters, primarily because memorandums have fewer formal parts and because they are usually directed to an audience within the same organization as the sender. In contrast, letters may have many parts and may be sent by the postal service or a commercial carrier to readers outside the organization.

All brief correspondence seeks the **goodwill** of readers and practices principles of good communication.

GOODWILL

Goodwill is the act of making a friend and then keeping the friend. Goodwill is like good vibes, a feeling of good intentions. Effective business correspondence fosters goodwill through its word choice and message. You can create goodwill in writing the same way you create the bonds of a friendship.

WARM UP

Imagine what the world would be like if people were not able to retain information or share ideas. For example, what would scientific knowledge be today if people had not been able to build on the discoveries of previous generations?

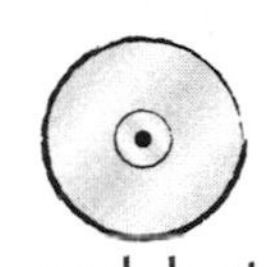

Complete the Sample Correspondence worksheet on the Data CD.

FOCUS

Warm Up

Use Warm Up to help students see the importance of written communication. They should understand that while talking might be more direct, records of ideas are valuable. Sharing written ideas gives people who work in different locations a means to think through a concept carefully and a way to respond efficiently.

TEACH

Introduce the following points about goodwill: goodwill in business is promoted by practicing good ethics, using proper manners, respecting others, accepting others as equals, being generous when possible, and providing high-quality service and products.

Have students complete

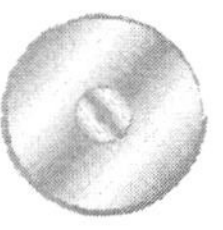

the Sample Correspondence worksheet on the IRCD.

TEACH

Ask students what destroys a good friendship. Many of the same things that destroy a friendship also destroy goodwill between business correspondents.

Students may be interested to know that goodwill can be bought and sold. When a business with an established name and reputation is sold, the company's goodwill increases its value.

Principles of good communication include being accurate, complete, and concise. Answering correspondence quickly in a professional-looking letter with no errors is also following good communication principles. Good communication promotes goodwill.

ENRICH

Conduct a discovery learning activity in which you give students an extremely bad handout—one with misspelled words, incomplete and illogical sentences, poorly organized and worded ideas, perhaps even coffee stains and torn edges. Then ask students for their impression of the handout and the person who prepared it. Ask them to evaluate the writer's performance based on the handout.

Goodwill, like friendship, is created by being honest and polite. Business friendships grow in an atmosphere of mutual respect and trust. You also foster goodwill by attending to correspondence as quickly as you can. In short, you generate goodwill by treating your reader as you would like to be treated.

PRINCIPLES OF EFFECTIVE COMMUNICATION

In addition to generating goodwill, brief correspondence should be helpful to readers. The list below suggests some of the characteristics of effective brief correspondence as well as traits to avoid in e-mails, memorandums, and letters.

Develops Goodwill	Hinders Goodwill	By
Concise language	Fuzzy, unnecessary words	Taking up readers' time with details they do not need
Accuracy, completeness	Inaccurate, incomplete information	Creating misunderstandings and problems to be solved later
Professional appearance	Sloppy appearance	Making you and your organization appear incompetent
Conventional format	Unfamiliar format	Confusing the reader, making your intent unclear
Logical organization	Illogical organization	Frustrating the reader
Standard English usage	Grammatical errors, misspelled words	Making you and your organization appear careless

Following conventional format and using standard English help make a positive impression on your reader. To ensure that the information in your correspondence is well organized, complete, and free of errors, reread the document before you send it. If you are unsure whether your message is clear, have a colleague read your correspondence and provide feedback.

E-mails, memos, and letters not only help to get the job done, but also serve as a way of evaluating the writer's performance. Managers and administrators can tell from an employee's correspondence whether that employee is solving or creating problems, communicating with or confusing readers, building or ruining relationships, getting the job done or making no progress.

CREATING A SUITABLE TONE

Brief correspondence usually has a conversational, informal tone. In fact, it is appropriate in this type of correspondence to use *I*, the first-person pronoun. "You're busy, so I'll be brief" is the opening sentence of an effective sales letter for a magazine. Note the focus on the reader, the use of first person, and the casual tone. Readers are more likely to cooperate when the message sounds as if a person, rather than a machine, wrote it. This informal writing style is similar to a conversation you might have with a friend, if that conversation were polished slightly.

USING HUMOR EFFECTIVELY

Use humor to create goodwill in difficult situations or with uncooperative audiences. For example, in Figure 5.4, Marissa McIntyre uses humor to convince students to volunteer to donate blood, even if they have not donated before or are a little afraid.

MEMORANDUM

TO: All Students 23 October 20—

FROM: Marissa McIntyre, Volunteer Club Chair

SUBJECT: Giving Up Your Blood!

The Volunteer Club again this fall invites you to give blood when we host the American Red Cross Bloodmobile on campus 28 October 20—. See Mrs. Liang in the main office to schedule an appointment for any free period on Bloodmobile Day. Please show your pride and sign up today!

Mr. DeLeone, the Volunteer Club sponsor, says not to worry if you are afraid of the sight of blood—especially your own. This year he offers blindfolds for the faint-hearted and a shoulder to lean on for those who just plain faint!

Figure 5.4 Using Humor Effectively

Writers, however, should be cautious about using humor. As useful as it can be, humor used carelessly may be harmful. For example, a manager is not likely to laugh when her quality assurance officer writes that the government safety inspectors "were going to kill us" if that manager's daughter had been involved in a fatal car accident. Consider audience, situation, and character of the relationship before deciding whether to use humor.

What is goodwill and why is it important? Is a formal tone ever appropriate for brief correspondence?

ENRICH

Collect sample correspondence or have students collect materials to compare tone and the effect it has on readers.

TEACH

Humor can provide an effective way to persuade or present difficult ideas. Ask students to share some of their experiences that show effective use of humor.

Remind students of the danger of using humor. Stress the importance of knowing and analyzing an audience before deciding to incorporate humor. For examples, you might use political cartoons from a newspaper. Students who are politically aware and know the issues are more likely to enjoy these cartoons than those who are not. They will see the importance of audience analysis.

ONGOING ASSESSMENT

Stop and Think

Goodwill is a positive feeling of trust and friendship. Create goodwill by behaving ethically and providing quality products and services. Effective communication promotes goodwill.

Writers should analyze their audience. If formality is expected and acceptable, then writers should meet those expectations. However, brief correspondence usually uses an informal but slightly polished tone.

WARM UP

Imagine writing an e-mail or a note filled with private jokes, insider stories, or juicy gossip to your closest friend. Now imagine that message being misdirected to your parent, guardian, or teacher.

FOCUS

Warm up

Use Warm Up to tune in to your students' experiences and dramatically show how important targeting an audience can be. Discuss the consequences of sending misdirected messages or failing to know your audience.

Ask students how they feel about spamming, the indiscriminate sending of electronic messages. If they respond negatively, they should understand how readers on the job will respond to e-mails that do not meet their needs.

AUDIENCE

Readers of e-mails, memorandums, and letters have some similar characteristics. All expect this type of communication to be brief, to target a specific reader or readers, to have a specific purpose, and to follow conventional format.

Some correspondence is sent to a multiple audience, and some is written with a very select audience in mind. If the reader is only one person, meet the needs of that person. Use language and information he or she will understand and answer questions that reader would ask if he or she were present. If an audience is made up of a group of readers, consider the needs of all of them.

Regardless of how well you know your readers, use Figure 2.3 in Chapter 2 on page 32 to help you focus on your audience. If you know little about your audience, learn as much as you can. Ask others what they know about your audience or read correspondence your audience has written. If you can't learn much about your audience, assume a serious or neutral tone.

Keep your language moderately simple and natural. Work especially hard to build goodwill.

AUDIENCE FOR E-MAILS

E-mail, for personal and professional correspondence, has become a common way to communicate. Readers may be within or outside the writer's organization. So writers will know some readers well and others not at all. Because readers frequently receive a lot of e-mail in a day, they expect writers to focus on a point and keep the message brief, without omitting essential information. Readers expect messages to be relevant and clear; they will not waste their time with messages that are incomplete, confusing, or unclear.

AUDIENCE FOR MEMORANDUMS

Memorandums are used only to correspond inside an organization. Therefore, the reader will be a member of the writer's organization, an **internal audience.**

Within an organization, everyone is likely to receive and read memos. For example, an employee might get a memo from a coworker explaining a procedure change. A memo outlining the facts—implementation time, date, actions, and checklist—provides a written record so the person receiving the notice does not become confused about the details of what is expected.

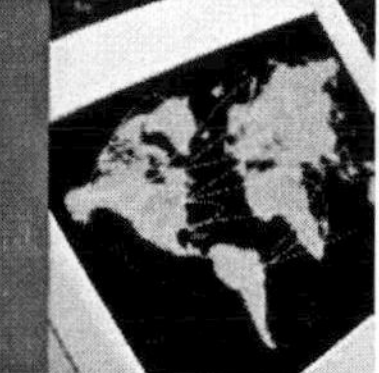

Communication Dilemma

You are sitting at your desk at Phoenix Fabrication when you receive an e-mail from your college dorm mate. He wants to know how you have been, what types of projects you are working on at work, and whether you plan to attend the class reunion. You want to send him an e-mail and boast a bit about the new product you are developing for your company. Since you haven't seen him in a couple of years, you also want to make plans to meet at the reunion.

Just when you are about to hit "reply," you remember that your boss cautioned you about using company time to conduct personal business. He also told you that if you reveal proprietary information about the company's products, you may be subject to legal action. That sounds pretty scary, you think, but maybe just one little personal e-mail will not hurt. After all, how will anyone know you sent it?

Should you reply to your college dorm mate?

COMMUNICATION DILEMMA

Use Communication Dilemma to initiate a discussion regarding good stewardship. Refer to the Focus on Ethics in this chapter to begin the discussion. Have students think of other situations that might be "stealing from the company." Ask students where they think the line should be drawn. This discussion may be extended to cover the ethics of making negative comments about a coworker or boss.

ONGOING ASSESSMENT
Stop and Think
E-mails may be sent to internal or external readers, memos typically target an internal audience, and letters generally address an external audience. However, in special circumstances when formality is needed, such as for a promotion, dismissal, or recommendation, letters may be sent to people inside an organization.

Even though memos are addressed to people inside a company, the writer must consider the audience carefully. The audience may consist of people with a variety of outlooks, backgrounds, opinions, interests, and levels in the organization.

Remember that the internal audience of an international company may have members in Los Angeles and Moscow. Once identified, each audience must be thoroughly studied to ensure that its needs are met.

AUDIENCE FOR LETTERS

While memos are for readers inside an organization (internal communication), letters are for readers outside an organization (external communication). Although you may know a great deal about members inside your organization, you may know very little about readers outside your company, an **external audience.**

A letter is an extension of your organization. The letter will be in the presence of your reader when you are not. If the letter is well written, you will make a good impression and inspire confidence in yourself and your organization.

What are the primary differences in audiences for e-mails, memorandums, and letters?

WARM UP

Think about the planning involved in hosting a party or preparing a meal. What kind of party or meal might result if you do not plan? Likewise, how effective can your correspondence be if you do not plan?

FOCUS

Warm Up

Use Warm Up to stress the importance of prewriting and planning.

TEACH

Share real-life disasters that resulted from going directly to final draft and omitting the important beginning phase. You probably know some illustrations of this fast-track writing, but here is one to help you get started:

A new personnel director decided to impress his supervisor with all he could accomplish on his first week at work. He sent memos to all 109 employees announcing the Service Awards given to people with ten or more years of employment and excellent service. While he specifically explained the requirements for being placed on the Service Awards list, he left out the names of the employees earning the honor. You will not be surprised to learn that his supervisor was impressed by the numerous calls requesting winners' names. Sadly, the impression was not a good one.

PREWRITING

Effective e-mails, memorandums, and letters depend on planning. After analyzing your audience, you need to make decisions based on what you have learned. Ask yourself these questions before you write:

- What do I want to accomplish with this message?
- What should happen after the receiver reads this correspondence?
- What is the main point?
- Does my reader need background information? How much?
- Do I need to make the message simpler for this audience? What definitions or explanations will the audience need?
- Is this reader familiar with the subject matter? Does the reader have previous experiences with this idea?
- What questions should my correspondence answer?

In addition to answering the questions above, you should take notes on the details you need for your correspondence. Gather the facts, such as the situation background, events that occurred, problems created, order/part numbers, accurate descriptions, or questions to ask. Find out the name, title, correct spelling, and correct address of the person you are writing to. Double-check to make sure the information you have gathered is accurate and complete.

Using the answers to these questions, put your ideas on paper. Some writers prefer a list, such as the kind you make for grocery shopping. Other writers like to use freewriting. As you learned in Chapter 4, freewriting is writing everything that comes to mind. Remember that this is the creative part of writing, so do not be critical of your ideas. Get all of the ideas, brilliant or otherwise, on paper.

Whichever technique you use will generate a collection of ideas you want to cover in the message or body. With all of the ideas before you, you can start to be critical. Cut the ones that are unnecessary and change those that do not communicate exactly what you want to say. Prewriting is also the time to rank ideas. Consider what you will place first, second, third, and so on.

PREWRITING E-MAILS

Prewriting for e-mail involves planning to communicate with readers who have diverse needs and expectations. First, remember that busy professionals may receive a great volume of e-mail. Thus, your SUBJECT line must be specific and descriptive; it should immediately show readers how the topic relates to them. If your SUBJECT line is poorly written, chances are the receiver will delete your message without reading it.

Second, consider the reader's expectations for formality and length. If you are sending an e-mail to people within your company or organization, you are likely to know the formality they expect by referring to other e-mails. For instance, the corporate climate may be formal, so readers might expect complete sentences, correct punctuation, and few or no abbreviations.

However, others with whom you communicate electronically may be more comfortable with informal e-mails—incomplete sentences; little punctuation; and the many abbreviations writers have developed to make online exchanges fast, such as *BTW* for *by the way* or *HAND* for *Have a nice day.*

In addition to level of formality, plan the length of your messages to meet readers' needs and expectations. Since people generally read e-mail from a computer screen rather than print hard copies, keep messages as brief as possible so that people can read the text without scrolling through several pages. Short messages also allow for easier response. If you have a long, involved message, send it as several different e-mails or create a document with a word processor and send the long document as an attachment.

Third, plan for differences in e-mail software. Avoid complex formatting, such as bulleted lists, tables, italics, or underlining, unless you know that the recipient's software can read them.

Fourth, clearly explain the context of your message so that all readers will understand. For example, when you respond to a question, make sure readers realize which question you are answering.

Finally, plan for handling emotions effectively. Do not flame. (When writers harshly criticize each other, they are flaming.) Avoid e-mailing when you are angry. Wait until you can handle the issue logically, rather than emotionally. Using all capital letters generally equates to shouting, so use this style only when you intend to shout. For emphasis, you can surround a word or phrase with asterisks or white space.

Another way to convey feelings is through the use of emoticons, symbols created on the keyboard to convey emotions, such as :-), the smiley face. Yet writers must carefully consider how readers will react to the feelings expressed in an e-mail because feelings can be misinterpreted or misunderstood.

To learn about writing processes for all types of correspondence, including business letters, e-mails, and memos, check out Colorado State's writing web site.

To view e-mail makeovers, articles about business writing, checklists to guide your writing, and more, log on to the E-write Online site. You can even take a quiz to test your e-mail know-how!

You can find the url for both sites in the web links on techwriting.swlearning.com.

SEE THE SITES

Set aside time in class for students to view the sites, which are full of information about technical writing. Students can then use the sites to improve an e-mail, a memo, or a letter they have written. Have them write a paper explaining how the information in the sites helped them improve their writing.

TEACH

Tell students to break long sections of text into short paragraphs. Readability improves with short paragraphs because the paragraph breaks help readers' spatial memory, the same way people find where a word or an idea is located and track where they are when reading from line to line.

Students can develop a glossary of emoticons with definitions or suggestions for use. Some emoticons they might include are :-) happiness, pleasure; :-(sadness, displeasure; >;-< anger.

TEACH

Explain that performance often is evaluated based on the memos employees write. The evaluation may be indirect, as when a manager hears about problems, questions, or second requests that resulted from an ineffective first memo.

RETEACH

Because memos are internal correspondence, remind students to consider their relationship with the audience. If the memo addresses more than one reader, students must plan to meet all of their needs and answer the questions all of them might have.

PREWRITING MEMORANDUMS

As with planning e-mails, prewriting memorandums requires writers to consider the audience's expectations. Readers usually expect memos to be brief and to cover one topic. However, the need to be brief should not override substance. Make sure the memo fully explains the topic, whether it offers a solution to a problem, outlines a change in procedures or policies, or deals with other business concerns.

© GETTY IMAGES/PHOTODISC

Furthermore, writers sometimes choose to write memos as documentation (proof) of discussions, decisions, or actions. Perhaps you or your company would like something more substantial or concrete than e-mail to back up an offer made during a meeting or a request for information or an action taken following a safety review.

You should plan to include all of the specific details—names, dates, times, locations, and other details—that your audience might need.

PREWRITING LETTERS

Memos as internal correspondence may, in some circumstances, be informal; and in others, formal. Letters, on the other hand, are almost always formal. Letters usually address external audiences, so letter writers should keep the reader informed.

For instance, the reader may not be as aware of history and background as others inside the organization are. The reader is not likely to know insider language or jargon. In addition, when a person is communicating with an unfamiliar audience, the writer should put his or her best foot forward, carefully choosing words, gauging tone, and focusing on the purpose of the correspondence.

When letters are used internally for special circumstances, such as promotions, dismissals, recommendations, or disciplinary matters, writers should plan for a higher level of formality because of the importance of the subject and the legal implications.

ONGOING ASSESSMENT

Stop and Think

The fact that e-mail is somewhat permanent, meaning that even deleted files can be retrieved and can be accessed or forwarded intentionally or accidentally, suggests that writers need to prepare for people other than the intended recipient to see the message. Such planning, even for remote possibilities, may prevent future problems.

Why are e-mail privacy and security issues important to consider in prewriting?

FORMATTING

Much as fancy type identifies a formal invitation, the formatting features of e-mails, memorandums, and letters help readers recognize the type of correspondence they are viewing. Specific elements are unique to each type. E-mails, for example, may look like memos, but they typically include e-mail addresses for the sender and receiver. Memos are recognizable by their headings (To, From, Date, and Subject) and the title *MEMO* at the top of the document. Likewise, the mark of a letter is the inside and return addresses, salutation, and complimentary close, features familiar to audiences.

WARM UP

Think about the information all readers want to know when they receive messages. What are their questions? Compare the answer to this question to the elements of formatting for e-mails, memos, and letters.

FOCUS

Warm Up

Use Warm Up to show students that the elements of formatting answer questions receivers ask. For instance, the receiver of a message usually wants to know 1) who sent the message, 2) who the intended receiver is, 3) when the message was sent, and 4) what the message is about.

FORMATTING E-MAILS

Writers usually do not need to be concerned about formatting decisions when they create e-mails because the e-mail software provider has already made most of the decisions. Most programs, such as Microsoft® Outlook Express®, shown in Figure 5.5, simply ask the writer to click on a light-colored line or in a blank box and type the intended receiver or subject line. Most programs insert the sender's name or address automatically.

Figure 5.5 Formatting E-mails

TEACH

Explain during discussion of the TO and FROM lines that writers should use job and courtesy titles based on the reader's need to know. For instance, in large organizations, an employee in one division may receive a memo from another part of the company sent by someone whom he or she has never heard of or met. Without a job title accompanying the sender's name, the receiver may not fully understand the message and its context.

RETEACH

Remind students to be consistent with titles throughout the memo. If a courtesy or professional title (Mr., Rev., Lt., Dr.) is used for one person, use a title for all names mentioned. The other option is to omit all titles.

FORMATTING MEMORANDUMS

The rough draft of a memo begins with a standard **format** of headings and is followed by the body or message. Like the addresses and salutation (Dear Mr. Roberio:) in a letter, headings make a document recognizable as a memo. Five elements usually appear at the top of a memo:

MEMO

TO:
FROM:
DATE:
SUBJECT:

However, the headings do not always appear in this order. When you begin work, your new employer will probably give you a style manual that shows you the format the company prefers.

Memo templates are included in most word processing software. Microsoft® Word, for instance, provides three memo templates and a wizard to help writers create memorandums. The advantages of working with memo templates are that they are simple to use (even for writers with no experience), are easily modified, and provide attractive document design.

At the same time, these familiar templates have a number of shortcomings, such as overused design (readers will recognize the template) and decisions made without the writer's input or consideration. Because writers do not need to think about design or headings, sometimes these "plug-and-play" templates encourage writers not to think about other decisions relating to their message. Ineffective communication may be the result.

Caption The word *MEMO* or *Memorandum* should be placed at the top of the page. Some preprinted memo forms and most computer software packages provide the caption for writers.

TO Line In the TO section, you name your audience. You can name one person, such as Joanna Jett, or you can name a group, such as the Employee Benefits Committee or the Sterile Manufacturing Division. On occasion, you may need to name several readers who are not connected by a unit or committee. In this case, you may simply list their names.

MEMORANDUM

TO:	Alec Abernathy	Hector Cruz
	Ruth Braxton	Bernice Spencer
	Wesley T. Crawford	Ann Ziegler-Lee
FROM:	Anita Delrio *Anita Delrio*	

Figure 5.6 Receivers' Names Listed in Columns

The list of receivers' names may be presented in several ways. For example, you can place all names on one or two lines and connect them with commas, as in the model memo at the beginning of this chapter. Another option is to place the names in one column or several columns, as in Figure 5.6. The number of columns you choose depends on how many names you list.

If you list several people's names, enter them in either alphabetical or hierarchical order. In hierarchical order, the people of greatest recognition and responsibility in the organization, such as the president and vice president, are listed first. Others are listed in decreasing order of rank within the organization. Remember, however, if the hierarchal list contains two employees of the same rank, such as two directors, you should place their names in alphabetical order so as not to offend either person.

FROM Line After the FROM heading, you list the name or names of the sender of the message. If you are the only person responsible for the message, your name appears. If the memo comes from a group, the group or unit name is listed, such as FROM: Jefferson Jazz Band.

Some memos are from several people not tied to a group. In this case, list the names of the individual senders in a line joined by commas or in columns, again in alphabetical or hierarchical order. Also, remember to write your initials or sign your full name after the typed name in the FROM section, as in Figure 5.6.

Initialing or signing is especially important on memos that deal with important legal or organizational matters. Memos become legal documents that can be used in a court of law when they are signed and dated. In

TEACH

Explain that job titles may be included after a name; however, job titles should not be used alone. If a name and a title are placed on the same line, a comma separates them. The job title also may be placed one line beneath the name. Writers might choose to include job titles for audiences who will not recognize the name alone.

Share with students the fact that the word "memorandum" comes from the Latin "memorare," which means "to remember."

FOCUS ON ETHICS

Tell students that using company time and equipment to conduct personal business can be equated to stealing from the company. In addition, workers may be embarrassed and worse, fired, if a personal e-mail ends up in a manager's in-box.

Sending a personal e-mail that reveals proprietary information (ideas the company owns) might cost you your good standing with your colleagues or even your job. It might subject you to legal action as well. Do not say anything in an e-mail that you would not say directly to a person and do not write anything that might embarrass you or your organization, regardless of who reads it. E-mail can be deleted, but it never really disappears and may be forwarded anywhere to anyone. Most networks (the sender's and the receiver's) archive and back up all e-mail.

In addition, some people might think that a simple e-mail reply to a friend outside the company is not so bad. If so, then you might ask, "Where do we draw the line?" and "Who draws the line?" If using the office computer to answer personal messages is fine, then is it okay to use the company car to pick up your dry cleaning or the corporate credit card to pay for the dry cleaning? Can you use the office copy machine to run off brochures for your weekend real estate business? Can you use time you have at work to order a gift online for your brother's birthday or pay your personal water bill? What about making a couple of long-distance phone calls to your grandparents on the company phone?

Using company time and equipment to conduct personal business is unwise; it could get your company in trouble legally, and you could be fired.

TEACH

Because communication today is often with people who are widespread culturally, international date style prevents confusion.

Reinforce the need for SUBJECT lines that are focused and specific. Well-written subject lines help writers and readers understand the message.

addition, your initials or signature tells your reader that you have reviewed the memo and accept responsibility for the message, especially if someone else typed the document.

DATE Line The DATE line usually appears after TO and FROM and before the SUBJECT line. It also can appear in the upper right corner across from the TO line. You can choose between two styles for writing the date: international (also called *military* in the United States) or traditional.

International date style is becoming increasingly popular in technical documents because of economy. International style requires no commas. In this style, the writer gives the day first, the month next, and the year last, as in 12 December 1996.

Traditional-style dates, as in June 4, 1955, or April 1, 2006, give the month, the date, a comma, and the year.

SUBJECT Line In most memos, the SUBJECT line logically appears as the last of the headings. It announces the point of the memo immediately before you develop that point. You may see terms such as *Reference*, *Regarding*, or *Re* (which comes from the Latin *res* meaning "thing" or "matter") used in the same way as the word SUBJECT. In addition to helping the reader predict the topic, the *SUBJECT* line distinguishes one message from another and focuses the writer on one main idea.

> **Predict.** The SUBJECT line should allow readers to predict what the memo will say; in other words, it reflects the main idea discussed in the body. Be as specific as you can when composing the SUBJECT line. A SUBJECT line that reads "Insurance" does little to help the reader predict what the memo will cover; the line is too general to provide insight. "Dental Insurance Open Enrollment Period Set for 20–27 June 2004" is precise enough to tell readers what to expect and encourage them to read the message. The SUBJECT line should not be a complete sentence, but a phrase or clause, more like a newspaper headline.
>
> **Distinguish.** In addition to helping the reader predict the subject of the memo, the SUBJECT line should make clear the difference between one memo and many others. For instance, servers at a restaurant may read many memos during the year that deal with menu items. Therefore, if the SUBJECT line says only "Menu Changes," the server reading it will not immediately know this message is different from last week's memo. Instead, specific SUBJECT lines, such as "Italian Items Added to Menu for June" or "Lobster Price Increase" or "Salmon Unavailable Until 20 April" tell the server exactly what to expect the message to cover.
>
> **Focus.** The SUBJECT line also aids the writer. Writing a SUBJECT line forces the writer to focus on the most important idea. It further allows the writer to check the message of the memo against the SUBJECT line. The message should cover the same idea that the SUBJECT line announces.

A memo should cover only one main point. Writers who have two messages for the same audience should write two memos. First, if a memo has more than one message, the reader cannot determine what is truly important. Second, the very busy reader may find the first idea, assume it is the only important information, and quit reading. Third, the memo might be so long that it intimidates readers. Readers generally expect memos to be one to four paragraphs. Finally, some messages are inappropriate to combine, as in Figure 5.7.

FOCUS

Figure 5.7
Stress that this model shows what NOT to do in memo writing.

Ask students to form groups and identify problems with this memo. Have each group create a list of revisions a writer would need to make. The list should include putting *MEMO* at the top of the page; placing names in the TO list in order, preferably alphabetical order; adding a signature or initials after Smith's name; and focusing the SUBJECT line and the body of the memo on one topic.

TO: Dr. Joyner Mr. Umezaki
Dr. Everest Ms. Shankowski

FROM: Hannah Smith, Personnel Officer

DATE: June 10, 20—

SUBJECT: 1. Vacation and Sick Leave Slips
2. Death of Mr. Martin's Mother-in-law

1. Please ensure that all vacation and sick leave slips for this fiscal year (July 1, 20— through June 30, 20—) are turned in to Tammie by June 27, 20—.

2. Dan Martin's mother-in-law and Selma Hale's grandmother, Mrs. Sadie Harper, passed away on Sunday, June 9, 20—. Funeral arrangements are being handled by Belevedere's Funeral Home. Services will be held at Belevedere's Funeral Home at 2 p.m. on Tuesday, June 11. Expressions of sympathy may be sent to

Dan at: 811 E. Cooper Street
Tylersville, SD 47934

Selma at: Route 1, Box 32
Tylersville, SD 47934

Figure 5.7 Ineffective Memo with Two Main Ideas

FORMATTING LETTERS

All letters share a similar format. They are constructed in basic parts and may be written in one of several styles. Two possible styles are **block style** and **modified block style.**

Letter Parts The letter model at the beginning of this chapter on page 110 and Figure 5.8 on the next page illustrate the basic parts of a letter: heading, dateline, inside address, salutation, body, closing, signature, and reference initials. Note the description of each part.

TEACH

Point out that people try to create a favorable impression by looking neat, using their best manners, working efficiently, and focusing on the person they are trying to impress. That is exactly what an effective letter does–it creates a good impression in the sender's place by looking attractive; being polite and efficient; and making the reader feel special, as though he or she has the sender's undivided attention.

Use Figure 5.8 to help students understand what information is contained in each part of a letter.

ENRICH

Share a collection of letters for students to review. Engage the class in a discussion of style choices and the resulting impressions they make.

Assign students to create personal letterheads to use in writing assignments.

Show the Parts of Letters Transparency on the IRCD.

Jefferson Gas and Appliance HWY 17 South P.O. Box 11 Washington, NC 27889	**HEADING:** complete address (no abbreviations) of the sender as a *return address* (personal business letter) or letterhead (company/organization letter).
13 July 20—	**DATELINE:** date the letter was written.
Ms. Rhea Tankard Manager Malloy's Manufacturing 1023 West Main Street Washington, NC 27889	**INSIDE ADDRESS:** professional (Dr., Rev., Capt., or others) or courtesy title (Mr., Ms., or Mrs.), correct name (first name/first initial and last name), title, and address of the person to whom you are writing (no abbreviations). Name here should match the name used in the salutation.
Dear Ms. Tankard	**SALUTATION:** exact name of the person you want to read your letter. May be written with or without end punctuation.
Subject: Contract for . . .	**SUBJECT LINE** (optional): focuses on the topic of the letter.
Xxxxxxxxxxxxxxxxxxx Xxxxxxx xxxxxxx xxxx Xxxxxxxxxxxxxxxxxxx Xxxxxxxxxxx xxxxxx x Xxxxxxxxxxxxxxxxx Xxxxxxxxxxxxxxxxxxx Xxxxxxx xxxxxxx xxxx Xxxxxxxxxxxxxxxxxxx Xxxxxxxxxxx xxxxxx x Xxxxxxxxxxxxxxxxx Xxxxxxxxxxxxxxxxxxx Xxxxxxx xxxxxxx xxxx Xxxxxxxxxxxxxxxxxxx Xxxxxxxxxxx xxxxxx x Xxxxxxxxxxxxxxxxx	**BODY:** usually two to five paragraphs long but can be several pages and may use headings similar to reports. The letter should look balanced on the page. The BODY of most letters is single-spaced with a double space (one blank line) between paragraphs. The organization depends on the type of letter you are writing. In standard block style letters, all lines begin at the left margin. In modified block style, all lines begin at the left margin except the date and the closing lines, which are centered. First lines of paragraphs may begin at the left margin or be indented.
Sincerely yours	**CLOSING:** friendly but businesslike ending. Common closings include *Sincerely, Yours truly,* and *Cordially* (never *Thank you*). Punctuate in *pairs:* Punctuate *both* the salutation and the closing OR punctuate *neither* the salutation *nor* the closing.
W. B. (Jeff) Jefferson President	**SIGNATURE LINE:** typed name and title with space for handwritten signature above.
WBJ/pjm	**REFERENCE INITIALS:** initials (in uppercase) of the person who dictated the letter followed by the initials (in lowercase) of the person who typed the letter. The two sets of initials may be separated by a slash or a colon.
Enclosures (3)	**ENCLOSURE NOTATION:** indicates additional documents in the envelope. Often the word *Enclosure* is followed by a colon and the titles of the enclosed documents are listed.
c: Pat Morgan Jon Reardon	**COPY NOTATION:** indicates a copy has been sent to other people.

Figure 5.8 Letter Parts

Letter Styles Letter styles vary. Usually, business letters are written on letterhead stationery in either block or modified block style. Personal letters include return addresses instead of letterheads and may be written in block or modified block style.

Block-style letters are easy to type but may look off-balance. Paragraphs are not indented, and every part (except the letterhead, which may be centered) is flush with the left margin. Modified block style is difficult to type but looks more symmetrical on the page. In this style, the dateline, return address (if letterhead stationery is not used), closing, and signature line are typed beginning at the horizontal center of the page. Paragraphs may be indented or typed flush with the left margin. Figure 5.9 illustrates basic differences in block and modified block design.

Two punctuation styles are commonly used in business letters: open and mixed. Open punctuation means no punctuation marks are used after the salutation and the complimentary close. Open punctuation is considered a time-saving style and is often used with a block format letter. When the mixed punctuation style is used, the salutation and complimentary close are followed by punctuation marks. The proper punctuation with this style is a comma after the complimentary close and a colon (for business letters) or a comma (for personal or informal letters) after the salutation.

Block With No Indents

Letterhead
Dateline

Inside Address

Dear Mr. Torres

Xxxx xxxxx xxxxxx xxxxx
xxxxxx xxx x xxxxx xx xxx
xx xx xxx xxxxxxxx xxxxx

Yours truly

Modified Block With Indents

Letterhead
Dateline

Inside Address

Dear Mr. Torres

Xxxx xxxxx xxxxxx xxxxx
xxxxxx xxx x xxxxx xx xxx
xx xx xxx xxxxxxxx xxxxx

Yours truly

Modified Block With No Indents

Personal Address
Dateline

Inside Address

Dear Mr. Torres

Xxxx xxxxx xxxxxx xxxxx
xxxxxx xxx x xxxxx xx xxx
xx xx xxx xxxxxxxx xxxxx

Yours truly

Figure 5.9 Letter Styles

In what order should the names of recipients be listed in e-mails or memos? Should a writer use *Thank you* as a complimentary close in a letter?

TEACH

Compare the block and modified block styles to see what advantages one has over the other. For instance, students will probably note that block style is easier to type because it involves fewer indentations and spacing issues.

ONGOING ASSESSMENT

Stop and Think

Names should be listed in alphabetical order or according to the hierarchy of the organization to avoid offending anyone.

No. Customary and acceptable closings include *Sincerely, Yours truly,* and *Cordially.*

WARM UP

Consider this opening line:

Dear Arnie, You're fired.

Does this message work? Will it build goodwill? Could the idea be presented more effectively?

FOCUS

Warm Up

Use Warm Up to show students that one composition plan does not fit all messages. Other possible uses for the Warm Up: role playing, an essay describing how Arnie might feel or react, or discussion of how to improve the delivery.

TEACH

Suggest that students test the organization of their good news messages by imagining that the reader has time to read only the first sentence before leaving the building due to a fire alarm. Does that one sentence provide the reader with the essential information? Is it the most important sentence in the document for the reader? If not, students should consider reorganizing.

Show the Illustrations of Organizational Strategies Transparency on the IRCD.

COMPOSING THE MESSAGE

Since all e-mails, memos, and letters begin with a specific purpose, writers must keep that purpose in mind when composing the message.

While formatting the document is important, the headings are only a means for conveying the ideas you want to share. The message or the body is the heart of the document.

The message section of correspondence should be organized for the reader, not for the writer. Employees are busy and cannot waste time, so correspondence should be organized accordingly. Imagine a busy decision maker opening an e-mail she expects to be one page, only to discover that the message is more than four pages. The receiver may decide not to invest the time to read four pages, especially when she expects e-mail to be brief. Writers who frustrate readers or fail to meet their expectations are not likely to be successful in achieving goals.

The message itself, along with readers' expectations, must be considered. Organize ideas according to the message. Some messages are best presented in a direct, straightforward way. Others, when presented bluntly and directly, are likely to offend readers. And others, such as persuasive messages, require more motivation than a direct approach provides. The strategies for informative and good news messages, negative or bad news messages, and persuasive messages are useful in writing e-mails, memorandums, and letters.

INFORMATIVE AND GOOD NEWS MESSAGES

Brief correspondence usually gives the audience information that is pleasant or at least acceptable. Pronouncements of good news, routine letters of inquiry, responses to letters of inquiry, and letters of appreciation all use a similar positive organizational structure.

You can expect the readers of a good news message to be in a receptive mood as they read your correspondence. Picture a smile, a HOORAY, or at least an affirmative nod from these readers. Because your news is responsible for the pleasant mood, these readers are easy to approach.

Therefore, the strategy is direct: present the main idea first. Explanations, background information, and supplementary ideas follow the main idea.

The model memo at the beginning of the chapter on page 109 and the memo message from the production manager at Imperial Waters, Inc., below are examples of the direct approach to organizing informative and good news messages.

MEMO

TO: All Lab Employees

FROM: Jamir Cayton, Production Manager *Jamir Cayton*

DATE: November 15, 20—

SUBJECT: Deadline to Turn In Leased Chemical Lab Garments

Please turn in by December 7, 20—, all leased chemical lab garments checked out to you.

We signed a contract and will receive service from a new cleaning company, D & W Garment Care Center, effective December 8, 20—. Benefits of the change you should notice are:

- Perfume- and starch-free garments.
- An additional coat each week.
- Immediate replacement of worn or damaged garments.

Main idea—what the writer wants the reader to do

Explanation and supplementary ideas—why the writer is requesting this action and what effect it will have on the reader

Figure 5.10 Memo Using the Direct Approach

TEACH

Use Figure 5.11 to review the strategy for good news messages as well as to review formatting.

Make students aware of current postal regulations regarding state abbreviations. See the Two-Letter Postal Abbreviations Transparency on the IRCD.

Introduce characteristics of positive messages by comparing them to how people give and receive good news in general. Point out that positive news is given quickly and is received well in good faith. Details usually follow the basic good news. Tone can vary from upbeat to enthusiastic.

Point out that the structure of each of the positive messages is essentially the same—general good news, necessary details, and a friendly close. Make sure students see this basic structure in all of the documents.

Figures 5.11 and 5.12 are examples of positive news letters. Figure 5.11 conveys good news to Regina Williams, the recipient of an $800 scholarship to a local community college. Here the tone is enthusiastic.

PITT Community College **Office Of The Dean Of Students**

Telephone **(919) 555-0139**
Fax Number **(919) 555-0140**

October 26, 20—

Ms. Regina Williams
P.O. Box 2453
Winterville, NCa 28590

Dear Ms. Williams:

I am pleased to award you an $800 PCC Student Government Association Scholarship to attend Pitt Community College for the 2004-2005 academic year. The selection committee recognizes your achievements and your need for assistance in attaining your chosen goal.

The funds will be disbursed during the upcoming academic year. These monies will be available for you to use during preregistration and registration for tuition and fees, as designated in the scholarship. Any remaining funds may be used to purchase books, supplies, or other school-related items in the PCC bookstore. Remaining funds will be given to you approximately four to eight weeks after registration.

I warmly congratulate you and wish you every possible success. We look forward to having you as a student at PCC. If you have any questions, feel free to contact Mr. Rudy Lloyd in Room 12 of our scholarship office in the Vernon White Building or call (919) 555-0164.

Sincerely,

Garrie Moore

Garrie Moore
Dean of Students

ta

P.O. Drawer 7007 • Greenville • North Carolina • 27835-7007
An Equal Opportunity/Affirmative Action Institution

Figure 5.11 Positive Message: Good News Letter

Figure 5.12 shows the body of a letter of inquiry. Correspondence of inquiry, while employing a more neutral tone, still represents positive messages because it shows an interest in a product or service.

Jamie Sitterson
1254 Littlefield Court, Johnson City, NM 40567-9903

3 February 20—

Mr. Robert M. Steiner, Director
William Faulkner Birthplace
P.O. Box 20
Oxford, MS 32145

Dear Mr. Steiner:

I would appreciate any information you can send me on William Faulkner's life as a young man in Oxford, Mississippi.

Specifically, I am interested in knowing:

1. Why Faulkner joined the Royal Air Force.
2. How old he was when he started to write.
3. Where he got the idea for Benji in The Sound and the Fury.

In addition, I would appreciate any brochures you have that show pictures of his birthplace, family, and life as a young man. I am working on a research paper for English and need this information by 12 December if I am to complete my research in time.

I would appreciate any information you can send.

Sincerely,

Jamie Sitterson

Jamie Sitterson

Figure 5.12 Positive Message: Letter of Inquiry

BAD NEWS MESSAGES

Occasionally the purpose of an e-mail, a memo, or a letter is to share negative news—information readers will not be pleased to get, such as employee layoffs or unpopular policy changes. Negative messages can range from serious to mildly disappointing. A letter with a negative message may refuse a request, delay an order, or register a complaint. In this case, the direct approach is not the best choice. If readers see the bad news immediately, the disappointment might be so great that they miss the explanation entirely. A bad news message must relay the bad news and still try to maintain the goodwill of the reader.

Therefore, the strategy of bad news messages is indirect. The bad news is softened by surrounding it with pleasant ideas in this way:

TEACH

Introduce negative news messages by comparing them to how people give and receive bad news in general. Point out that bad news is often given slowly with plenty of explanation. Often the explanation is given before the bad news. People generally try to console the receiver in some way after giving the bad news. Perhaps students can tell you of instances when bad news was given "well," with the bearer of the bad news showing compassion and concern for the receiver.

TEACH

The indirect approach sandwiches the bad news in the middle of good news. The indirect approach is psychologically sound because the message begins on a positive note. Close a negative letter by suggesting alternatives, looking toward the future, or offering something. In complaint letters, you may ask for something that will rectify the situation or satisfy you.

1. Open with a positive statement, or **buffer,** generally some idea about which the writer and reader agree.
2. In the next section of the message, clearly announce the bad news, but place it in the middle or at the end of the section, not at the beginning. Writers may choose to explain the reason for the bad news. Sometimes the explanation is unnecessary or even counterproductive.
3. Close the message on a pleasant note by offering an alternative solution or a different perspective, making a constructive suggestion, or looking positively to the future.

The following memo body written by the owner of Precision Cuts Hair Studio shows how the bad news in the middle is buffered by pleasant ideas in the opening and closing.

Precision Cuts Hair Studio

Memo

To: All Stylists

From: Monza Hairston *MH*

Owner and Manager

Date: 6 June 20—

Re: Fashioning a Positive and Professional Image

Positive statement–creativity, something about which reader and writer agree

Being creative folks, we enjoy expressing our individuality in the way we dress. It is stylish and fun to dress flamboyantly.

Bad news statement–new policy that is likely to be unpopular

Some of us, using those creative energies, have been talking about ways to improve our professional image. Toward this end, the shop will adopt a uniform dress policy beginning on the first working day of next month. You may choose from solid navy and solid white outfits or outfits combining the two colors.

Positive close–benefits employees may enjoy

Besides enhancing the shop's professional image, the new policy will save you money because your personal clothes will not be subjected to the chemicals you use every day. Any creative energy you have left can be spent on clients to make our shop the most popular one in town!

Figure 5.13 Bad News Memo with Buffer

The opening buffer protects the reader from the bad news, a friendly close ends on a positive note, and the bad news is strategically sandwiched in between.

Figure 5.14 shows a negative news letter. Abraham Bizmark of Bizmark Gold Studio writes La'Neice Jackson, president of D'Oro Jewelry Stores.

TEACH

Note that the bad news occupies the least amount of space. Likewise, writers should not dwell on the negative part of the message.

Help students see that each of the negative news messages uses a variation of the indirect approach.

Bizmark Gold Studio
123 Front Street Rivervale, ND 99743
Telephone 709.555.0110 Fax 709.555.0111

30 September 20—

La'Neice Jackson, President
D'Oro Jewelry Stores
P.O. Box 4091
Tabor City, ND 99712

Dear Ms. Jackson:

Thank you for your recent order from Bizmark Gold Studio. We know you are preparing for the busy holiday season.

Buffer

However, the recent trucking strike has made it difficult for us to deliver customers' orders in the southwest region of the state. Therefore, your order for 250 rings (100, #3567890; 100, #7865301; and 50, #9956541) and 300 serpentine necklaces (150, #7643781; 100, #3215431; and 50, #9799773), which would normally reach you in ten working days, will be delayed until the trucking crisis has been resolved.

Explanation

We appreciate your understanding and apologize for any inconvenience. The trucking strike has caused similar delays with other businesses in the region.

Bad news

We know that gold jewelry says so much more than other gifts for many of your customers; it represents life connections. Since our designs in 14-karat gold are such an important element in your preholiday inventory, we will make sure that your order is on the first truck out of our Missoula studio when the new trucking contracts are signed.

Friendly close—what the writer CAN do

Sincerely,

Abraham Bizmark
Abraham Bizmark
Vice President, Marketing and Distribution
c:Ricardo Batista, Shipping and Receiving

www.bizmarkjewelry.com

Figure 5.14 Negative Message: Bad News

Letters of complaint are also examples of correspondence containing negative news. When an individual has a legitimate complaint, the challenge is to present the complaint without alienating the reader. Most complaint letters also include a request to make things right, sometimes a refund, an exchange, extra service, or at least an assurance that the problem will not recur. Figure 5.15 shows the body of a complaint letter to Luigi's Restaurant.

76 Old Tar Road
Homestead, FL 83713
March 19, 20—

Manager, Luigi's Italian Restaurant
Ocean Boulevard
Key Largo, FL 83725

Manager:

Buffer

I have enjoyed dining at Luigi's for a number of years. My parents have visited your restaurant to celebrate special occasions—birthdays, anniversaries, graduations—ever since I can remember.

Last Saturday night I took my date to Luigi's for an elegant meal before our senior prom. However, instead of receiving the special treatment my date and I were expecting, we were treated unfairly.

Explanation and complaint

My 7:40 reservation, made well in advance three weeks ago, was not honored. Instead, I saw the host give the corner table I had requested to another couple. As a result, my date and I had to wait 45 minutes (a very long and hungry 45 minutes) before another table was ready. I was embarrassed, and our late dinner caused us to miss the opening toast at our senior prom.

Request for action

I would like to know that I can look forward to other special dinners at Luigi's. Would you please talk to your host and convey my disappointment? Please let me know that the next time I bring a friend to eat at Luigi's, the service will be improved.

Respectfully,

Zane M. Brecht

Zane M. Brecht

Figure 5.15 Negative Message: Letter of Complaint

PERSUASIVE MESSAGES

A persuasive message is any correspondence in which the sender attempts to convince the receiver to agree with the writer. Persuasive messages are most typically used to sell products or services. Persuasive messages also include requests for assistance, support, or participation, such as a request for an employment recommendation or an invitation to participate in a telethon to raise money for a charity. The memo below written by a sales director shows a persuasive strategy at work.

ENRICH

Assign groups of students to analyze television commercials and print ads for motivational techniques. Ask each group to report its findings to the class. As a class, determine the most effective appeals.

Have students write a paper in which they describe a time when someone else successfully persuaded them to do or agree to something. Talk about what their descriptions say about persuasion.

Point out that writers of sales literature must know a great deal about their readers and competition to write successful sales letters.

Ask a business instructor or a local sales professional to talk about his or her skills and experiences.

Share with the class your own collection of sales letters.

Interoffice memorandum

to: All Sales Representatives

from: Jordan Smithwick, Sales Director JS

date: 12 November 20—

subject: Using the Board to Help Yourself OR
Putting Your Schedule to Work for You and Others

Would you like the IRS to be able to find you in order to deliver your tax refund check? Would you like customers to be able to find you when they want to place an order?

Hook—uses humor and direct questions to grab attention

If these possibilities are important to you, please help me to help you. Just today I have had five calls for sales representatives I could not locate. That could be five orders that will not be placed, as well as commissions that will not go into your paycheck. To avoid this problem, check in and out on the board. It is still on my office door, and a brand-new marker is attached for your use.

Sell—gives details to convince the reader

Please remember to sign in when you arrive at work and to sign out when you leave for the day, but especially mark times when you leave the building for lunch or sales calls. If you do, I can tell your callers when to call again or when to expect your return call. And I'll even hold your refund check until you return!

Motivate—calls the reader to action

Figure 5.16 Persuasive Memo

Communication Update

You are now in the midst of a worldwide intelligent network that can do some amazing things. Communication tools are wireless and much smaller today than they were just a couple of years ago. Handheld computers allow you to fax, call, e-mail, and surf the World Wide Web and to send graphics, videos, and instant messages to anyone in the world. The use of such devices, such as AT&T's Blackberry™ handheld computer and Palm's™ TREO™ 600, allows you to conduct business and communicate with people anywhere at any time.

COMMUNICATION UPDATE

Use Communication Update to generate a discussion about how today's communication devices are changing not only the way business is conducted, but also the ways personal lives are led. How does being able to communicate and conduct business any time, anywhere increase the busyness of people's lives? Or has it? What do students see as the future for communication in their business and personal lives?

Sales Letters Sales letters, because they must convince readers that the product or service is worthy of their time and money, are one type of persuasive message. Many employees write sales letters as a part of their responsibilities. Some sales letters target only one reader, while others target a large audience. Think, for instance, of the junk mail, or direct sales mail, you receive. Many products—magazines, books, vinyl siding, music, videos, seeds and plants, tools, and others—are sold by these mass mailings of sales letters.

Who Reads Sales Letters? Today's sophisticated marketing techniques make it possible to target select audiences for certain products. Knowing your audience's needs and interests is vital to writing sales letters.

Consumers make buying decisions based on a number of psychological and sociological factors. Abraham Maslow, in his work on human motivation, said people try to satisfy the following basic needs and higher-order needs. His system is known as **Maslow's Hierarchy of Needs:**

Physiological. Physical needs for food, water, and air; the need to be free from pain; and the need to have a family

Safety. Protection from the environment by adequate shelter

Love and Belonging. The need to receive and to give affection, to feel accepted by others

Esteem. The need to be respected by others and by themselves; the need for recognition, status, and prestige

Self-Actualization. The highest of needs, attained by only a few people; after satisfying the first four needs, self-actualized people fulfill their potential

Basic needs must be met before higher-order needs can be met. For example, individuals must have food and shelter and feel physically secure before they can seek love and belonging. They must feel love and belonging before they can seek esteem.

When writing a sales letter, ask which needs on Maslow's Hierarchy you are addressing. Meet the lower needs first and remember that people's buying decisions can be more complicated than they appear. Wanting particular brand-name shoes may have more to do with a need for acceptance than with a physical need for footwear.

Consider **sociological influences** and buyer involvement. Present circumstances, social class, culture, and family influence buying decisions. Also, some consumers may be more involved in buying decisions than others. Highly involved consumers search for information and evaluate alternatives. Less-involved consumers may be indifferent, buying what is on sale or what is convenient.

Know what your competition has to offer so you can counter with convincing proof of your product. Try to find out how much your reader is willing to spend.

Use these questions to analyze your sales audience:

- What psychological needs does my reader have? (Use Maslow's Hierarchy as a starting point.)
- What sociological factors may influence my reader's buying decision?
- How involved is my reader likely to be?
- What is my competition offering, and how is my offer better?
- What objections will my reader have to my product?
- How much is my reader willing to spend?

Organizing and Composing Sales Letters Persuasion means you make your product or service look appealing. Presenting false information is unethical, but it's considered good business sense to present a product's strengths in a sales letter. To make a product or service look appealing, write sales letters according to the following organizational plan:

- HOOK your reader's attention.
- SELL your product or service.
- MOTIVATE your reader to action!

HOOK Your Reader's Attention. Hooks are attention-getters designed to make you open the letter and start to read. They often start on the envelope itself and continue after the reader opens the letter.

Sometimes an announcement written in boldface precedes the letter itself. The first line of the body sounds exciting. Throughout the letter, the writer "pulls out all the stops": some information is boldfaced, underlined, bulleted, shadowed with color, or set apart from the text. Some letters use headings and different fonts. Some have borders, pictures, or graphics—anything to capture the readers' attention. Figure 5.17 illustrates some familiar attention-getters.

Figure 5.17 Hooks in Sales Letters

The appeals of the attention-getters vary. Some appeal to the desire to get something for nothing. Some appeal to your sense of compassion, need for security, or desire for prestige. Some appeal to your curiosity.

SELL Your Product or Service. Advertisers describe their product (sometimes including pictures) to help you understand, but also to give you a favorable impression of the product. It is unethical (and illegal) for an advertiser to lie, but the words are usually written to sell—to create a favorable impression and a desire for the product or service.

A sales letter should offer convincing evidence of the merits of the product or service. Facts, figures, and statistics can provide objective proof. **Testimonials,** endorsements from real people (often famous people), provide personal stories that the product or service worked for them. Sometimes the advertisers try to compel the reader to try their product free for a limited time. This way they hope the product itself will convince the reader to keep it and pay for it. Often enclosures are included, such as brochures with pictures, order forms, or more testimonials. Sometimes a sales letter is not just a letter; it is a whole packet of materials!

MOTIVATE Your Reader to Action. Finally, the writer must try to motivate you to do something—go to the phone and dial a number, get into your car and drive to the store, write a check, or fill in a credit card number. To move you to action, advertisers make this part as convenient as they can. You have probably heard motivators similar to the ones listed in Figure 5.18.

An operator is waiting to take your call.

COME ON DOWN to Barton's Building Supplies.

Buy **now** and save **15%** off the cover price.

Send your tax-deductible contribution and help a homeless person find shelter from the cold.

Figure 5.18 Motivating Statements in Sales Letters

Figure 5.19 is a sales letter from West Winchester University trying to convince Jennifer Nelson to apply for admission. Using testimonials, a strong focus on Jennifer's needs and interests, and facts, the letter is persuasive. In addition, the use of an enclosed reply card makes it easy for Jennifer to say yes.

WEST WINCHESTER UNIVERSITY

1203 South Leming Road, Alexandria, Virginia 22314
Phone 202-555-0171 • FAX 202-555-0190

April 17, 20—

Jennifer L. Nelson
764 Lord Fulford Drive
Boling, NC 27878-7873

Dear Jennifer:

We've heard great things about you from the Student Search Office. Based on what we've heard, we thought you would be interested in West Winchester University, one of Virginia's most progressive universities specializing in technology, teaching, and public service.

Here is what others are saying about us:

"WWU trains its students to tackle the tough problems of a technological age."
-EDUCATION WEEKLY

"WWU's academic program is impressive ... Its professors rank teaching as their number one priority."
-HOW TO GET A GOOD EDUCATION AT A STATE UNIVERSITY
by Shireen Straker

WWU offers programs under the College of Arts and Sciences and five professional colleges-Architecture, Business Administration, Engineering, Education and Allied Professions, and Nursing. Classes averaging 33 students encourage individual attention. Laboratories are equipped with the most up-to-date facilities. Our 940-acre campus is located in the largest urban area in Virginia.

Want to learn more? Send us the enclosed card, and we will tell you more. Find out why WWU is the right decision for your education.

Sincerely,

Marilyn L. Zavala

Marilyn L. Zavala
Director of Admissions

Figure 5.19 Example of a Sales Letter

Complete the three Persuasive Writing worksheets on the Data CD.

TEACH

Point out the testimonials in Figure 5.19.

Ask students to locate the Hook, Sell, and Motivate elements in this persuasive message.

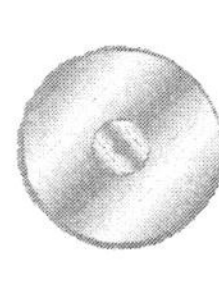

Have students complete the three Persuasive Writing worksheets on the IRCD.

ONGOING ASSESSMENT

Stop and Think

Since the direct approach would begin with the main idea, the bad news, readers would be overwhelmed by the negative information. Such bluntness does not help to build and maintain goodwill. Imagine how many customers a store would lose if it offended everyone it had to say no to for special orders, for products out of stock, for credit applications, for employment, for donations, and more.

A call to action appears at the end of persuasive messages, in the Motivate section. In a call to action, the writer tells the reader exactly what the reader should do.

In the Warm Up, you read the following statement: "Dear Arnie: You're fired." Why is the direct approach not effective for bad news messages? What is a call to action in persuasive messages?

TEACHING RESOURCES

IRCD

Chapter Activities, Ch. 5

Work Is A Zoo!, Ch. 5

PowerPoint® Slides, Ch. 5

Exam*View*®, Ch. 5

techwriting.swlearning.com, Ch. 5

CLOSE

Summary

Use the summary to review main ideas covered in this chapter. Ask students to identify one or two things they learned that they can use immediately.

Ask students to write a composition in which they explain how they might use what they learned in this chapter in their future careers.

Chapter 5 Review

SUMMARY

1. Three types of brief correspondence—e-mails, memorandums, and letters—are essential tools in the business world.
2. Maintaining goodwill, following principles of effective communication, creating a suitable tone, and using humor effectively are important factors in brief correspondence.
3. Writers must analyze and appropriately address the audience in all three types of brief correspondence.
4. Considering audience needs and expectations, determining goals, thinking about technology and the situation, and freewriting are prewriting steps to successful brief correspondence writing.
5. Each type of correspondence uses specific formatting that distinguishes it from other correspondence.
6. The body must be organized with the type of message and the reader's needs in mind. Writers share good news messages using a direct approach. However, bad news messages require an indirect approach to buffer the unpleasant news. Persuasive messages are best presented with a "Hook, Sell, Motivate" strategy.

Checklist

- Have I identified and analyzed my audience? If I am addressing a multilevel audience, have I planned to meet the needs of each group or type of reader?
- Did I establish my purpose or goal in this correspondence?
- Did I use freewriting to generate the information I want to share with the audience?
- Did I develop an organizational plan? Does it take into account a good news, bad news, or persuasive message?
- Does my correspondence follow the correct format and use consistent style? Does it contain correct parts?
- Is the tone and level of formality appropriate to the audience?
- Have I asked a respected peer to read my correspondence and give specific feedback on the impact and effectiveness of my message? (Ask this editor if he or she has questions after reading the correspondence. Also, ask if any part is unclear or inappropriate.)
- Did I proofread the headings for completeness and accuracy?
- Did I proofread the message for errors in spelling, typing, grammar, and punctuation?
- When the correspondence was acceptable, did I sign my name or, if appropriate, write my initials to the right of my typed name?

Build On What You Know

1. Here are eight parts to a good news letter announcing that Terrence Heilig has won a cruise to the Caribbean. The parts, however, are mixed up. Rewrite the letter, putting the sentences in proper order. Several combinations may be possible.
   a. To claim your prize, you must call 1-800-CRUISES before April 18 and provide the operators with proof of your identity.
   b. You have just won an all-expenses paid cruise to the Caribbean!
   c. Congratulations, Terrence. We look forward to helping you arrange the vacation of your life!
   d. Enjoy a variety of on-board recreational activities, delectable meals, and superb entertainment at our expense.
   e. Your name, Terrence Heilig, was drawn out of 456,897 entries to be our top-prize winner in the Colombo Publishers Sweepstakes.
   f. Colombo has reserved four nights and five days for you and a guest.
   g. You must schedule your trip between 1 June and 21 September 20—.
   h. Pack your bags, Terrence, and include lots of sunscreen!
2. Read the following writing situations. Select the details you need; then write the headings for each memorandum.
   a. You are manager for your school's soccer team. Normally you coordinate the packing of equipment and supplies for traveling to away games. However, for the next conference game to be played at Midland, you will be out of state attending your cousin's wedding. Therefore, you are writing a memo to Coach Marsh Rivers and your two assistant managers, Brent Abene and Deborah Johansen, to remind them of what needs to be done in your absence.
   b. You are Janice Fitzsimmons, manager of A Helping Hand, a residential cleaning service in San Alto, New Mexico. Six full-time and fifteen part-time employees are under your supervision. To thank the entire staff for their service, you plan to hold a picnic in your backyard. The event will take place on October 1, 20—, from 5 to 8 p.m. You are writing a memo today to invite all employees and their families to the picnic.
3. Mac Erwin of the ABC Detective Agency has just located Nina Reddenberger's car, stolen three months ago from a shopping mall. List information you would include in a letter to Nina from Mac announcing the good news. Make up the addresses. Before making your list, use your imagination to answer these questions: How can Nina get her car back? When can she get her car back? How did the detective find the car? How does Nina feel?
4. If you are currently working on a research project in another class, compose a letter of inquiry to ask for some of the information you need. Begin thinking about this assignment by listing things you want to know.

ASSESS

Build On What You Know

1. Here is one effective version: h, b, e, g, f, d, a, c.

2. **a.** To: Marsh Rivers, Coach; Brent Abene and Deborah Johansen, Assistant Managers; From: Student's name; Date: Month 1, 20–; Subject: Packing Duties for May 9 Game in Midland **b.** Date: September 6, 20–; To: All Employees; From: Janice Fitzsimmons, Manager; Subject: Invitation to Company Picnic October 1, 20–

3. Lists will vary depending on the circumstances the students make up. You could have students work on the lists in groups. Refer students to the checklist at the end of the chapter.

4. Be sure to have students use the checklist at the end of the chapter.

ASSESS

Apply What You Learned

5–7. Allow students to compare their memos. Since one version of each memo is on the IRCD, you may further compare choices that different writers made. Also, discuss the effect those choices are likely to have on readers.

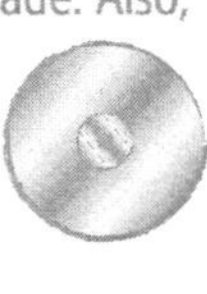

8. **a.** Managers will be concerned about coordinating several people responsible for doing one job and determining who will be responsible for that coordination. Some managers may have experience with this type of program. Others may worry that supervising three people for one position will take more time and paperwork. **b.** Employees who hope to use the program are likely to be pleased, while those opposed to it may need to be convinced or reassured.

9. Students may complete this assignment individually or in small groups. They may need time in your school's library or computer lab to conduct research and send e-mails. Letters of inquiry are usually developed as informative or good news messages; the writer is saying that he or she is impressed enough with a product, a service, or an organization to want to know more.

Apply What You Learned

5. Write a memo from Cheryl Brinkdopke, chief of installation services for Fox Cablevision, to Eric Monroe, an employee under her supervision. Eric has just completed 25 years of service with Fox Cablevision, and Cheryl wants to show her support for his work. Eric has had perfect attendance for the last three years, and his customer evaluations are consistently positive.

6. As assistant to your Quality Assurance Team at World Wide Insurance Association, you are in charge of scheduling meetings. The chair, Janine Leone, has asked you to call a meeting for Monday afternoon, April 24, 20—. She wants the group to discuss a recent employee concern regarding unsafe exercise equipment in the Employee Wellness Center. Janine would like the Quality Assurance Team to gather in Room 124-C at 4:15. She expects the meeting to end at 5 p.m. Write a memo announcing the meeting.

7. You are chief food scientist for Leigh Bakery in Anderson, Wisconsin. Matthew Carlson, president of the Logan Dairy Cooperative, a farmer-owned and -operated sales organization under contract to sell its entire production to your company, has invited you to speak to his members regarding the effect of certain veterinary medicines on the taste of dairy products. On the date the Cooperative requested, Thursday, January 18, 20—, you are already scheduled to attend a meeting of the American Association of Bakers. Write a memo declining the invitation to speak to the Cooperative.

8. Plan and draft an e-mail that announces a new flextime program at Bauman Industries. The program will allow all workers to share the responsibilities of one position among two or three people. Print the e-mail to give your instructor or share it with your classmates or team.

   a. One e-mail should target and address the managerial staff within the company. Consider the needs, concerns, questions, and biases of this audience before composing the e-mail.

   b. The second e-mail should target and address all employees of the company. Remember that you will need to meet the needs and answer the questions of all readers without offending anyone.

9. Conduct an Internet search for the web site of a business or an industry related to a topic you are interested in. Search until you find a web site that provides an e-mail address for contacting the organization.

   a. Write an e-mail requesting information or materials from the company. Before you send it, print the e-mail to give to your instructor or to share with other students. Consider which strategy (good news, bad news, or persuasive message) to use for organizing the body of your e-mail.

   b. Analyze the e-mail you receive in response to your request and share your analysis and the e-mail with your class.

Work Is A Zoo!

Next Friday you and Tyrone will meet with the entire Marketing Department (which includes the public relations division).

You hope to present information from other zoos with similar programs. You also are trying to talk to a local science instructor for her thoughts. If you speak with her, you will present your findings from that conversation as well.

Additionally, you are developing a survey that will go out to science instructors in the area.

It is important that the rest of the staff buy in to the ZiPS program because they will be involved in various aspects of it. Their ideas and input are valuable at the start of the program.

Send a memo to the staff telling everyone about the meeting and what it is going to be about. Remember that all memos:

- Include a heading. List the recipients according to rank, starting with the highest. For example, Nevil Kaplan is the head of the entire department, so his name should come first.
- Are accurate and brief. Don't get off track going into all of the details of the presentation; the goal of this memo is to tell people about the meeting.
- Cover one subject only. Now is not the time to invite people to a potluck for the July 4 weekend.
- Explain any actions to be taken. If you need to know how many people are coming, include that in your memo.

Use the Work Is A Zoo! worksheet and checklist on the Data CD to help guide you through this activity.

WORK IS A ZOO!

Use this Work Is A Zoo! activity to practice writing memorandums to different audiences. Before starting this activity, have students review the information in this chapter about writing memos. Use the Work Is A Zoo! worksheet and

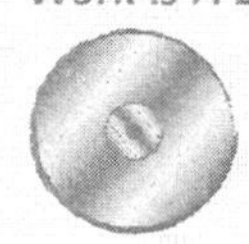
checklist, *Write a Memo about ZiPS Meeting*, on the IRCD.

DOCUMENT DESIGN AND GRAPHICS

GOALS

DESIGN an effective document for your audience and purpose

DETERMINE the audience and purpose of graphics

FORMAT graphics to make them easy to understand

CONSTRUCT graphics for your audience and purpose

See the Data CD for Write-to-Learn and In The Know activity worksheets.

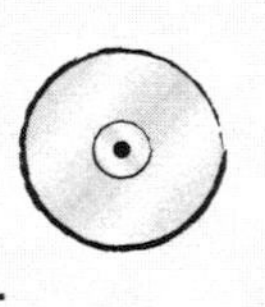

TEACHING RESOURCES

IRCD
- Lesson Plans, Ch. 6
- Chapter Activities, Ch. 6
- PowerPoint® Slides, Ch. 6
- Sample Documents, Ch. 6

techwriting.swlearning.com, Ch. 6

Exam*View*® CD, Ch. 6

CHAPTER OVERVIEW

Covers elements of page design and use of graphic aids.

See the IRCD for Write-to-Learn and In The Know activity worksheets.

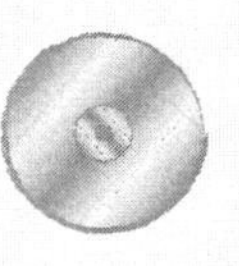

WRITE-TO-LEARN

Using words only, write directions from school to your residence. Then draw a map with arrows to show the same route. Which is easier to understand, the written directions or the map? In a short journal entry, explain why.

In The Know

bar graph a graph using a horizontal axis and a vertical axis to compare numerical data, drawn with heights or lengths of rectangular bars

call outs the names of specific parts of a diagram, connected to the diagram or drawing with lines

chart a drawing with boxes, words, and lines to show a process or an organizational structure

design elements considerations in writing a document that affect page layout; the way a document looks

diagram a line drawing

double bar graph a graph using a horizontal axis and a vertical axis to compare pairs of numbers, drawn with heights or lengths of rectangular bars

double line graph a graph using a horizontal axis and a vertical axis to compare trends and show relationships between two sets of data, drawn with lines

flowchart a drawing with lines and arrows to show a process or series of steps

formal table numerical information set up in rows and columns and drawn with rules; used to present figures

graphics information presented in a visual form, such as tables, graphs, and diagrams

informal table a simple table with two or three items, drawn without rules and stubs

line graph a graph using a horizontal axis and a vertical axis to show a trend or relationship between numbers, drawn with lines

multiple bar graph a graph using horizontal and vertical axes to compare data, drawn with two or more bars for each measurement

multiple line graph a graph using more than one line to compare data

organizational chart a drawing with boxes, words, and lines to show how an organization is structured

pie graph a circular graph showing how parts relate to the whole; the whole equals 100 percent

verbal table information given in rows and columns; uses words instead of numbers

Writing@Work

Dorinda Gunther is a freelance graphic designer and creative director. She has expertise in interactive multimedia design, including Web and CD-ROM, set design, video, corporate identity, printed materials, exhibits, and business meetings. She takes a versatile and integrated approach to design and communications, sales training, and consumer education.

As a freelance designer, Dorinda must communicate with clients to update them on their projects and to earn new business. She mainly uses e-mail to communicate with clients about current projects. To earn new business, she has created several tools that she uses to promote her work. One of these tools is a web site. She uses the web site to promote herself and her work, but she also uses it to upload work in progress for her clients to review.

In addition to the web site, Dorinda has created a letter of introduction and a PowerPoint® presentation to promote her work. Using these tools, she effectively communicates her abilities to prospective clients. Without effective communication, Dorinda would have difficulty obtaining new business.

In the graphic design industry, it is possible to encounter a client who wants a designer to use graphics to intentionally mislead an audience. Dorinda feels strongly about this issue and says, "I don't believe I have ever stretched the truth through design. I would not feel comfortable misleading the audience in any way."

Another ethical issue in the design industry is using pictures from someone else's web site or using pictures whose source you have forgotten. Dorinda is careful about this issue. She uses stock photography when original photography is not available, and she always instructs clients on the rights and usage guidelines of purchased photography.

Dorinda has a bachelor of science degree in design. She has worked for companies as an art director and as an associate creative director. She has been freelancing since 2001.

APPLY

Writing@Work

This profile may surprise some students. Those interested in design and the arts may think they will not need good communication skills. Have students create a self-promotional tool. Students can choose from creating a web site, a PowerPoint® presentation, a sales packet, or a letter of introduction. Be sure they include the skills and benefits that they will be able to bring to potential clients.

Dorinda mentioned that she uses stock photography. Have students visit some stock photography web sites to see the kind of artwork that is available for designers. You also may suggest that students visit web sites such as Quark and Adobe, since these companies all have software packages available to help designers create professional-looking graphics. Links to these web sites are available at techwriting.swlearning.com.

MEMO

TO: Teachers and Students

FROM: Principal Oden

DATE: October 6, 20—

SUBJECT: Parking Reassignments for Friday, October 14, 20—

On Friday, October 14, 20—, 16 marching bands from area high schools will be arriving to compete in the Holbrook High School Annual Band Classic. To help our school sponsor this important event, we ask teachers and students with Area A, B, and C parking permits to park in the garment factory parking lot across the street to make room for the 30-35 buses that will be arriving on that day. Please note the following parking reassignments for Friday, October 14, only:

Area A	move to parking lot to the north of the factory
Area B	move to parking lot to the south of the factory
Area C	move to parking lot northeast of the factory
Administration	move to Austin Avenue in front of the factory

The map reproduced here and posted on bulletin boards throughout the school will help you locate the proper parking areas:

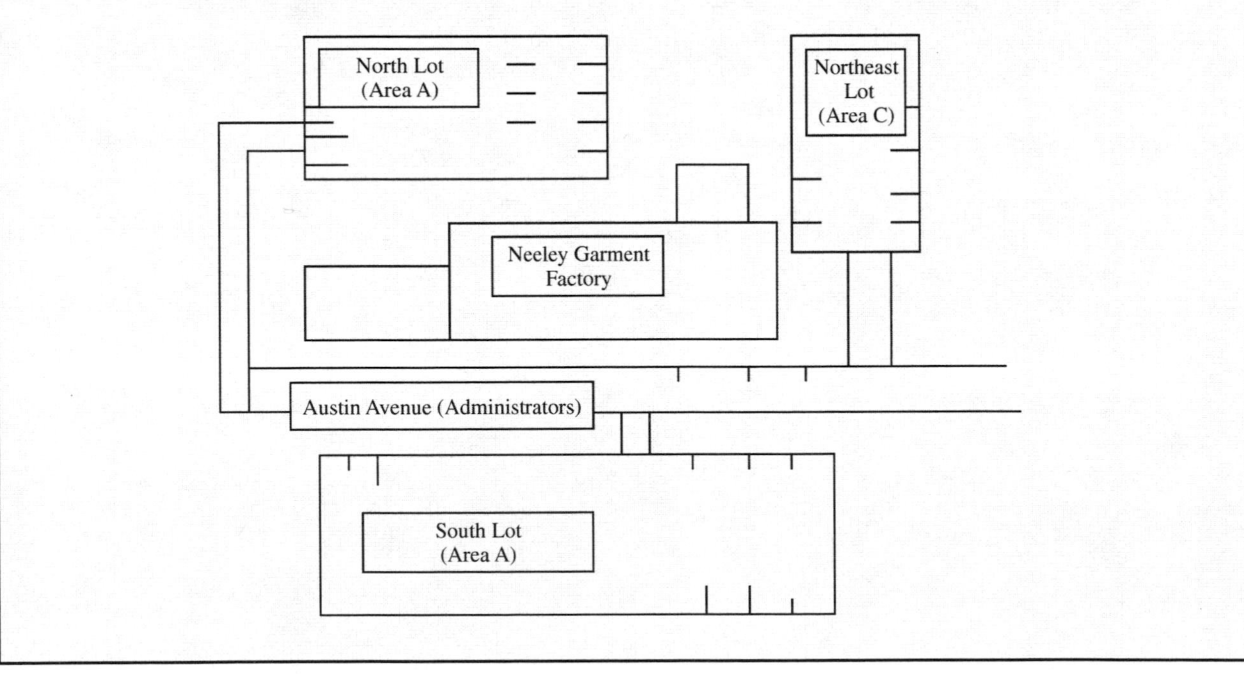

Figure 6.1 Document with Graphics

DESIGNING THE DOCUMENT

When you write, you make many decisions. For example, you decide what to write, how to organize, which words to use, and whether the words reflect standard usage. Indeed, words are important to any writer, but in technical writing, how the words *look* on the page is just as important as what the words say.

A cluttered room with poorly designed lighting can make you feel overwhelmed. A cluttered document with poorly designed elements can make your readers feel the same way. Readers may be discouraged if they cannot find the information they need quickly and easily. Good technical writers must learn to design pages that are visually friendly if they want readers to stay focused.

For example, the 3″ × ½″ plastic tab inserted into Lorenzo's potted rosebush included six steps for planting and 57 tiny words squeezed onto the tab. Lorenzo could not read the directions, so he threw out the tab and dug a hole deep enough to plant the root ball of the bush several inches below the ground. Stephanie, the next-door neighbor, showed Lorenzo the 2″ × 3″ set of instructions that came tied around a branch of her newest rosebush. With the instructions having room for an illustration and print big enough for Lorenzo to see, Lorenzo read the caution against burying the root ball too deeply and adjusted the hole he had dug. In a few months, both neighbors had beautiful roses, thanks to Stephanie's better-designed instructions. Figure 6.2 shows two sets of instructions, one poorly designed and the other designed with the reader's needs in mind.

Tea Rose

Find an area that will receive full sun. Use rich, well-drained soil that contains organic matter. Dig a hole slightly wider than the root-ball. Plant the bush so that the top of the root-ball is exposed. Do not cover the root-ball. Water the area thoroughly and fertilize twice a year: in spring and late summer.

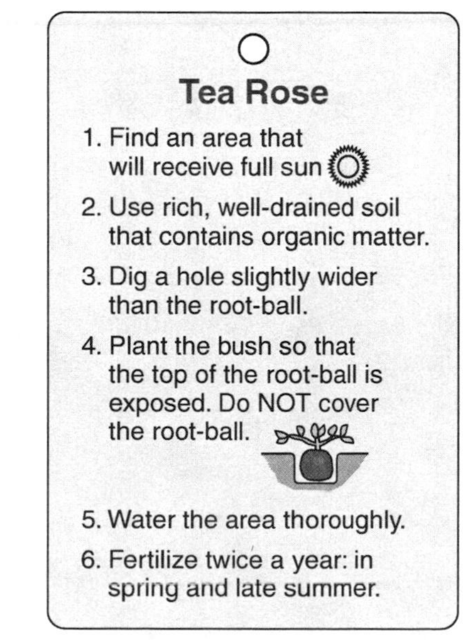

Tea Rose

1. Find an area that will receive full sun
2. Use rich, well-drained soil that contains organic matter.
3. Dig a hole slightly wider than the root-ball.
4. Plant the bush so that the top of the root-ball is exposed. Do NOT cover the root-ball.
5. Water the area thoroughly.
6. Fertilize twice a year: in spring and late summer.

Figure 6.2 Examples of Poorly Designed and Improved Instructions

WARM UP

Recall a time you went to the library to choose a book for a book report. After looking through several books, how did you make your final choice? Did some books look more inviting than others? Why or why not?

FOCUS

Warm Up

Use the Warm Up to emphasize how document design affects our reactions to the words we see. Bring several books to illustrate how some look more inviting than others. Point out how elements such as font size, pictures, white space, and color affect the reader's psychological reactions to a document.

FOCUS

Figure 6.1

Use Figure 6.1 to illustrate how a document is easier to read when it follows design principles. Point out the boldfaced headings, the indented list for parking, and the map. Compare the figure with the original model on the IRCD in the sample documents.

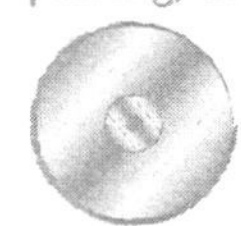

Figure 6.2

Use the two sets of instructions for planting rosebushes to illustrate how the larger one is user-friendly and the smaller one is not.

TEACH

Use the Cluttered Page Layout Transparency on the IRCD to reinforce how proper page design makes a document easier to read.

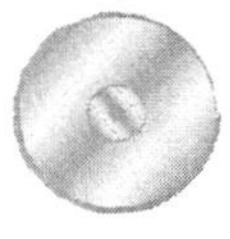

SEE THE SITES

The American Institute of Graphic Arts web site gives many tips on how to use design elements to make your document stand out. It also gives information about careers in document design.

To learn how to build a web site that is user-friendly and that incorporates good document design, go to the Usable Web web site. You will learn how to design effective web pages using the design elements mentioned here.

You can find the URL for both sites in the web links on techwriting.swlearning.com.

SEE THE SITES

Encourage students to think visually as well as verbally by following the recommendations on the sites for document design.

TEACH

Use the Examples of Line Justification Transparency on the IRCD to show the differences in left, right, aligned, and centered justifications.

Use the Four Popular Fonts Transparency on the IRCD to illustrate the difference between serif and sans serif fonts and the different sizes.

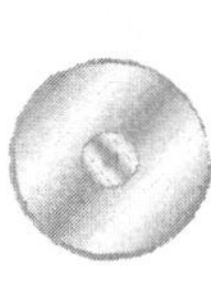

DESIGN ELEMENTS

In addition to words, writers can use **design elements** to aid comprehension and keep the reader's interest. Elements to consider when designing are white space, text, headings, graphics, and physical features.

White Space White space is space that is white or blank. White space rests the eyes, separates chunks of information, and makes a document look inviting. Writers can create white space in margins, between paragraphs, before itemized lists, and around graphics.

Text Text refers to the words printed on the page. Readers read text more quickly if it is left-justified with ragged-right edges. Left justification means that the text is flush with the left margin of the page. Ragged right means that words lie unevenly along the right margin. This page is set up with left justification and ragged-right edges.

Two differences between fonts, or letter design, are serif and sans serif. (*Sans* is French for "without.") Serif refers to letters with distinguishing lines or "tails" (like this sentence) that make it easy to see the differences between one letter and another. Sans serif refers to letters with fewer distinguishing lines and no "tails" (like this sentence) and is appropriate for something short, such as a title or a heading. The major headings in this textbook use a sans serif font.

Size is measured in points, with a large point number (14 or 16) used for a larger letter. Text in 10 or 12 points can be seen easily. For paragraphs, choose a 10- to12-point serif font that mixes capital and lowercase letters. Do not write an entire document in all capitals; all capitals are hard to read and should be used only for emphasis, for a title, or for a major heading.

Highlighters are print styles that focus the reader's attention on something important. **Boldface**, underline, *italics*, and CAPITALS are effective highlighters, with **boldface** being the most effective and CAPITALS the least effective. Use highlighters sparingly: overuse clutters the page and distracts the reader, drawing attention *away from* the text instead of *to* the text.

Another effective tool for highlighting is an itemized list. To itemize a list, set up a list separate from the text and indented from the left margin. Bullets (•) often precede each item in the list to highlight the information.

For example, Mr. Gorham wrote his students a letter, giving them last-minute instructions for their trip to France. He used a bulleted list to draw attention to the five important items for his students to pack.

The items below are essential for a smooth, trouble-free trip. Be sure to check and double-check that you possess the following items:

- Your passport—you will not be allowed on the plane without it
- Your money—credit card, traveler's checks, and some currency
- Your insurance card
- Any medication you routinely take
- Your driver's license

Headings Headings are short titles that introduce the main idea of a selected portion of text. Like a formal outline, headings help your reader see the organization of a document in one glance. Most reports use a system of two headings (first-degree headings and second-degree headings) but can use more. For example, this textbook uses a system of four headings.

Graphics **Graphics** are visual representations of data or information. They include many familiar visual aids such as tables, line graphs, pie graphs, and diagrams, but they also include more sophisticated and less familiar aids such as schematics, pictographs, decision charts, and Internet graphics.

Graphics are used in technical writing any time information can be expressed better in a visual form than in words alone. Sometimes a graphic is used by itself, as in the traffic signs posted on your way to school. For technical writers, the graphic is often used along with text to fully convey meaning.

Whether you use graphics alone or with text, considerations of purpose and audience guide your decision and influence which graphic is appropriate for your document. The last section of this chapter will introduce you to some of the most familiar and easy-to-design graphics.

Physical Features In addition to considering white space, headings, and graphics, writers choose the best physical features, or medium, to use for their document. Possible choices include paper media (heavy stock, 8½ by 11 inches, or a trifold brochure) or electronic media (e-mail, CD-ROM, or web pages). Again, purpose and audience determine which medium you choose. In turn, the medium also will influence the design.

For example, Washington Research Associates (WRA) sent a one-page marketing survey to photography enthusiasts to determine potential customers for a photography supply store. WRA wanted to encourage readers to complete the survey quickly and return it promptly. Because the survey was only one page and the target population was small, the graphic artists decided to use heavy-stock paper with the survey on one side and the return address with prepaid postage on the back. This way, readers could simply refold the document after completing the survey, use the enclosed sticker to seal the "envelope," and put the survey in the mail. The purpose (receiving completed surveys quickly) influenced the medium (the envelope design). Likewise, the envelope design (the medium) influenced placement of the address, the prepaid postage, and the sticker to seal the envelope (the format).

Why do white space, ragged-right edges, serif font, and headings make text easier to read? What is the purpose of highlighters?

Complete the Practicing Systems of Headings Activity worksheet on the Data CD.

TEACH

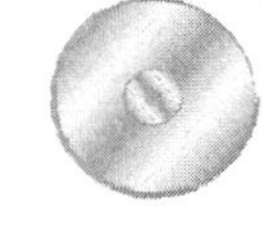

Have students complete the Practicing Systems of Headings Activity worksheet on the IRCD to apply concepts in this section.

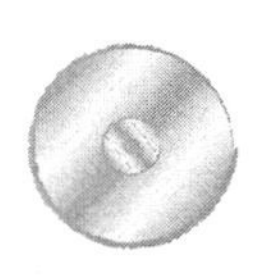

Use the Three Levels of Headings Transparency on the IRCD to illustrate systems of headings.

Help students see that a system of headings is like an outline. Instead of Roman numerals, capital letters, and Arabic numerals to show subdivisions, the size and placement of headings show the organization.

Ask students to turn the headings in this chapter into a formal outline.

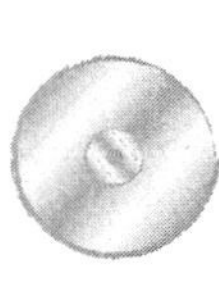

Use the Document Design Guidelines Transparency on the IRCD to review the guidelines.

ONGOING ASSESSMENT

Stop and Think

White space makes text easier to read because the extra space relaxes the eye. Ragged-right edges make the text end naturally along the right margin. Because the words are evenly spaced, ragged right is easier on the eye. Serif font is easier to read because the "tails" on the letters make them more noticeable. Headings make the organization more apparent.

Highlighters draw attention to particular words, phrases, or lists by making them stand out in some way from the text.

WARM UP

What is being described here?

A circle, 3 inches in diameter, contains three items. At the bottom of the figure, approximately ¾ of an inch from the bottom, is a single line, approximately 2 inches long curved in the shape of the bottom half of a small circle. At the top of the 3-inch circle, approximately ½ inch from the top and 1 inch apart, are two small circles, ¼ of an inch in diameter. A perfect square encloses the 3-inch circle, the four sides of the square barely touching four points of the circle.

FOCUS

Warm Up

Ask students to draw the graphic. Then ask them which is easier to understand, the instructions for the graphic or the graphic itself. See the Who Reads Graphics Warm Up Transparency on the IRCD for a drawing of the graphic.

TEACH

Help students see that the more information a graphic contains, the harder it is to read. An experienced reader with a strong background and interest in the subject will read graphics more easily than a less experienced reader. Show the Visual Scale of Difficulty Transparency on the IRCD.

WHO READS GRAPHICS?

A picture is indeed worth a thousand words. Graphics can clarify information quickly. At one glance, your readers can perceive more information than they would with words alone. Most complex technical material can be simplified with a graphic: a table, a drawing, a diagram, or a graph. Where academic readers rely heavily on words to understand meaning, technical readers often rely on words *and* graphics to convey meaning.

AUDIENCE

Technical subjects, such as engineering, marketing, and medicine, rely heavily on data that is presented visually, so readers of technical documents expect to see graphic aids in their reading. However, readers vary in their ability to understand graphics. As with decisions about text, decisions about graphics depend on what your readers are able to understand and what they already know.

Generally, the more data that is included in a graphic, the more difficult it will be to read. When deciding which graphic your audience will best understand, you should always be sure to ask these questions about your reader(s):

- How much does my reader know about the subject?
- How interested is my reader in the subject?
- Do my readers include a technical audience? In other words, do my readers need or expect technical information or figures?
- Will my audience be confused by technical information or figures?
- Does my audience's reading level tend to be higher (tenth grade or higher) or lower (ninth grade or lower)?

PURPOSE AND OBJECTIVES

Audience is only one consideration in deciding what kind of graphic to use. You also must consider the purpose of your graphic, how much information you have, and what type of information there is.

To choose graphics that relay your meaning most effectively, you can ask yourself 1) what the objectives of your writing are and 2) how graphics can help you achieve those objectives. Then choose the graphic that best meets those objectives.

To help you decide which graphic to use, look at the purpose column in Figure 6.3. Turn each purpose statement into a question that begins with an understood "Do I want . . .?" For example, "Do I want to show my readers how to operate a digital camera?" If so, drawing the mechanism of the camera with clearly labeled parts would help achieve that purpose.

Purpose (Do I Want . . .?)	Type of Graphic
to show a mechanism or part of a mechanism?	line drawing or diagram
to show how the whole is divided into parts or how the parts relate to the whole?	pie graph
to present a small amount of data in an easy-to-read format?	informal table
to compare sets of data; to present differences; to depict a trend?	bar graph
to compare several sets of data; to depict a trend?	double bar graph
to show a trend; to show how data is related?	line graph
to show several trends; to compare trends; to show how data is related?	multiple line graph
to present information, especially many numbers, in an easy-to-read format?	formal table
to present a process?	flowchart
to present the structure of an organization?	organizational chart
to show the details of what something actually looks like?	photograph

Figure 6.3 Graphics Purpose

What are some questions to ask about your audience to help you select an appropriate graphic? Using Figure 6.3, name three graphics you see frequently in textbooks. Give the purpose of each.

FOCUS

Figure 6.3

Use Figure 6.3 to show how to match the writer's purpose and objectives to a graphic. Ask students to turn the purpose statements into questions to help them decide which graphic to use. For example, a writer may ask: "Do I want to show my readers how our tax dollars are spent, pointing out specifically what parts of all revenue collected are spent on education, Medicare, defense, national disasters, etc.?" For this example, a pie graph would help readers understand how tax revenue is divided among different programs.

ONGOING ASSESSMENT

Stop and Think

Ask what the audience knows and does not know about the subject. What are the audience's expectations?

Students will mention a variety of graphics but will probably tell you that they see tables, pictures, and diagrams most often.

WARM UP

Take a close look at the graphics in the following sections of this chapter. What do you notice about each graphic? What do the graphics have in common? Notice some of the differences. In what graphics do the differences occur?

FOCUS

Warm Up

Preview the graphics. Ask students what the graphics have in common. Help students see that the graphics in the chapter follow the guidelines for creating graphics in this section.

RETEACH

Remind students that the most important factor affecting whether a graphic is read is how it looks on the page. Graphics must be neat and uncluttered.

Tell students to refer to this section when they design their own graphics.

Show the Guidelines for Formatting Graphics Transparency on the IRCD.

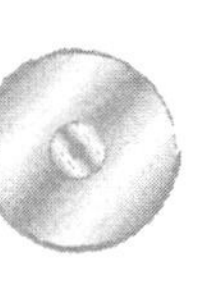

FORMATTING GRAPHICS TO MAKE THEM EASY TO UNDERSTAND

Graphics add critical information to your text and become part of the overall appearance of your document. Good writers create a flow between words and graphics that unifies a document so that readers move along without interruption. To help your reader interpret graphics quickly and easily, you should keep graphics simple and neat, integrate graphics with text, give credit for borrowed graphics, and use color effectively.

KEEP GRAPHICS NEAT AND SIMPLE

The quality of a graphic is a factor in how carefully it is read. A neat, clean graphic is easy to read and interpret. Leave enough white space to make the graphic look uncluttered and make the graphic large enough to see all parts clearly. Align decimals when they are presented in columns, as shown in the figures below:

8.3
0.525
98.6

In general, a graphic should have one main point. Using two uncluttered, simple graphics to illustrate two concepts is better than using one cluttered graphic to illustrate too many concepts.

Figure 6.4 is an example of a cluttered graphic. Its many lines make it look more like a robotic weapon from a *Star Wars* movie than a line graph predicting trends in community college majors.

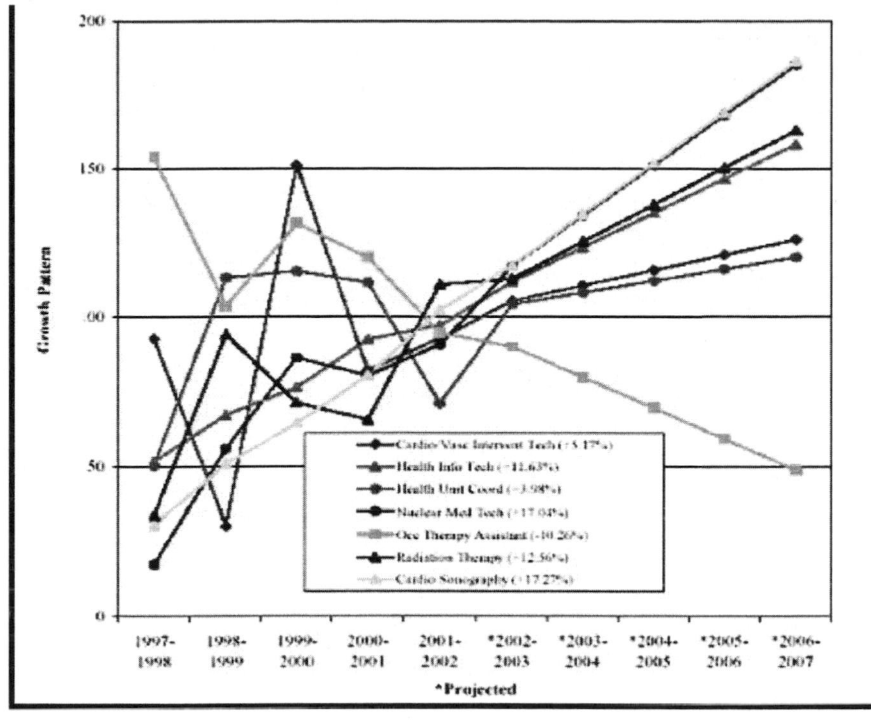

Figure 6.4 Cluttered Graphic

FOCUS

Figure 6.4
Use Figure 6.4 to illustrate how difficult it is to read a cluttered graphic.

TEACH

Ask students to look closely at the three ways to refer to graphics. Which way do they prefer and why? Some will think incorporating the reference in their text makes the reference less obtrusive and effectively directs the reader's attention, but others will prefer the use of parentheses because for them that style seems less obtrusive. Some will prefer the stand-alone sentence because it seems more direct.

INTEGRATE GRAPHICS WITH TEXT

Refer to each graphic clearly in the text BEFORE you place it on the page. Refer to the graphic when you think your reader will look at it for the first time. Use the word *Figure* to refer to any graphic that is not a formal table. Use the word *Table* to refer to a formal table (a table with rules and titles). Call your reader's attention to figures or tables by 1) incorporating references into your text, 2) using parentheses, or 3) creating stand-alone sentences:

1) Table 1/Figure 1 shows the amount of rainfall in Idaho over the past three years.

2) The rainfall in Idaho over six years varied substantially (see Table 1/Figure 1).

2) The rainfall in Idaho over six years varied substantially (Table 1/Figure 1).

3) The rainfall in Idaho over six years varied substantially. See Table 1/Figure 1.

Choose one method and refer to all of your figures and tables the same way. Informal tables need not be referred to as a table or a figure. **Verbal tables** are not always referred to as a table or figure but are often integrated into the text with an appropriate introduction.

Place each graphic in a convenient place for the reader to see. If the graphic is small enough (⅕ to ½ page), try to place it on the same page as its reference. If the graphic is large (¾ to 1 page), you may need to place it on the page immediately following your reference. For graphics used in reports, explain the graphic's significance in the report as you introduce the graphic. Explain in words the relationships you want your reader to see. For

RETEACH

Stress to students the importance of integrating graphics with the text. Students must refer to the graphic and discuss the significance of it the same way they would integrate a quote and discuss its significance.

Remind students that some graphics are used by themselves without text. Road signs, the instructions for replacing a print cartridge, or instructions for using a fire extinguisher may use graphics only, without words. However, for graphics used with technical documents, it is important to use the guidelines mentioned here.

ENRICH

Ask students to bring page designs from brochures, magazines, and newspapers that they think are attractive. Ask them to share their findings with the class. Create a bulletin board of the best designs.

COMMUNICATION DILEMMA

Ask students to research the psychological meanings associated with certain colors, or how different cultures associate meanings with colors. Students can use a search engine to locate this information on the Internet. Students should learn that white is associated with death and mourning in China, so the color white was not a good choice for this audience.

example, point out parts of a diagram, trends in a line graph, or important numbers in a table. You need not discuss every part of the graphic, but do point out what is important for the reader to know. Generally, explanations are presented in the introduction preceding the graphic. More complex graphics may require discussion before and after placement of the graphic.

Provide a title for every graphic. Table titles may be centered above the table and figure titles centered below the figure; however, placement may vary. Choose a placement and be consistent throughout your document. Use titles that are specific so the readers can understand what they will learn from the graphic. For example, use

Salary Distribution for 1955-1956	NOT JUST Salaries
Regal Powerboat Model OTY-453	NOT JUST Powerboat

Informal tables do not need titles. Number figures consecutively throughout. Number tables consecutively, but separately from figures, throughout.

GIVE CREDIT FOR BORROWED GRAPHICS

Give credit for a graphic if you do not compile it yourself or if you compile it using borrowed data. Place the word *Source* below your figure and give the bibliographic reference for the source as you would a footnote or an endnote.

You work as a wedding planner for I Do Wedding Consulting. Your manager, Rachel, is proud of the way you communicate with clients to find out and provide exactly what they want for their wedding day. The company has recently expanded to include international clients, and Rachel has put you in charge of marketing the company's services to Chinese couples who want a "westernized" wedding.

You decide to create a brochure that shows pictures of weddings you have planned in the past. You personally believe the most beautiful weddings have been "all-white" weddings, so you include pictures that show arrangements of white roses and other white flowers on the cover of your brochure. Several weeks after the brochures are distributed, Rachel is upset with you because not a single Chinese couple has called to make an appointment.

Why do you think the brochure was not effective for the target audience? You may need to research color associations in other countries to learn why the brochure was not an effective marketing tool.

USE COLOR EFFECTIVELY

Color draws a reader's attention often before the reader pays attention to the words. Color is a powerful design tool that can be used to:

- Indicate a document's organization. By using the same color for major headings, you give your readers visual cues to the overall organization of a document and help them scan quickly for information.
- Emphasize or clarify an important point. By using a color for a key word, a phrase, an idea, or a part of a graphic, you draw your reader's attention to important information. You also can use color to signify a change or to guide readers through a process.

- Support your text's meaning. By using certain colors consistently to convey specific information, your reader begins to associate the color (red with danger, for example) with the meaning and therefore understands text more quickly.
- Make your document attractive. By using colors to break up black and white text, your page will be more appealing.

Color, like any technical writing tool, can be misused. To use color effectively:

- Avoid overusing color. More than three or four colors (including black and white as two colors) can overwhelm a reader, and using one color too often can be distracting.
- Apply color consistently to elements throughout your document. For example, if you set major headings in red and key words in black boldface, do not suddenly switch a major heading to blue or a key word to red boldface.
- Remain sensitive to cultural identifications with colors. International audiences associate colors differently from American audiences. For instance, green is associated with go (traffic lights) to an American audience, and red is associated with danger (a firetruck or stop sign). On the other hand, green is a holy color to a Muslim, and red is a sign of mourning to a South African.
- Avoid unusual combinations of colors. Some colors, such as purple on a blue background or orange on a red background, are simply too difficult to read.

Why should graphics be neat and simple?

You can get thousands of free images from a variety of sources to add to your documents. Many web sites have images, graphics, and photographs that are free and do not require permission to use. You also can purchase CD-ROMs that store thousands of images on a disk. These disks are organized by categories, such as business, wildlife, or travel images. Once you purchase the CD-ROM, you may use the images without copyright permission.

COMMUNICATION UPDATE

Have students download free images from the Internet to use in future publications. Have them set up a folder and give them a category of images to download. Links to web sites that have free images are located at techwriting.swlearning.com.

ENRICH

Ask an art instructor to visit your class to talk about color associations.

ONGOING ASSESSMENT

Stop and Think

Graphics are easier to read when they are neat and simple.

WARM UP

When you look at a page with text and a graphic, which do you read first, the text or the graphic? Do you ever read the text without looking at the graphic or look at the graphic without reading the text? Why?

FOCUS

Warm Up

Use the Warm Up to make students aware of their attitudes toward reading graphics. Visual learners probably look at graphics before they look at text. Verbal learners probably look at text first. Some students tend to skip the text or graphics altogether. Note that such reading habits mean that writers must put forth extra effort to plan, create, and integrate graphics.

RETEACH

Thoroughly explain Theresa's writing assignment and make sure students understand the differences between the two audiences for whom she is writing. The *Fitness* readers are younger, less capable, and less interested readers. The *Mind and Body* readers are older, more knowledgeable, more capable readers, and they are more motivated. This ongoing scenario will help illustrate why different graphics are chosen.

CONSTRUCTING GRAPHICS FOR AUDIENCE AND PURPOSE

As a composer of graphics, you have many choices available to use in your documents. You must make choices about which graphics are most appropriate to use for different audiences and purposes. This section will show you how one writer selected graphics for two articles she wrote on the topic of fitness for two different magazines.

Theresa has been asked to share the secrets of her successful fitness program with two very different audiences. One article will appear in *Fitness,* a magazine for junior high school students just beginning an exercise program. These readers have little knowledge of fitness and only a moderate interest in improving their health. As younger readers, their reading level is lower, and their experience reading graphics is limited.

The other article will appear in *Mind and Body,* a magazine for college students majoring in physical education. These readers are different from the readers of *Fitness*: they have a solid background in physical education, a keen interest in the subject, a higher reading level, and more experience interpreting graphics. This section will take you through Theresa's decision-making processes as she decides how to present her fitness expertise to the different audiences of *Fitness* and *Mind and Body.*

CONSTRUCTING TABLES

Tables are used to present words or numbers that can be organized into categories of columns and rows. Tables are one of the most popular graphic aids and can be informal or formal. A verbal table, often called a chart, is a variation of the formal table, categorizing words instead of numbers into columns and rows.

Informal Table An **informal table** is a graphic that uses rows and columns drawn *without* rules (lines) or stubs (column headings). In an informal table, the information flows with the text. The explanation of the graphic is a brief summary of the information presented in the graphic.

Theresa wants to motivate the younger readers of *Fitness* to begin their fitness program. Theresa thinks that beginners could benefit from seeing how quickly she saw results. To present her own progress after two months on a workout regiment, Theresa uses an informal table. The informal table is a good choice because the information is simple (only three items to consider) and appropriate for her younger audience. See Figure 6.5 for the informal table and its written introduction.

Over the next two months, Theresa lost a total of 4.2 pounds. For every pound of fat she lost, she gained approximately ¾ pound of muscle.

Fat lost	14.0 lbs.
Muscle gained	9.8 lbs.
Total pounds lost	4.2 lbs.

Figure 6.5 Model of Informal Table

FOCUS

Figure 6.5
Point out that the informal table is one of the simplest graphics. It uses no title or number and is used to show a few numbers placed in one or two columns.

FOCUS

Figure 6.6
Use the formal table to point out the features of a properly constructed table. Make sure that students notice the title, the stubs, the rules, the footnotes, and the source. Point out that tables do not need rules drawn across every part, that too many lines can clutter a table. Make sure students understand that the table is appropriate here because of the need for numbers presented in consistent categories.

Formal Table A **formal table** is a graphic that presents numerical information in rows and columns with rules (lines drawn). It is typically used to organize numbers in a consistent format.

Theresa wants the readers of *Mind and Body* to know at what rate they should exercise to burn fat. She uses part of a table from a published book. The older and more knowledgeable audience of *Mind and Body* will understand the detailed numerical data. They also will be motivated to locate their own heart rates and will appreciate the information given in the footnotes. Figure 6.6 is part of the formal table Theresa reproduced from *Exercise and You* along with her brief introduction.

Table 1 shows the recommended heart rates by age during exercise. The athlete's training rate is for only the most fit athletes. The average training rate is recommended for a healthy person beginning a fitness program.

Table 1. Recommended Heart Rates During Aerobic Exercise

TRAINING RATES[a]			
Age	Maximum Heart Rate	Athlete, 85%[b]	Average, 80%
20	200	170	160
22	198	168	158
24	196	167	157
26	194	165	155
28	192	163	154

[a]Based on average heart rates of 72 beats per minute for males and 80 beats per minute for females

[b]Percentages represent percents of maximum heart rates in Column 2

Source: Alan Grayson and Susanne Brazinski, *Exercise and You,* Clearview, ND: Mountain Press, 1994.

Formal table is labeled *Table*

Superscript letters direct attention to footnotes

Stubs

Rules

Footnotes explain parts of the table

Source provides bibliographic data

Figure 6.6 Model of Formal Table and Introduction

Complete the Formal Table Activity worksheet on the Data CD.

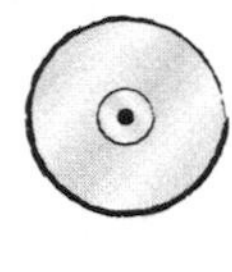

Have students complete the Formal Table Activity worksheet on the IRCD to apply the concepts in this section.

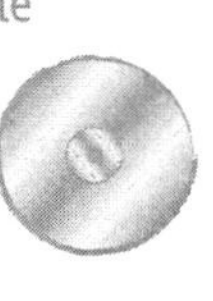

TEACH

Remind students that verbal tables typically do not use the reference "See Table XX." More often they are introduced in the text. In other words, they look like a graphic, but because they are composed of words, they are considered to be part of the text.

Ask students to think of information that could be placed in a verbal table. Troubleshooting tables, parts guides, and job titles and responsibilities might use a verbal table. Verbal tables could contain more information than this one does and could be several pages long.

All of the graphics presented in the chapter are on the IRCD as transparencies. Use the overheads to point to specific features as you discuss the graphics.

A formal table is appropriate here because the many different numbers make the information more difficult to read. By presenting numbers in columns, the formal table helps to simplify the information.

Theresa decides to use only a few rules because more would clutter the graphic. The columns are named with stubs. Notice the "a" and "b" superscripts next to the column titles. They direct the reader's attention to the footnotes that give additional information about the table. Underneath the graphic, the word *Source* appears with a footnoted bibliographic entry. Notice that the introduction tells what kind of information is included in the table, but it does not explain every item. The table, with a short introduction, is self-explanatory.

Verbal Table A **verbal table,** also known as a **chart,** is similar to a formal table with its rows and columns. Like a formal table, it uses stubs and may include footnotes and bibliographic information if taken from another source. It is different, though, in the kinds of data included. Formal tables use numerals; verbal tables use words.

Theresa wants to emphasize to both audiences the dangers of poor eating habits and little or no exercise. She needs a graphic appropriate for both audiences. She could write this information in a paragraph but decides that a chart presents the information more efficiently. So Theresa uses the simple verbal table in Figure 6.7 and writes a short introduction.

The following chart shows that some diseases have possible causes in poor eating habits.

Eating Habits	Diseases from Poor Eating Habits
Too much fat	Some cancers, heart disease, strokes
Too much salt	Heart disease, high blood pressure
Too much cholesterol	Heart disease, high blood pressure
Too much sugar	Diabetes, hypoglycemia
Lack of fiber	Some cancers, gallstones
Lack of calcium	Osteoporosis

Source: Marion Newberry, *Nutrition*, New York: Medical Press, 1992, 12.

Figure 6.7 Model of a Verbal Table with Introduction

Theresa believes strongly that both audiences need this information. To avoid overwhelming her younger readers, she does not add data that might interest only the older audience. She knows that the older audience is already aware of the health risks of an inactive lifestyle and needs to be reminded only of possible health consequences. She designs the chart to be simple enough for a younger audience who, she believes, will make the effort to relate to the information.

TEACH

Help students see that graphs are mathematical. Help them understand the difference between a horizontal axis and a vertical axis.

ENRICH

Invite a math instructor to talk about the importance of graphs, to explain the relationship of the X axis and the Y axis, and to bring examples of different graphs.

CONSTRUCTING GRAPHS

A graph is a visual that shows the *relationships* between numerical data. Three types are bar graphs, line graphs, and pie graphs.

Bar Graph The **bar graph** is a graphic using a horizontal axis and a vertical axis to compare numerical data presented in rectangular bars.

Theresa wants to show the readers of *Fitness* how much fat she lost per week for the first two months. She has already given these readers the total amount of fat she lost and wants to follow that information with more specific data. The bar graph is relatively easy to read and is therefore appropriate for the *Fitness* readers. Figure 6.8 shows the bar graph she designed, along with the introduction that tells Theresa's readers which numbers to pay attention to.

Figure 1 shows the progression of fat loss per week for eight weeks. Notice that the greatest amount of fat loss occurred during weeks 1 (3.6 pounds lost) and 2 (2.7 pounds lost). Weeks 3 (1.5 pounds lost) and 4 (1.1 pounds lost) show the least amount of fat loss. Typically, the body will lose more weight at first because of sustained metabolism and significant water loss. Several weeks into the weight-loss program, the metabolism slows down the amount of loss to protect the body from harm. Notice also that after seven weeks on the program, Theresa's weight loss stabilized at a loss of a little more than a pound a week.

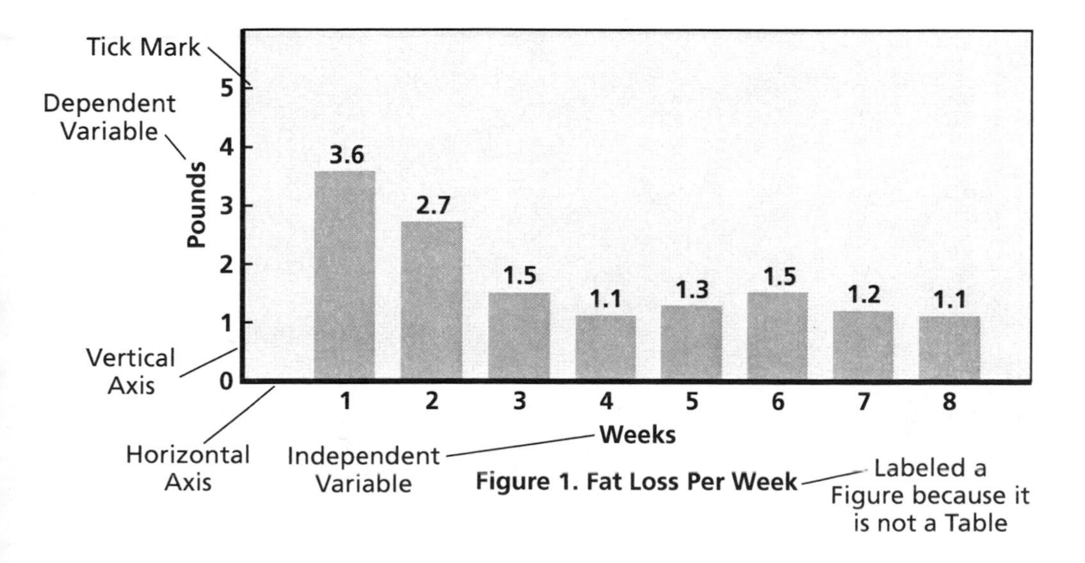

Figure 6.8 Model of Bar Graph with Introduction

TEACH

Ask students to tell you what their first impression is when they look at a bar graph. They will likely tell you that they notice differences in the height of the bars. Tell them this perception is the strength of the bar graph—it is ideal for pointing out differences.

Make sure students understand the different variations of the bar graph: to use specific numbers atop the bars or to leave them out; to create more tick marks or fewer. Each decision depends on the purpose of the graphic and what the writer wants the reader to pay attention to.

Point out that the double bar graph and multiple bar graph need a key to designate heights of the bars.

In her bar graph, Theresa used the horizontal axis for the independent variable and the vertical axis for the dependent variable. In this case, the independent variable is the number of weeks and the dependent variable is the amount of pounds lost. The independent variable (the variable that changes automatically) effects changes in the dependent variable. Typically, the vertical axis represents the dependent variable, and the horizontal axis represents the independent variable. Often the horizontal axis depicts time or distance.

Here, the number of weeks, which pass automatically, has something to do with the amount of weight lost. Put another way, the dependent variable, weight lost, is affected by the independent variable, the passage of time.

Notice that the specific number of pounds has been added atop each bar for easy reference. To do so is not necessary, but helpful. In fact, Theresa could have left out the numbers next to the tick marks, since the actual numbers were placed atop the bars. The decision to add specific numbers depends on your readers and how specific they need you to be. Additional tick marks between pounds to mark individual ounces or half pounds were not added because the graph was understandable without them. Additional lines would have cluttered the graphic. Note that the bars are the same width and that the space between the bars is one-half the bar width.

Multiple Bar Graph To compare how much fat she lost to how much muscle she gained, Theresa uses the **multiple bar graph,** a bar graph with more than one bar, in Figure 6.9. With just two bars, this **double bar graph** is easy for both audiences to read and offers the *Mind and Body* audience more information than a single bar graph. However, Theresa decides to use the multiple bar graph for only the *Fitness* readers because she wants a graph that emphasizes the *difference* in fat loss and muscle gain in the first weeks.

Figure 2 compares the amount of fat lost to the number of pounds gained. Notice that the amount of muscle gained is small compared to the amount of fat lost during the first weeks. However, as the fat loss stabilized during weeks 7 and 8, the amount of muscle gain is slightly higher. Muscle is denser than fat. As the body converts more fat to muscle, the net effect is to actually gain weight while still losing fat.

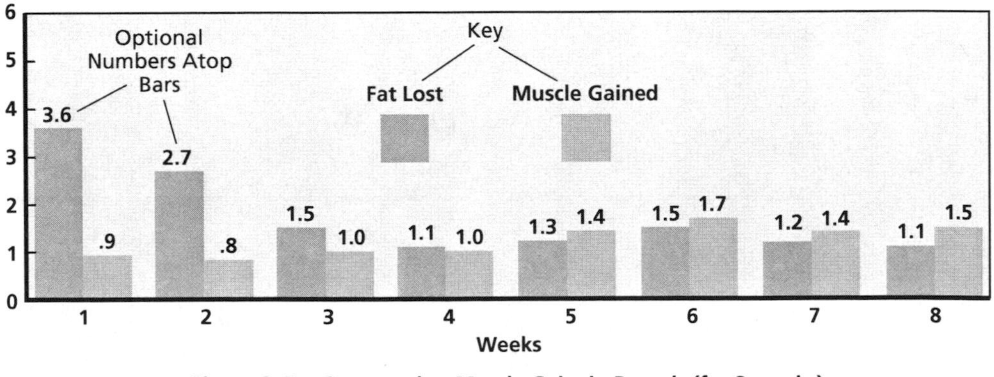

Figure 2. Fat Compared to Muscle Gain, in Pounds (for 8 weeks)

Figure 6.9 Model of a Double Bar Graph with Introduction

Focus on Ethics

Writers have a responsibility to present data accurately without creating distortions that may be misleading. When constructing graphs drawn on horizontal and vertical axes, be careful to begin the quantitative scale at zero and to keep horizontal and vertical axes proportional. In the following graphs, note how misleading the approval ratings for a political candidate can be: Figure 1 minimizes the trend by spreading the horizontal axis out. Figure 2 exaggerates the trend by shortening the horizontal axis. Figure 3 minimizes the trend by taking away the zero point. Figure 4 is the most realistic of all.

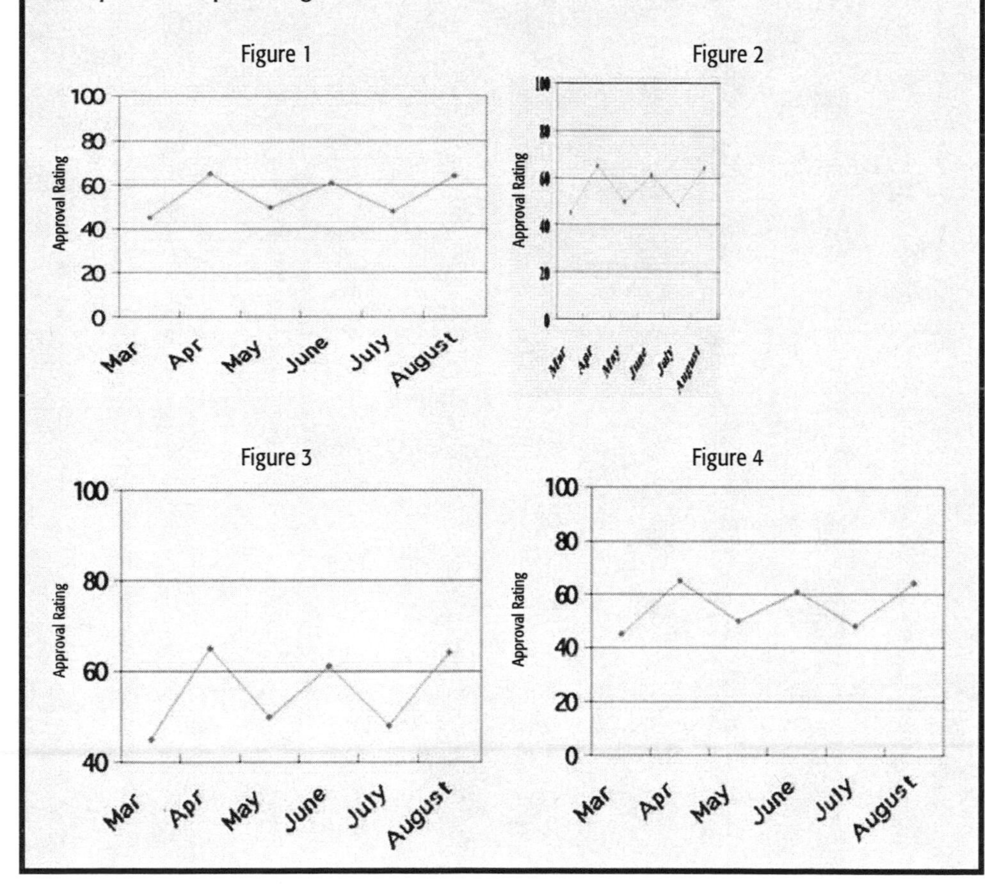

FOCUS ON ETHICS

Use the Focus on Ethics feature to discuss the responsibilities writers have to readers to represent data accurately with no distortions. Spend time asking students to describe their perceptions of each figure in the Focus on Ethics feature.

TEACH

Because the bar graphs and line graphs in this chapter present the same data, it is helpful to compare the two graphics and the impression each makes on the reader. Ask students what their first impression is when they look at the line graph. Notice how this graph is depicting a *trend over time* rather than *revealing dramatic differences.* Also, note that in showing the trend, the writer gives up the ability to show the *details* of the specific numbers written atop the bars.

Ask students to explain Theresa's decision to use two bar graphs for the readers of *Fitness* and one double line graph for the readers of *Mind and Body.* Students should realize that the younger audience is better able to handle the data in two different sets and that the older audience is better able to handle the two sets of data in one graph.

The double bar graph uses two sets of bars on a horizontal and vertical axis to compare several sets of numerical data. With some bars taller than others, the bar graph dramatically depicts differences. Again, the introduction points out what is most important to the reader.

The bars for fat lost are shaded differently from the bars for muscle gained. A **key** is provided to explain the shading. Also, Theresa considers adding the specific pounds atop each bar as she did in the single bar graph. This way, her readers can see the specific amount easily.

Line Graph The **line graph** is similar to a bar graph in that it uses a horizontal axis and a vertical axis to compare numerical data. Instead of bars, however, this graph uses a line that depicts a trend.

TEACH

The double bar graph and double line graph, or multiple line graph, present the same information. Using the transparencies of the double bar graph and double line graph on the IRCD, lay one transparency over the other to show students the similarity of the data. Where the bars show differences, the lines show a trend. Furthermore, the double line graph shows how the two sets of data interact with each other. It actually shows what happens to fat loss as the muscle loss increases. A multiple line graph can show the interactive relationships of two sets of data.

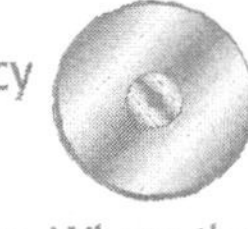

Point out that the double line graph needs a key to identify each line.

Theresa can use a line graph to show the same data she used in the bar graph and must decide which graph is more appropriate for her readers. To experiment with a different graph, she plotted the same eight-week fat-loss data on a line graph. Figure 6.10 shows the same data in a line graph that Figure 6.9 shows in a bar graph.

Figure 3 shows how the fat loss peaked in the earlier weeks, dropped remarkably during the middle weeks, and plateaued during the last four weeks.

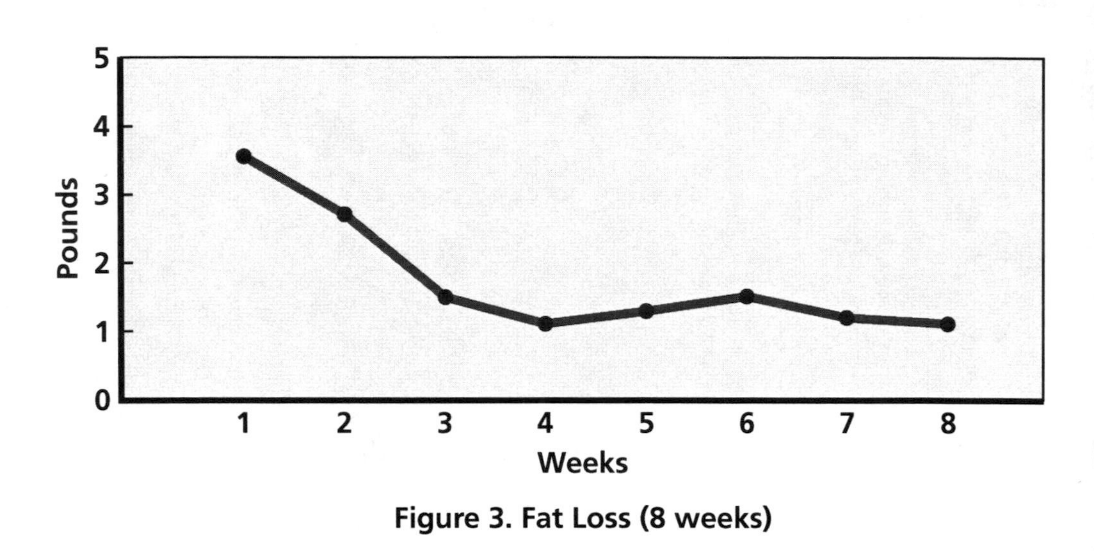

Figure 3. Fat Loss (8 weeks)

Figure 6.10 Model of Line Graph with Introduction

Theresa's line graph illustrates the fat loss over a period of time. Even though it shows the same data as Figure 6.9, it plays up the general trend, not the individual numbers. The introduction focuses on the overall trend: the fat loss "dropped remarkably" and "plateaued." It plays up relationships between weeks instead of the differences between them.

This graph would be appropriate for either audience because the trend is easily interpreted, but Theresa decides not to use this line graph for either article. She believes that the bar graph is more appropriate for the inexperienced readers of *Fitness* because she wants to highlight differences in the fat lost. Instead, Theresa considers using the multiple line graph below for her *Fitness* audience.

Multiple Line Graph Theresa's Figure 6.11 puts the same information as the double bar graph in Figure 6.9 into a **multiple line graph,** a graph using more than one line to compare data. Because Theresa's graph compares two sets of data, think of it as a **double line graph.**

The relationship between fat loss and muscle gain is more closely matched after the first weeks of the fitness program (see Figure 4). During the first two weeks, the amount of muscle gain is minimal and fat loss is at its maximum. As the fat loss plateaus, the muscle gain stabilizes, surpassing fat loss by a few ounces.

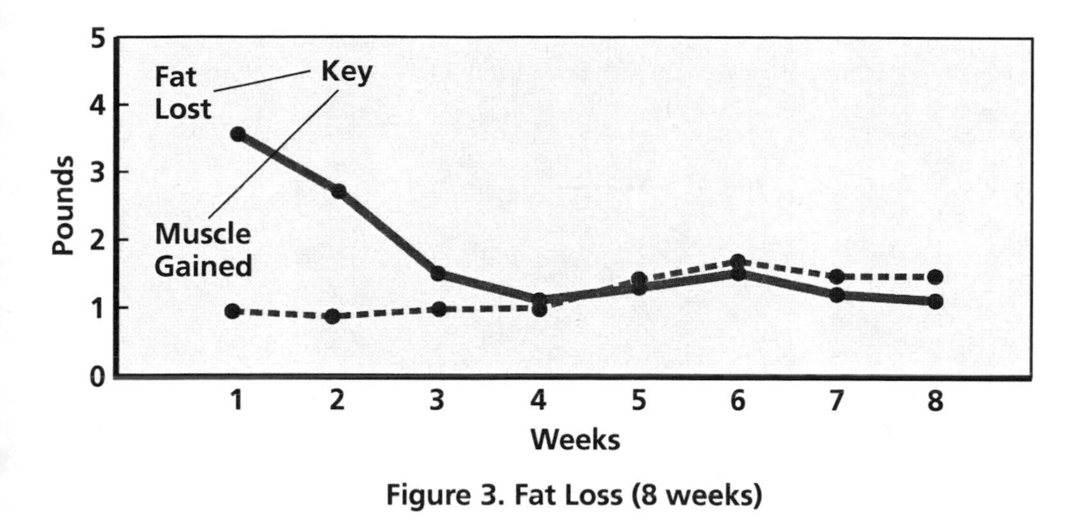

Figure 6.11 Model of Multiple Line Graph with Introduction

Theresa decides that the physical education majors would be interested in seeing how the two sets of data interact with each other and would have the educational background to understand how muscle gain affects fat loss. While she will present her *Fitness* readers the same information in *two* bar graphs, she will present her *Mind and Body* readers the same information in *one* multiple line graph.

Notice how the double line graph illustrates the *relationship* between fat loss and muscle gain rather than the *differences* between fat loss and muscle gain. Again, the introduction emphasizes this relationship.

Pie Graph To represent what percentage of her total daily food intake consisted of fat, protein, and carbohydrates, Theresa draws a **pie graph** in Figure 6.12. A pie graph is a circular graphic that shows how the parts relate to the whole.

Complete the Pie Graph Activity worksheet on the Data CD.

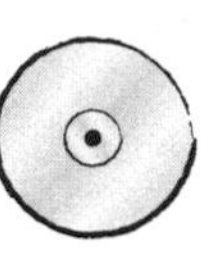

FOCUS

Figure 6.12
Tell students that the purpose of the pie graph is to show how parts relate to the whole. The pie graph is just what its name implies: a whole pie divided into different-sized pieces. The pie represents 100 percent. The pieces of the pie represent varying percentages that total 100 percent.

TEACH

Tell students that a pie graph divided into more than seven parts has too many pieces. Rather than having this many divisions, combine smaller pieces into one category.

Explain the importance of labeling pieces. Smaller pieces may require call outs instead of labels directly on the pie.

Have students complete the Pie Graph Activity worksheet on the IRCD to apply the concepts in this section.

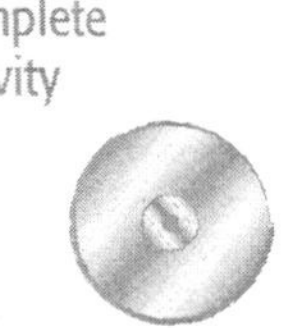

The whole totals 100 percent, with each piece of the pie representing a percentage of the whole. Notice that the pie pieces move clockwise from the twelve o'clock position from the largest to the smallest. A pie graph should contain no more than seven sections.

Figure 5 shows the amount of protein, carbohydrates, and fat a person on a fitness plan needs in one day. Surprisingly, the human body needs more carbohydrates (65%) than protein and much less fat than previously thought.

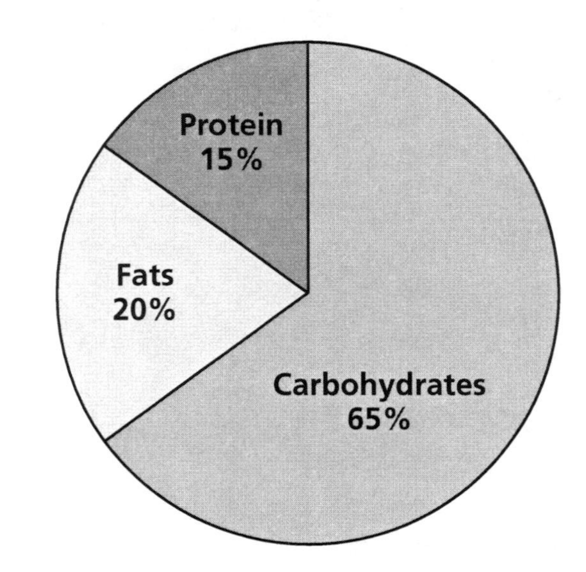

Figure 6.12 Model of Pie Graph with Introduction

The introduction repeats the actual percentages in the pie and points out the significance of those numbers. The readers of *Mind and Body* already know these percentages and do not need to be reminded of them, so Theresa decides not to use the pie graph for this more sophisticated audience. The readers of *Fitness,* who include people just beginning fitness programs, may need this information.

CONSTRUCTING CHARTS AND DIAGRAMS

A **chart** is a drawing with boxes, words, and lines to show a process or an organizational structure. Two popular charts include the **flowchart** and the organizational chart. A **diagram** or drawing shows what something looks like or how it operates.

Flowchart Theresa wants a quick way to show the complex process of converting glucose to fat. She knows the readers of *Mind and Body* already understand what happens to food the body does not use, but the readers of *Fitness* are unaware of this process. She chooses a flowchart, Figure 6.13, to illustrate this process to her less knowledgeable readers. In the flowchart, the arrows lead the reader through the process, and the introduction summarizes the process.

Figure 6 shows what happens when sugars and starches are digested to glucose. The glucose not used by the brain or the muscles is converted to fat.

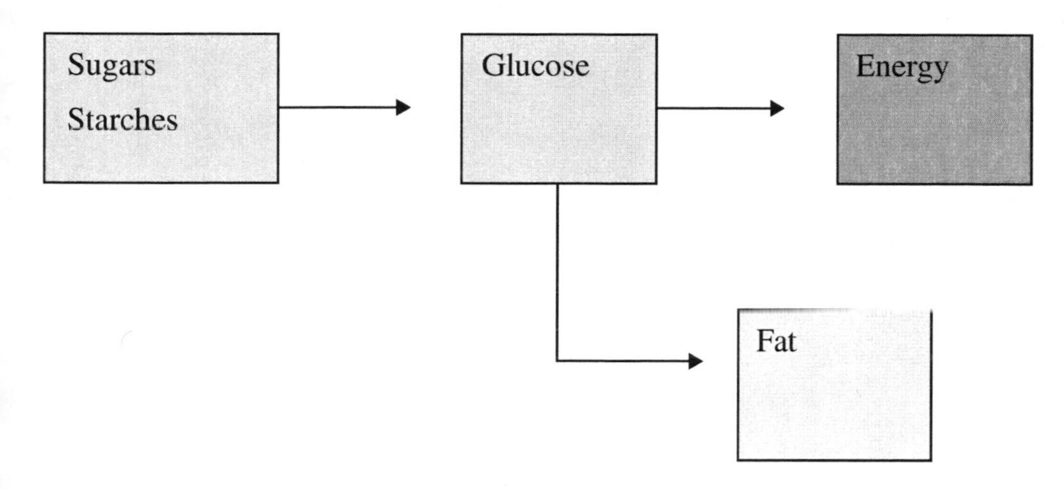

Figure 6.13 Model of Flowchart with Introduction

Organizational Chart Theresa was asked to present her research to the student body during assembly. To make students aware of the school's fitness center, she creates an **organizational chart.** The chart shows the hierarchy of the fitness center employees. Theresa creates her organizational chart using boxes, words, and lines in Figure 6.14.

The following chart shows the organization of the school fitness center.

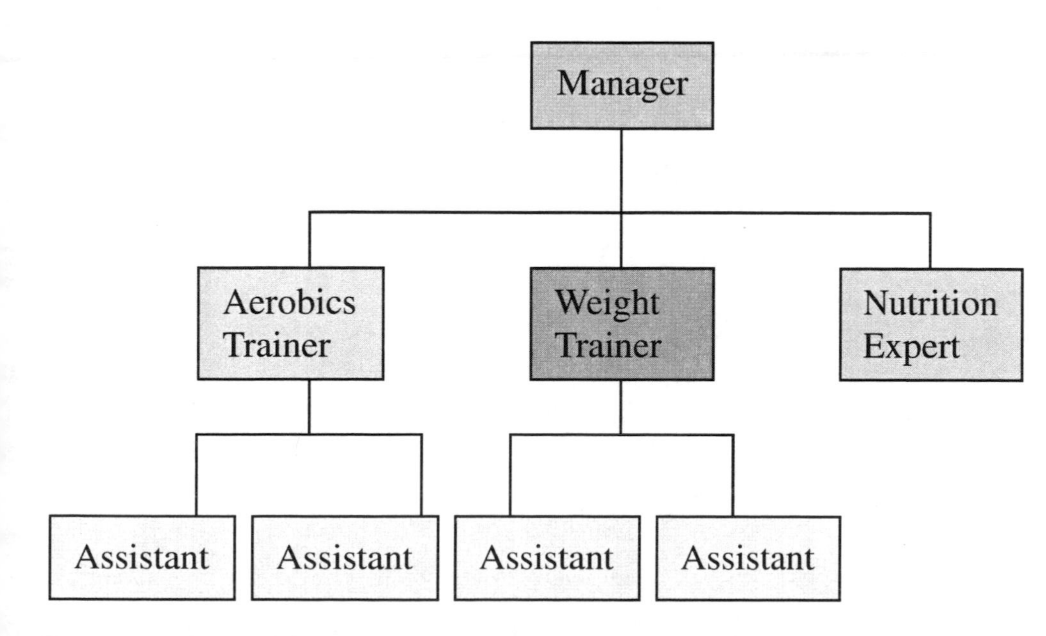

Figure 6.14 Model of Organizational Chart with Introduction

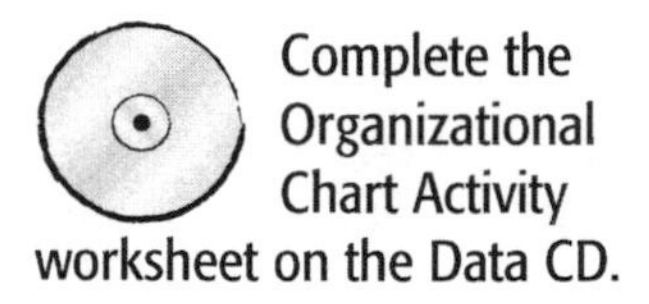
Complete the Organizational Chart Activity worksheet on the Data CD.

FOCUS

Figure 6.13
Use the figure to explain the construction of a flowchart. Point out that the direction of the flow is reflected in the direction of the arrows. In each box, short names describe stages in the process.

ENRICH

In groups, ask students to create a flowchart of a process they know well; for example, the writing process, the drop/add procedure at school, the election procedure for school or another organization, or the procedure for some hobby.

FOCUS

Figure 6.14
Use the figure to explain an organizational chart. Point out that boxes contain job titles and that the hierarchy is top-down: the person at the top oversees more people and has more responsibility for the entire organization than the person listed at the bottom. Connecting lines show who supervises whom. Notice how the short introduction refers to the graphic.

TEACH

Emphasize that the purpose of a flowchart is to present a process and the purpose of an organizational chart is to present the hierarchy of an institution.

Have students complete the Organizational Chart Activity worksheet on the IRCD to apply concepts from this section.

FOCUS

Figure 6.15

Use the figure to explain the construction of a diagram. Point out that diagrams are simple depictions or representations of what something looks like, but they are not as realistic as a photo. Draw attention to the use of call outs. Remind students that the introduction refers to the graphic.

The blocks contain the job titles. At the top of the chart is the highest position. The lines show who is responsible to whom. The introduction describes information in the chart.

Diagram or Drawing For her *Mind and Body* article, Theresa uses a diagram, or drawing, in Figure 6.15 from *Good Health* to show what triglycerides (fat) look like in the bloodstream. She believes her *Mind and Body* readers have the background for this information and hopes the diagram will reinforce the dangers of a diet too high in fat.

Notice the use of **call outs,** names of parts with lines drawn to the appropriate place. The drawing represents a simplified version of the blood arteriole and capillaries. Adding other particles in the bloodstream would complicate the graphic. Here, the author drew only what was needed to make the point.

Figure 8 shows how the blood cells clump together abnormally after a dinner high in triglycerides (fat). Notice that when the triglycerides create sludging, blood flow to the capillaries is impeded.

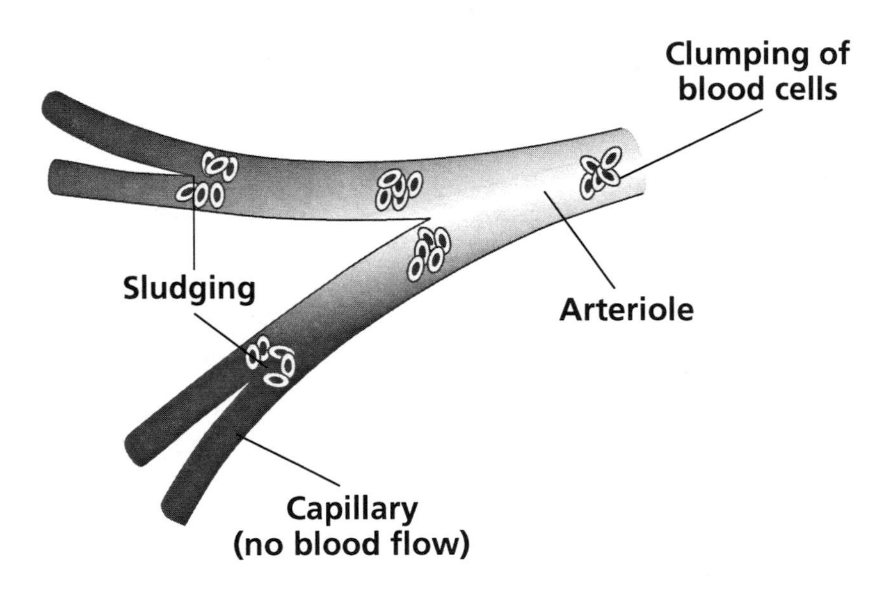

Figure 6.15 Model of a Diagram with Introduction

Photograph A photograph can be inserted into a document when it is important to show what something actually looks like. Photographs include a lot of detail, however, and are not always an appropriate graphic aid to use. To be effective, the photo should be clear and should focus on a particular idea or message.

Theresa decides to set up a web page to promote a healthy lifestyle. Because she thinks exercising with others encourages people to keep up their fitness regime, she decides to post a photograph of friends engaging in a power walk at lunch. Her photo also helps create the mood she is after, that is, to depict fitness in a fun and positive way. Figure 6.16 shows the photo she chose.

FOCUS

Figure 6.16
Use the figure to point out how photos differ from other graphics. Photos are realistic and can capture a mood, but unless they are of good quality, they may have too many details to be clearly seen. Note that this graphic still needs to be introduced.

The workers at Sampsun Marine Industries, shown in Figure 6.16 below, get together every day for a walk around the grounds.

Figure 6.16 Photograph of Empoyee Power Walk

ONGOING ASSESSMENT

Stop and Think
Flowchart

Organizational chart

Diagram, drawing, or photograph

A photograph's advantage is its realism and attention to detail. A photograph's disadvantage is that it may show too many details without focusing on a central idea. If the photo is of poor quality, it will not be a good choice for the graphic.

Stop and Think

Which chart shows a process? Which chart shows an organizational hierarchy? Which graphic shows what something looks like? What is the advantage of using a photograph? What is the disadvantage of using a photograph?

TEACHING RESOURCES

IRCD
- Chapter Activities, Ch. 6
- Work Is A Zoo!, Ch. 6
- PowerPoint® Slides, Ch. 6

Exam*View*®, Ch. 6

techwriting.swlearning.com, Ch. 6

CLOSE

Summary

Ask students to divide into groups and devise a group pop quiz based on the summary. Reproduce the quizzes and distribute them to other groups to see whether they, as a group, can answer the questions. You could actually grade the group quizzes or give prizes to the groups with the best score.

CLOSE

Checklist

Ask students to use the checklist when they design reports and construct graphics. See the IRCD for additional guidelines.

Chapter 6 Review

SUMMARY

1. To create effective document design, 1) use adequate white space, 2) use left justification with ragged-right edges, 3) use a 10- to 12-point serif font that mixes capitals and lowercase letters, 4) determine a workable system of headings, 5) use highlighters to draw attention to important information, and 6) consider appropriate physical features.
2. Graphics should adhere to basic principles. They should be neat, use figure labels and numbers to refer to anything that is not a table, use table labels and numbers to refer to formal tables, and be located in a convenient place for the reader (usually right after the referral phrase). They also should use specific titles, give credit when necessary, use words to explain, show decimals aligned, and use color effectively.
3. Each type of graphic has a purpose that can be matched to writing objectives and audience needs.
4. Effective graphics include informal, formal, and verbal tables; bar graphs and line graphs; flowcharts, organizational charts, and diagrams; and photographs.

Checklist

- Have I determined my writing objectives and found a graphic to match?
- Have I designed my page effectively with adequate white space, left justification and ragged-right edges, a 10- to 12-point serif font, capital and lowercase letters, a workable system of headings, and appropriate highlighters?
- Have I selected appropriate graphics?
- Have I selected appropriate physical features and an appropriate medium for my writing objectives?
- Have I constructed the graphic neatly?
- Have I referred to the graphic properly as a table or figure?
- Have I placed the graphic in a convenient place for the reader?
- Have I provided a specific title for every graph, every chart, and every formal table?
- Have I numbered the graphics consecutively? Table 1, 2, etc. or Figure 1, 2, etc.?
- Have I given credit for the graphic found in an outside source?
- Have I explained the significance of the graphic?
- Have I kept the graphic as simple as possible?
- Have I used color effectively?
- Have I constructed each graphic according to the criteria required by that graphic?

Build On What You Know

1. Examine several of your textbooks for design features. Describe each design. Which book has the best design and why?
2. Read local newspapers and magazines. Cut out an example of each type of graphic presented in this chapter. Identify the parts of the graphic. Using your checklist, determine whether the graphic designers presented data effectively.
3. Look for graphics that are different from the ones presented in this chapter. Note what is different about them. What has been added or changed? Even though the graphics are different, they will likely fall into one of the categories described in this chapter. Which category do they fall into?
4. Suggest the best graphic to use for presenting the situations below. As a bonus, try to construct the graphic.
   a. Lamar wrote to his father and listed his last test grades in calculus: Chapter 1 Test, 83; Chapter 2 Test, 79; Chapter 3 Test, 92.
   b. Carrie wanted to know how many miles she walked as she went about her everyday activities during a regular five-day school week opposed to how many miles she walked during the first five days of summer vacation. She used a pedometer and estimated her mileage each day on a chart. Here are her figures: School in session: May 25, 1.3; May 26, 1.9; May 27, 2.7; May 28, 1.6; May 29, 2.5. Vacation: June 1, .6; June 2, 1.2; June 3, .9; June 4, 1.4; June 5, 2.0.
   c. Ichiro wanted to show his parents that he had wisely spent the money they gave him for the first month of college. They gave him $800 to buy books and set up his dorm room. In his letter, he rounds his figures to the nearest dollar and uses a graphic with the following information: $562, books and educational supplies; $36, eating out; $115, dorm accessories (rug, poster, sheets, etc.); $25, entertainment; $40, parking fine (which he assures them will not happen again!); and $22, unspent funds.
   d. Crystal is head cashier for a grocery store. She must show her coworkers the procedure for gaining approval for a customer check over $200. The procedure is as follows: politely tell the customer it is store policy to have checks over $200 approved; verify the identity of the customer with a picture ID; make sure information on the check is correct; get two phone numbers from the customer; put your initials on the check; call the manager to the checkout to meet the customer and approve the check.
   e. Alessandra must show her physics instructor the structure of a hydrogen atom and the location of protons, neutrons, and electrons.
   f. Patrick is designing a travel brochure for future Peace Corps volunteers. He wants to show how eager students were to learn English in a Phillipine village where current volunteers recently spent time.

ASSESS

Build On What You Know

1. Encourage students to think about the differences in page design.
2. Students will see the importance of graphics in print media.
3. Use this exercise to make students aware of the variety of graphics available.
4. **a.** Informal table. The informal table should be introduced by a few sentences. **b.** Bar graph or line graph. She could even devise a double bar graph or double line graph and call different bars or lines School Week and Vacation Week. **c.** Pie graph **d.** Flowchart **e.** Diagram **f.** Photo

ASSESS

Apply What You Learned

5. This exercise gives students an opportunity to design graphics based on activities they are familiar with.
6. Students are invited to make up details, but the percentages and the associated expenditures should be the same as what is shown in the solution presented on the IRCD.
7. Be sure students use the guidelines for constructing graphs.

Apply What You Learned

5. Select a photo of you or a friend that you are especially proud of. Write a brief article explaining the significance of the photo and insert the photo. Be sure to title the photo, number it, and refer to it in your article.
6. Convert this survey information into a pie graph. You surveyed 450 clients of Iron Works Gym to determine their preferences for new equipment, facilities, or services. Results were as follows: 175 clients want more weight-lifting equipment, 50 clients want child-care services, 75 clients want a sauna, 50 clients want more trainers, and 80 clients want a juice bar.
7. Use the information from the table below to generate graphics.

Commodity	1980	1985	1990	1995	1996	1997	1998	1999	2000
Milk (plain and flavored)	27.6	26.7	25.7	24.0	24.0	23.6	23.2	23.1	22.6
Whole	17.0	14.3	10.5	8.6	8.5	8.3	8.2	8.2	8.1
Reduced-fat, light, and skim	10.5	12.3	15.2	15.4	15.4	15.3	15.1	14.9	14.5
Bottled water	2.4	4.5	8.0	11.5	12.3	12.9	15.7	17.7	(NA)
Fruit juices	7.4	7.8	7.9	8.7	8.7	8.7	8.5	9.3	8.4
Fruit drinks	(NA)	(NA)	6.3	7.7	7.9	8.2	7.7	7.7	(NA)
Vegetable juices	(NA)	(NA)	0.3	0.3	0.3	0.3	0.3	0.3	(NA)

All measurements are in gallons.

Source: U.S. Dept. of Agriculture, Economic Research Service, Food Consumption, Prices, and Expenditures, annual; *Agricultural Outlook,* monthly; and online at <http://www.ers.usda.gov/data/sonsumption>.

- A bar graph to illustrate the *total* amount of milk consumed from 1996-2000
- A double bar graph to show the amount of whole and reduced-fat milk consumed from 1996-2000
- A line graph to illustrate the amount of bottled water consumed from 1990-2000
- A double line graph to illustrate the amount of whole and reduced fat milk consumed from 1980-2000
- A table of milk, bottled water, fruit juices, and vegetable juices consumed from 1996-1999
- An informal table of *total* milk and *total* vegetable juices consumed in 2000

Work Is A Zoo!

You have gathered your information, and the presentation is taking shape. But you will be presenting a lot of ideas at once, including numbers and comparisons to other zoo programs. Tyrone is worried that people will be overwhelmed.

You mention this problem to Anya, and she says, "Guys, why not make some attractive graphics to help the listeners? I like being able to see numbers presented in graphs. You could even give us some ideas about the kinds of logos that other zoos are using on their promotional materials." Great idea, Anya.

Now your task is to produce graphics to enhance your presentation. You may want graphics to show:

- Logos and promotional material from other zoos.
- Number of zoos with similar programs.
- Overall cost of the program.
- Success rates of the program.
- Information from interviews.

Think about these things as you plan your graphics:

- Complicated and unclear graphics add no value to a presentation.
- Your audience and purpose should determine the kind of graphic you use.
- Graphics should provide *needed* information.
- The size of the graphic should not be too big or too small.

Be sure to use the graphic that best presents the information. You might choose from the following graphics:

- Tables
- Bar graphs
- Line graphs
- Flowcharts
- Organizational charts
- Diagrams
- Photographs

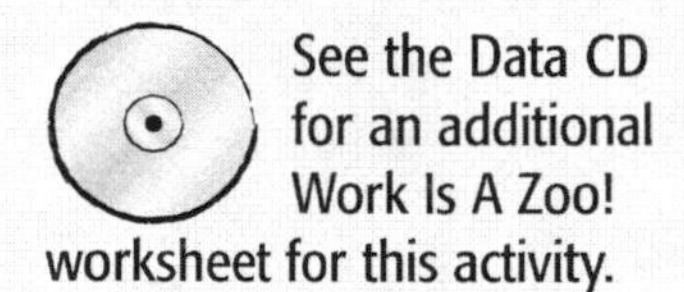

See the Data CD for an additional Work Is A Zoo! worksheet for this activity.

WORK IS A ZOO

Have students research various business aspects of zoos, concentrating on the topics here. Then have students graph the information they find using the best graphic for the information. Students can choose from the list presented here, or they can graph everything in the list, creating separate graphics. This assignment also makes an excellent team project, with each person responsible for graphing different information.

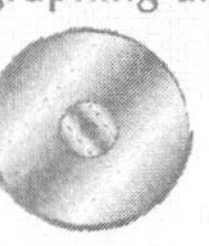

See the IRCD for an additional Work Is A Zoo! worksheet for this activity.

INSTRUCTIONS

GOALS

ANALYZE your audience's expectations and the steps required for instructions

DETERMINE an appropriate format for instructions

PREPARE a clear, concise set of instructions

DETERMINE how to write online instructions

See the Data CD for Write-to-Learn and In The Know activity worksheets.

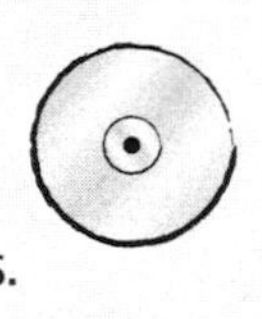

TEACHING RESOURCES

IRCD

Lesson Plans, Ch. 7

Chapter Activities, Ch. 7

PowerPoint® Slides, Ch. 7

Sample Documents, Ch. 7

techwriting.swlearning.com, Ch. 7

Exam*View*® CD, Ch. 7

CHAPTER OVERVIEW

Tells how to write instructions.

See the IRCD for Write-to-Learn and In The Know activity worksheets.

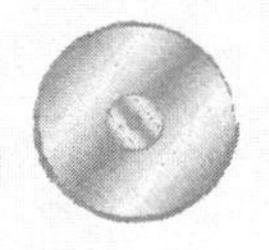

Use the Write-to-Learn activity to discuss the importance of a well-written set of instructions.

WRITE-TO-LEARN

Think of the last time you followed instructions. Maybe the instructions were from an instructor, a parent, an employer, or a manual. In a short journal entry, answer these questions: What were the circumstances under which you followed the instructions? Were the instructions easy to follow? If so, why? Were the instructions hard to follow? If so, why? How did you handle any problems created by poorly written instructions? Did the instructions use graphics? If so, what kind? Were the graphics helpful? What kind of medium was used: verbal, paper, or online?

In The Know

active voice refers to a verb whose subject performs the action of the verb

cautions statements designed to keep a person from harming the mechanism he or she is working with

concurrent testing determining the usefulness of a product or an activity by observing someone's performance while he or she is using the product or engaging in the activity

explanations information coming after a step and providing additional data to clarify the step

field test checking your instructions with a small sample of people to see whether the instructions are clear

imperative mood the form of a verb that signals a command or instruction; the subject is "you" or understood "you"

online instructions instructions using computer technology as the medium; some types include help menus, CD-ROMs, or web-based instructions

retrospective testing checking the usefulness of a product or an activity after someone has used the product or performed the activity

second person use of "you" or an understood "you"

set of instructions a step-by-step list of actions necessary to complete a task

step one action in a set of instructions

warnings statements designed to keep a person from being harmed

Writing@Work

Sara Coers is a technical communicator for RDS, a financial software company in Indianapolis. In her position, she is responsible for planning, writing, and editing instructional materials, including tutorials and online help, for her company's software products.

As a technical communicator, it is essential that Sara's written communication be absolutely clear. The clarity of her communication is so important because, before Sara's employment with RDS, the company had a history of documentation that did not meet users' needs. Sara's challenge is to create documentation that is user-friendly. Sara also strives for minimalist writing—she wants to use as few words as possible and still have people understand. And to ensure consistency among her written documents, she tries to reuse as much material as possible.

Sara writes for a wide range of audiences. Not only does she write for external clients, such as credit union employees, but she also must write for internal audiences, such as RDS trainers and developers. Although she will generally write different information for these different groups, she must always consider each group's level of understanding.

Because of the number of users Sara writes for, she must be able to effectively relay information to people of varied educational backgrounds. Her rule is to present information in such a way that the people with the least amount of education or lowest level of comprehension of the product will still be able to understand clearly.

RDS has some clients who base their businesses on different ethnic populations. Sara must consider this when she is writing her instructional materials. She makes sure that her communication is not confusing to any group of users. She also uses what she calls "equal-opportunity examples." When using examples in her writing, she makes sure they will make sense to people of all different cultures.

Sara has a bachelor of arts degree from Indiana University and a master's in technical and scientific communication from Miami University in Ohio. She served two internships with Peregrine Systems, primarily writing user guides and online help, before obtaining her current position with RDS.

APPLY

Writing@Work
This profile emphasizes the importance of technical writing skills. Have your students choose a product they know a lot about. This may be anything from a software product to a miter saw to a sewing machine. Have them write detailed instructions for using the product. Stress the importance of making the information understandable for people with no prior knowledge of the product.

At Home Operation

Recording Your Outgoing Announcement

Before using your new answering system telephone, you should record an announcement. This is what callers will hear when the system answers a call. Your announcement may be up to 2 minutes long.

1. Prepare your announcement.

   Example: "Hello. I can't come to the phone right now. Please leave your name, telephone number, and a short message after the beep. I will return your call as soon as I can. Thank you."

2. Hold down ANNC, located under the cassette cover (Figure 1). Continue to hold don ANNC while recording. The system will beep once to indicate that it is ready to record.
3. When the system beeps, speak toward the front of the unit in a normal tone of voice.
4. Release ANNC when you are finished. The tape will reset automatically.

> **NOTE:** Your system cannot record an announcement when messages are on the tape. If you have messages and the MESSAGES light is blinking, first listen to your messages and then let your system clear them. (See page 14, "Listen to Your Messages.") When the MESSAGES light is lit steadily, you can record your announcement.

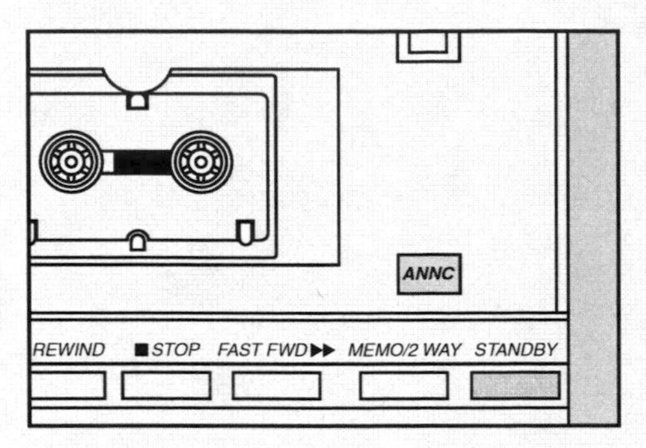

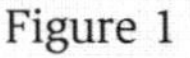
Figure 1

Playing Back Your Announcement

1. If the tape is rewinding, wait for it to stop moving.
2. Set the message VOLUME control (on the right side of the system) to the middle.
3. Tap (quickly press and release) ANNC

> **NOTE:** Be sure that you release the button quickly. If you hold it down for more than a second, your announcement will be erased.

To change your announcement

Follow Steps 1–4 under "Recording Your Outgoing Announcement." Your new announcement will be recorded over the old one.

Figure 7.1 Instructions Model

GETTING STARTED ON INSTRUCTIONS

Imagine that you just purchased a new entertainment center for your television and stereo. You want to assemble the entertainment center quickly because you invited some friends over to watch a movie. Your friends will be arriving in two hours, and you must put together your entertainment center before they arrive. Since you are on a tight schedule, you start to assemble the entertainment center without looking at the instructions. "It cannot be that hard," you think. You are certain that reading the instructions will slow you down. An hour and a half later, you are still trying to connect the parts. You are frantic because your guests will be arriving in 30 minutes, and the entertainment center is still in pieces on the floor. Finally, you look at the instructions.

WARM UP

Do you always read instructions before you attempt a procedure? Why or why not?

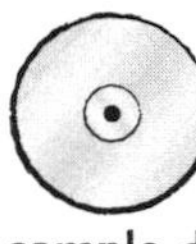

You can view various sample instructions in the sample documents on the Data CD.

FOCUS

Warm Up

Some students will say that they read instructions carefully; others will say that they do not. Use this question to help students understand how unpredictable readers can be. As writers, students must encourage readers to read the steps.

If you have examples of poorly written instructions, share them with the class.

FOCUS

Figure 7.1

Refer to this model as you discuss information in the chapter. Please note, though, that while this is a good set of instructions, not all instructions use this format.

Show the additional sample

instructions in the sample documents on the IRCD.

WHO READS INSTRUCTIONS?

People who read a **set of instructions** need to perform a task or understand how someone else performs that task. The server who is asked to close a restaurant at night needs to know the procedure for doing so. The surveyor measuring a road for underground pipes needs to know traffic patterns. You, assembling your newly purchased entertainment center, need to know how to set it up as quickly as possible.

You can empathize with a reader trying to follow a set of instructions. Instructions, with their graphics and technical language, can be intimidating. Consequently, some readers will read instructions carefully, paying attention to every word.

On the other hand, a lot of readers, like you in the situation above, are impatient, trying to go through the steps without reading them first. Some readers, thinking they are familiar with the procedure already, will read only a few steps and think they know what to do. Other readers rely more on the graphics for information and less on the words.

To see how your audience affects the way you write instructions, see the Instructions for a Pre-Schooler and Teenager in the Sample Documents on the Data CD.

TEACH

Show students the Instructions for a Pre-Schooler and Teenager in the Sample Documents on the IRCD.

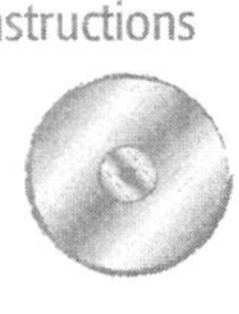

TEACH

Ask students to put a simple process such as their daily class schedule, their extracurricular activities, or their exercise routine on a flowchart. You can use the Sample Flowchart Teaching Master to help them get started.

Whatever their attitude, readers trust the writer of a set of instructions to give them accurate, precise information in the proper sequence. Some instructions—electrical installation and medical procedures, for example—can be matters of life or death. In these cases, readers trust writers with their lives and with the lives of others.

© GETTY IMAGES/PHOTODISC

Because your reader trusts you, make sure your procedures are accurate and include enough detail. The amount of detail depends on your audience's knowledge about the process. A beginner, for example, needs more detail than someone with experience. Good instructions keep readers motivated to read carefully.

PREWRITING

Before writing your own instructions, you must understand the sequence of events in the procedure you are writing about. That way, your explanations will be clear to someone reading them. If you do not understand the procedure, your readers probably will not understand it either. Use these suggestions to analyze the process and to better understand the steps involved:

1. Create a flowchart with steps to the process. Write what someone should do first, second, third, etc. Try not to skip any steps. Add steps or remove steps as needed.
2. In your mind, work the process backward. What is the purpose of the procedure? What is done last, next to last, third to last, etc.?
3. Watch a person who is a member of your target audience performing the task for the first time. Take notes. What is the very first step? What is the most difficult step? What steps does the person misunderstand? Would additional steps help this person? Do any of the steps need to be explained?
4. Interview this person about the procedure after he or she has finished. What additional suggestions can he or she give you for improving your instructions?

ONGOING ASSESSMENT

Stop and Think

Use responses to show how audience level and prior experience affect what you include in instructions. Four-year-olds might have to be told to use a butter knife (for safety reasons), to use a small amount of peanut butter and jelly, to wipe off the utensils when they finish, and to spread ingredients evenly with the broad side of the knife.

What would you tell a four-year-old about making a peanut butter and jelly sandwich that you would not tell a person your age?

ORGANIZING AND FORMATTING INSTRUCTIONS

Now that you have analyzed the steps for your instructions, organize your information into sections for your reader. Then place that information in an easy-to-read format.

© GETTY IMAGES/PHOTODISC

ORGANIZING INSTRUCTIONS

All instructions include steps of procedures and appropriate **explanations;** however, instructions often contain other parts as well. Whether to include these parts depends on the audience and the purpose of the instructions.

Instructions usually include an introduction, but some do not. Manuals contain an introduction at the beginning but may not contain introductions for one of the parts. Telling someone how to use an appliance would require only familiarity with the appliance, not a list of materials. But telling someone how to make pancakes would require a list of materials and ingredients. Explaining how to answer questions on a job interview would require a different structure from suggesting ways to deal with depression.

Some instructions might require **cautions** against actions that would harm the mechanism. Others might require stronger **warnings** to prevent serious injury to someone using the instructions. When you delete a file from your computer, a message appears to ask whether you really want to send this file to the recycle bin. The instructions telling you how to administer flea and tick protection for your cat warns about the dangers of swallowing, coming in contact with skin and eyes, and using near an open flame. Even your bag of popcorn warns you: "HANDLE CAREFULLY—CONTAINS HOT AIR AND STEAM." You are responsible for including proper cautions and warnings with any instructions you write.

WARM UP

Look at the instructions model that opens this chapter on page 172. What do you notice about how the instructions are laid out on the page? What special features do the instructions use? What have the writers done to make the instructions easy to follow?

FOCUS

Warm Up

Help students become aware of their formatting choices. Point out special features such as numbered steps and headings.

RETEACH

Make sure that students understand why one set of instructions may require all of the headings and another set may require only two.

TEACH

Make sure that students understand the importance of safety. Written warnings and cautions are important to the safety of people and equipment.

FOCUS

Figure 7.2

Point out the differences between the last two items: More Explanation of Each Step and Less Explanation of Each Step. Remind students that the document changes when the writing situation and audience needs change.

ENRICH

Ask students to form groups and think of instructions that would need a list of definitions, a list of materials (tools or ingredients), warnings, etc.

Ask two or three students to write a set of simple instructions in class. One student can depict the written instructions visually. Students could tell how to solve a math problem, how to get from one part of campus to another, or how to apply for graduation.

Ask two extroverted students to come to the front of the class. One of them should be wearing shoes that lace up and tie. Tell that student to untie his or her shoes. Ask the other student to teach the first student how to tie his or her shoes. Tell the student tying the shoe to follow the directions precisely with no variation. See what happens. The results are funny and enlightening. This exercise shows students that telling someone how to do something is harder than they think.

Use Figure 7.2 to determine what sections to add to basic steps.

PROVIDE...	IF...
Introduction	Your reader needs any or all of the following information: background, context, purpose (what readers will be able to do when they finish), whom the instructions are for, scope (what the instructions do and do not cover), organization, something special about how to read the instructions, assumptions about readers' knowledge or ability, motivation to read the instructions carefully.
Definitions	Your reader must learn new terms to perform the procedure. Place six or more terms in a separate list or glossary; define fewer than six terms as you write.
List of Materials, Tools, or Ingredients	Your reader should gather materials, tools, or ingredients before following your instructions.
Graphics	A picture, diagram, or flowchart would make the instructions easier to follow. Also include graphics if the instructions are complicated or dangerous.
Warnings	Your reader could get hurt if he or she overlooks a step or does it incorrectly. Place warnings before the reader is likely to do anything dangerous. Often a symbol or graphic that signifies danger accompanies the warning.
Cautions	Your reader could damage equipment if he or she does a step incorrectly. Place cautions close to where readers need them before they are likely to do anything dangerous. Often a symbol or graphic accompanies the caution.
Notes	Additional information would aid your reader's understanding. This information is not an essential step. Include it immediately after the step to which it is most closely related.
More Explanation of Each Step	Your reader is performing the process for the first time, the procedure is complicated, or the reader needs to know more to perform the procedure correctly.
Less Explanation of Each Step	Your reader has performed the process before or the procedure is simple. You also should provide less explanation for steps in an emergency procedure where reading explanations would prevent the reader from acting quickly.

Figure 7.2 What to Include in a Set of Instructions

FORMATTING INSTRUCTIONS

Because readers are unpredictable and often impatient, format instructions so they are easy to read. Use plenty of white space to make instructions look accessible. Number your steps with Arabic numerals and align the steps in a list.

Another effective way to make instructions easy to use is by incorporating graphics, such as flowcharts and diagrams. Graphics simplify a process and are especially useful for an intermediate reader, one who has performed the process before and needs to be reminded only of the steps. Sometimes different parts of a mechanism are shown at different times during the steps. (See Chapter 6, *Document Design and Graphics,* for help making decisions about your graphics.) Refer to your graphics with an explanatory statement, such as "Refer to Figure 1 to see the location of buttons on the DVD player." Instructions that include these referral statements remind the reader to look at the graphic at the proper time.

Formats can vary. For example, simple instructions may include only a one-sentence introduction and a list of steps. Some may contain pictures only. More complex instructions require several sections and graphics. Figures 7.3 and 7.4 illustrate two simple instruction formats.

Figure 7.3 Instructions Using Pictures Only

ENRICH

Try the "gossip" game by whispering instructions in one student's ear. Ask this student to whisper to the next person, continuing around the room. The students can say the instructions only once. No one can take notes or ask questions. See what happens to the instructions by the time they make their way around the room.

Make up your own instructions or use one of these: "When you leave this classroom, turn left, walk eight steps, wait five seconds, and turn completely around. Take a sheet of notebook paper, fold it in half lengthwise, draw a half moon on it, and pass it to the person behind you." Use this activity to show how easily misunderstandings occur and that having something written helps readers review what they did not understand. Point out that many instructions at work are oral—just like this and can be misunderstood. Ask students what would make the "gossip" game work more accurately. They will probably say writing the instructions, taking notes, asking questions, or repeating the instructions.

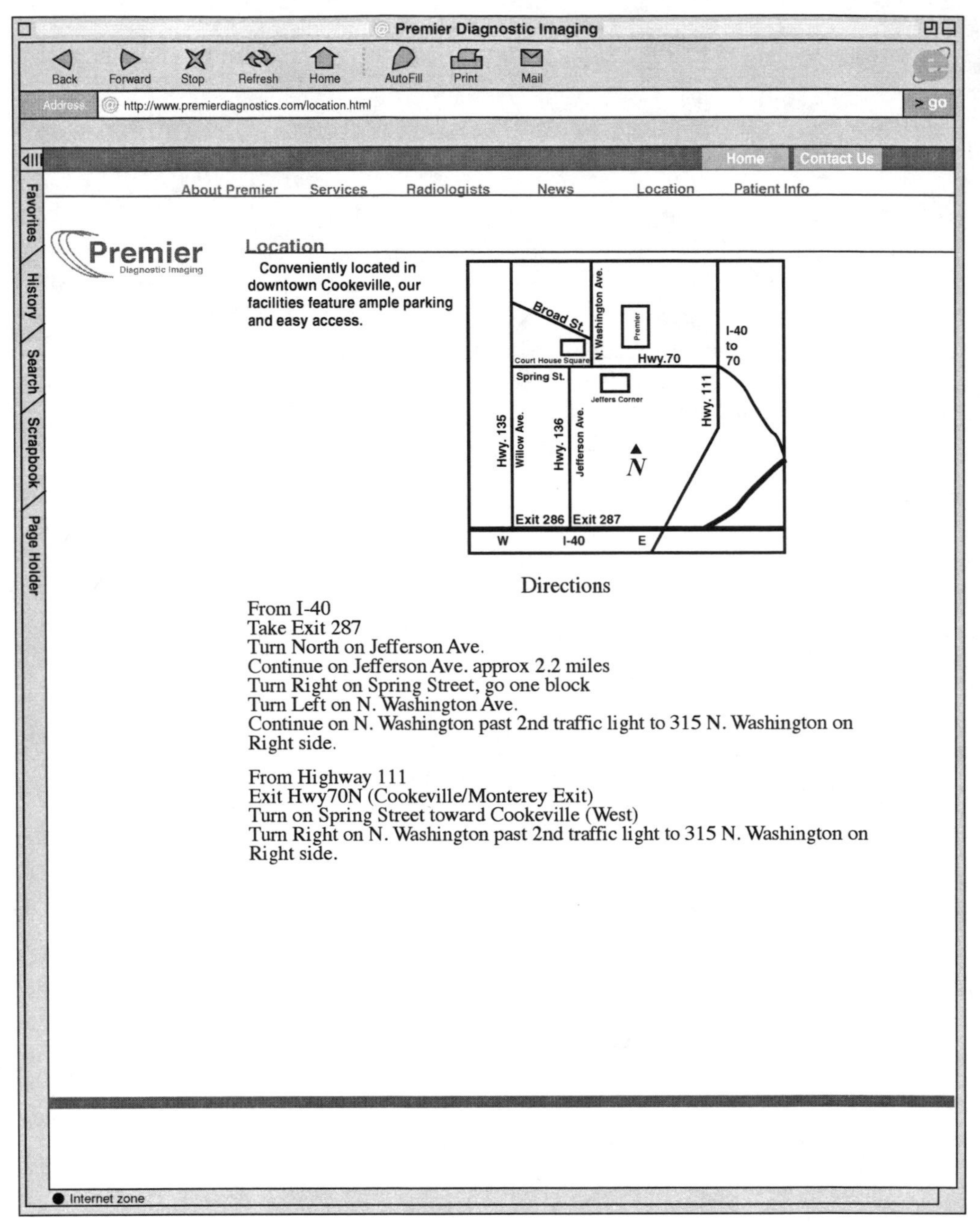

Figure 7.4 Simple Instructions with List of Steps

ONGOING ASSESSMENT

Stop and Think

The organization for instructions varies because the subject and requirements of the instructions change. Some instructions call for a list of materials, some call for cautions, and others call for definitions.

Numbered steps and white space help readers follow the sequence.

Diagrams and flowcharts can help readers see the process.

Why does the organization of a set of instructions change from one set to another? How can page layout help someone read and follow instructions more effectively? Name some graphics that help readers understand instructions.

COMPOSING INSTRUCTIONS

Organization, format, and graphics may vary, but all instructions require chronological steps. Except for instructions written for experienced readers, most instructions require explanations to accompany the steps.

WARM UP

Look at Figure 7.1 at the beginning of this chapter on page 172. Determine the sentences that actually tell the reader to do something. What do you notice about the wording of these sentences? What do the other sentences tell the reader?

FOCUS

Warm Up

Read the model closely, demonstrating that the step-by-step instructions provide two things: steps (action) and explanations of steps. Have students describe what the explanatory sentences actually explain about the steps.

TEACH

Discuss how the examples under "Steps" illustrate the guidelines.

RETEACH

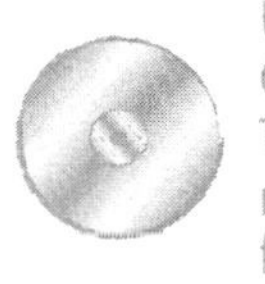

Use the Word Choice: Steps Teaching Master to review guidelines for writing steps.

STEPS

A **step** is the action a reader performs, what he or she actually does. Steps have a consistent and unique structure. Use the following guidelines for writing steps:

1. Make sure steps proceed forward in time, with no backtracking to pick up a step that was forgotten.
   - Incorrect (Backtracking):
     a. Insert the key into the ignition switch.
     b. Turn the key forward until you hear the engine hum.
     c. Buckle your seat belt before you turn the key.
   - Correct (Forward in time):
     a. Buckle your seat belt.
     b. Insert the key.
     c. Turn the key forward.
2. Begin each step with an **active voice** verb in **imperative mood** (a command: verb + what) using **second person.**

- Incorrect (No verb to start): The system needs to be cleaned with a tape cleaner.
- Correct (Action verb to start): Clean the system with a tape cleaner.

NOTE: Sometimes it's necessary to begin with a modifying word or phrase, as in "Thoroughly clean the system . . . ." OR "If the sound is garbled, clean the system . . . ."

3. Use short sentences.
   - Incorrect (Too long): Slide the brake lever(s) as close as possible toward the grip without limiting the operation of the brake levers or causing the end of the brake lever to extend beyond the end of the handlebar.
   - Correct (Shorter sentences): Slide the brake lever(s) as close as possible toward the grip. Do not limit the operation of the brake levers. Do not cause the end of the brake lever to extend beyond the end of the handlebar.
4. Write only one instruction for each step.
   - Incorrect (More than one step): Buckle your seat belt and depress the brake.
   - Correct (One instruction per step):

     a. Buckle your seat belt.
     b. Depress the brake.

EXCEPTION: If two steps are closely tied to each other in time, reading them in the same step might be easier for your reader: Release the clutch. At the same time, press the accelerator.

5. Make sure each step is truly a step, something to do.
   - Incorrect (Not a step): The rope will come back to you.
   - Correct (Step): Grasp the rope when it comes back to you.
6. Keep the natural articles *a, an,* and *the.*
   - Incorrect (Without articles): Send electrician notice to connect power to house.
   - Correct (With articles): Send the electrician a notice to connect power to the house.
7. Place explanations after the step (if you need an explanation).
   - Incorrect (Explanation before the step): Make sure there is an equal distance between each chain stay tube and the wheel. Securely tighten the axle nuts.

NOTE: Even though *Make* is a verb, it is not a step. It explains how to securely tighten the axle nuts.

   - Correct (Step beginning with the action): Securely tighten the axle nuts. Make sure there is an equal distance between each chain stay tube and the wheel.

EXPLANATIONS

An **explanation** is an extension of the step it explains. Explanations use the same number as the step they follow and are written immediately after the step.

1. Write the step. *Then* write the explanation.
2. Write the step. *Then* write the explanation.
3. Write the step. *Then* write the explanation.

The number and type of explanations depend on your reader's previous experience. Typical explanations include:

What not to do and why Do not place stray pencil marks on the answer sheet. The computerized scanner may read the stray mark as an error.

Significant details to help the reader understand why something is important Rinse the boiled egg with cold water as soon as you remove it from boiling water. The cold water will cause the egg to contract from the shell, making it easier to peel the shell off the egg.

How to make a decision Wrap a small section of hair around the curling iron. If you want curls to flip up, wrap the hair backward (away from the shoulders). If you want curls to curve under, wrap the hair down (toward the shoulders).

NOTE: This step and explanation also could be written using the following format:

1. Wrap a small section of hair around the curling iron.
   a. If you want curls to flip up, wrap the hair backward.
   b. If you want curls to curve under, wrap the hair downward.

What will happen when the reader does something 1) Press PROGRAM on the remote control. The MENU will appear on the TV screen. 2) To autoscan for a channel, press CHANNEL SCAN on the remote control once. The tuner scans the channels stored in the tuner's memory, stopping on each channel for about two seconds.

More details on how Tighten the axle nuts. Make sure they are tight. There must not be any space between the inner nut, the wheel slip, and the axle nuts. If there is space, tighten the axle nuts more securely.

Quick definitions Beat the eggs until frothy, or until they look like sea foam. OR The antenna is the "signal receiver" that picks up TV broadcasts.

NOTE: If you have six or more definitions, you need a separate section labeled *Definitions* or *Glossary.* If you have fewer than six, define them as you write or place them in the introduction.

Because some readers need more details than others, you must think carefully about how much explanation to add. Consider the answers to these questions:

- What should readers not do? Why? (What did you do wrong the first time you performed the process?)

Many companies use interactive video to train employees. This choice saves companies money by avoiding costly travel expenses incurred when employees must go somewhere else for specialized training. Interactive video places instructional material on a CD. Employees load the CD, study it at their own pace, and interact by typing answers or comments. Training is available on a host of topics, including sales techniques, museum operations, and information technologies.

COMMUNICATION UPDATE

Interactive video teleconferencing allows companies to set up distance learning environments in multiple sites for training sessions over the Internet on phone lines. The instructor and participants can see each other on big screens or TV monitors and can talk to each other using microphones. Ask students to talk about the pros and cons of video teleconferencing. If you have access to instructional materials on CD in your library, give a demonstration of the materials.

To apply the concepts in this section, complete the Formatting Instructions Activity worksheet on the Data CD.

RETEACH

Review these questions using the How Much Explanation to Include Teaching Master on the IRCD.

You also can use the Word Choice: Explanations Teaching Master to review what to include in explanations.

Have students practice formatting instructions using the Formatting Instructions Activity worksheet on the IRCD.

FOCUS ON ETHICS

Talk about the ethical responsibilities that pharmaceutical companies have to their customers. Bring an insert to show students how this information is presented.

- Would readers be more likely to perform the steps correctly if they knew the significance of the action, the reason for performing the step, or more about the process?
- Would pointing out what should happen when readers execute a step help them? (The first time you performed the process, how did you know you had performed a step correctly?)
- Does the reader need help making a decision? Should some steps be subdivided? Refer to the curling iron example in this chapter:

  1. Wrap a small section of hair around the curling iron.

     a. If you want curls to flip up, wrap the hair backward.

     b. If you want curls to curve under, wrap the hair downward.

- Would the reader benefit from a quick definition?
- What questions will readers have? (What questions did you have the first time you performed the process?)
- What are the most crucial steps, the steps that absolutely must be done correctly?

PRECISE DETAILS

Make sure you have included enough precise, specific details to show your reader what to do. Details might include distances, sizes, places, or time.

Focus on Ethics

When you pick up a prescription from the pharmacy, you receive an insert that gives you information about the drug–instructions for use, proper doses, and risks. By giving patients and doctors more information on which to base judgments about good health, drug companies accept an ethical responsibility to protect their consumers. Warnings appear on the inserts in order of the risk severity:

- Contraindications
- Warnings
- Precautions
- Adverse reactions

In addition to these four risk categories, the Food and Drug Administration (FDA) requires another category for selected drugs to indicate special problems that could lead to serious injury or death. These problems are displayed prominently in a box as a warning to consumers and physicians. Based on clinical data, the black box warning alerts physicians to carefully monitor the health of patients taking these drugs.

- Incorrect (Insufficient): The bike chain should have correct tension. Make sure there is some movement, or "give," in the chain.
- Correct (Sufficient): The bike chain should have correct tension. Make sure there is 3/8″ of movement, or "give," between the front and rear sprockets.
- Incorrect (Insufficient): Connect the short wire from the TV/Game Switch Box to the antenna terminals on your television set.
- Correct (Sufficient): Connect the short twin-lead wire from the TV/Game Switch Box to the VHF terminals on your television set.
- Incorrect (Insufficient): Switch the computer on.
- Correct (Sufficient): Turn on the power switch. The power switch is a ½″ wide black oval button under the CD-ROM drive on the front of the central processing unit.

FIELD TESTS

Always **field test** your instructions by asking several people to try them before you send your final copy. Your field testers can provide you with valuable feedback by noting wording that is not clear, steps that are out of sequence, or steps that have been left out altogether. To administer a field test, also called a usability test, you must select a test method, design the test, select test subjects, and make revisions based on the data.

Concurrent testing and **retrospective testing** are two field tests used to evaluate how well users perform your instructions.

Concurrent testing Concurrent testing evaluates a product or an activity while it is being used or performed. In a concurrent test, you observe your subjects reading and performing your instructions. You measure such things as their accuracy, speed, recall, and attitude.

Rhonda adapted an informal method of concurrent testing to evaluate instructions she wrote. Her instructions told AmeriCorps volunteers how to find the campsite for their training retreat. To make sure that all 50 volunteers would find the site, she asked three of her classmates to follow her directions using a map she had drawn. Two classmates did not arrive at the campsite because they turned onto Riverview Lane instead of Riverview Road. As a result, Rhonda knew she needed to revise her instructions to emphasize the name of the correct road and to caution drivers against making the wrong turn. Because of the information Rhonda learned from the field test, none of the AmeriCorps volunteers got lost.

Concurrent testing for longer instructions involves a more formal procedure. For example, Arturo, service manager for Satellite Dish Subsidiaries, wants to know that his instructions for installing a satellite dish for TV and Internet service are clear. He selects five test subjects in a rural community, ranging in age from 21 to 41, since these are the people who will most likely install the dish themselves. He then watches each one install the dish, taking careful notes on the errors they make, the comments they make, the questions they ask, and frustrations they show. After watching the five subjects perform the satellite dish installation, he knows that two subjects had difficulty mounting the dish in the right

Check out the College of Wooster library web site to find an online field test. The purpose of this field test is for the creators of an online literacy tutorial to learn how to improve the tutorial.

The University of Wisconsin-Eau-Claire has an online help collection that gives tutorials about various computing and technical resources. Browse this site and find examples of effective online instructions on a variety of subjects.

You can find the URL for both sites in the web links on techwriting.swlearning.com. You also will find a worksheet for activities.

SEE THE SITES

Have students complete an online tutorial at the second web site. When students complete a tutorial of their choice, they can critique it: What steps helped them complete the task? What graphics were useful? Were any steps confusing? How would they improve the tutorial? Did the tutorial follow guidelines mentioned in this chapter?

Practice conducting a field test using the Field Test Activity worksheet on the Data CD.

TEACH

Stress to students that concurrent testing observes someone performing the instructions and that retrospective testing asks for feedback after someone has performed the instructions. Questionnaire writers should remain neutral, not leading participants to say or write something they would not think of on their own. Have students refer to Chapter 3, *Technical Research,* for more information on writing neutral quesionnaires and surveys.

Where the field test easily shows a problem with instructions, it does not always reveal an obvious solution. Tell students that they may try many times before they implement a solution that works.

Have students practice conducting a field test using the Field Test Activity worksheet on the IRCD.

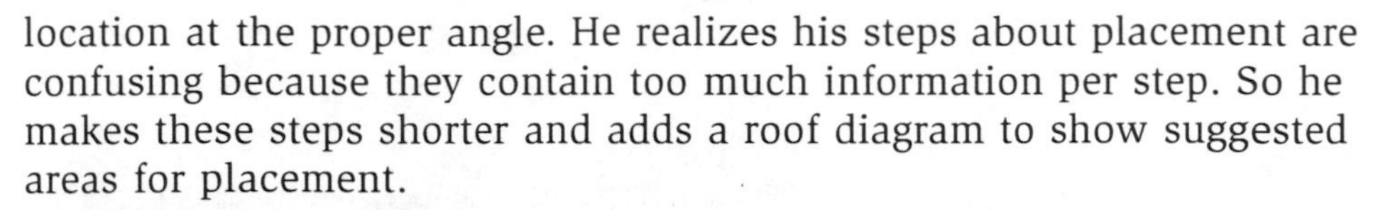

location at the proper angle. He realizes his steps about placement are confusing because they contain too much information per step. So he makes these steps shorter and adds a roof diagram to show suggested areas for placement.

© GETTY IMAGES/PHOTODISC

To design a useful conconcurrent study, decide whether your subjects should complete the whole procedure or selected tasks. Rhonda and Arturo asked their subjects to perform the entire task. On the other hand, one usability study of a web site advertising cars asked users to perform only selected tasks. These tasks included finding the sale of the day, descriptions of used models, and information on warranties.

As you observe your test subjects, ask yourself these questions:

- Were the subjects able to do what the instructions told them to do?
- How long did the subjects take to complete the task?
- How many mistakes did the subjects make?
- What steps were the most difficult? the least difficult?
- Were the subjects frustrated at any time? If so, explain.
- What did the subjects remember about the task 15 minutes after completing it?
- What did the subjects remember about the task 24 hours after completing it?

You also can ask subjects to think aloud, reading the instructions aloud and saying whatever comes to mind. Through this window to subjects' thoughts, you see how they are reacting to every step. If possible, videotape or audiotape their performance to review more closely later.

Retrospective testing A second way to test instructions is by retrospective testing—asking subjects to complete a questionnaire or to answer questions about a task after they perform it. Many field tests use a concurrent test along with a retrospective test. This way testers gain additional insights into test subjects' behavior.

Surveys are often used with retrospective testing. As you learned in Chapter 3, *Technical Research,* a survey can include different types of questions. Figure 7.5 shows questions Kelsey plans to ask his loan officers after they have field-tested his procedure for completing a car loan application.

Question Types	Questions
Multiple Choice	Was the introduction informative? Yes__ No__
	After filling in the applicant's name, address, Social Security number, and telephone number (steps 1-4), the next step was to
	a. enter the amount of money requested.
	b. include the value of the car.
	c. enter the current interest rate.
Likert Scale	Rank on a scale of 1-10 (with 10 being the most satisfied and 1 being the least satisfied) your satisfaction with the completeness** of this document.
	1 2 3 4 5 6 7 8 9 10
Short Answer	Describe the first step you performed.
	After reading step 6 *(maybe a critical step such as entering gross income)*, what did you think you were supposed to do?
Open	What suggestions do you have for improvement?
	What was the most difficult section and why?

** Kelsey could ask about clarity of the wording or usefulness of the graphics.

Figure 7.5 Survey Questions for a Retrospective Field Test

Regardless of the test method you use, select a reasonable sample of subjects. To ask senior accountants to test instructions for using a machine lathe is not practical because they would not use the instructions. You would ask senior accountants to test instructions for new accounting software and machine shop technicians to test instructions for the machine lathe. Some experts say to use at least five testers, but others think five is not enough—especially for a longer document such as a manual or for more interactive media such as a web site. After completing your field test, compile your data, list problems from most frequent to least frequent, and devise solutions.

How are steps written? What kind of information do explanations contain? What kind of information makes instructions precise? Why is field testing important? How can a writer field-test instructions?

ONGOING ASSESSMENT

Stop and Think

Steps proceed forward in time; use active-voice verbs and imperative mood; are written in short sentences; include only one instruction per step; show action; keep the articles *a, an,* and *the;* and have explanations placed after them.

Explanations tell what not to do, help the reader understand why something is important, tell the reader how to make a decision, describe what happens when a step is done, and provide quick definitions.

Specific details make information more precise and easier to follow.

Field testing assures accuracy.

Writers can use concurrent testing (observing what happens while someone actually uses the instructions) or retrospective testing (asking directly or using a questionnaire to learn what the person thinks about the instructions after trying them).

WARM UP

How are computer screens similar to and different from pages in a book?

FOCUS

Warm Up

Discuss how computer media are different from print media and how these differences can affect online instructions. When you talk about the guidelines for online instructions, remind students of these differences: With print media, pages can be flipped through, shuffled, and left in piles on a desk. Portions can be highlighted and underlined for future reference. Computer screens are one-dimensional and cannot be moved. However, the document can be printed.

TEACH

Tell students that specialized software aids the creation of computer-based instructions. The help menus they are familiar with were probably created using RoboHelp® software. This software is specifically used to create help systems for desktop and web-based applications. Toolbook is used to create interactive instructions, for example, taking a patient's blood pressure or injecting radioactive dye.

WRITING ONLINE INSTRUCTIONS

No doubt you have used **online instructions**—perhaps to order concert tickets, track a UPS special delivery, or complete a job application. Online instructions allow users to find out something, get something, or learn something quickly. Online instructions sometimes offer immediate feedback, too. For example, you might learn before you click the Submit button that you forgot to include your Social Security number on a job application.

© GETTY IMAGES/PHOTODISC

TYPES OF ONLINE INSTRUCTIONS

Online instructions, also called computer-based instructions, include help menus, CD-ROMs, and web-based instructions. Help menus are one of the most popular types of online instructions. Most computer programs feature a help menu, typically in the upper right side of your screen. Examples include the Macintosh balloon help (the call out that appears when you point to a menu item) or the animated paper clip in Microsoft® Word (the smiley-faced paper clip that provides a gateway to the help topics). When you use your Hotmail™ or Yahoo® e-mail accounts, or when you log onto AOL® Instant Messenger™, you probably used the help feature to set up addresses, send attachments, or add names to your buddies list.

Think back over your educational career, and you may recall using tutorials (over a network or on CD-ROMs) to teach yourself everything from grammar to math to keyboarding. Your school or community library may have online instructions to the online catalog. Now wireless classrooms at colleges and universities provide students with Internet access to an instructor's syllabus and handouts. As a result, students take laptops instead of books to class. Some classes are taught entirely on the Internet, and students access a teacher's instructions for the class from home through programs such as Blackboard™ or WebCT™.

Communication Dilemma

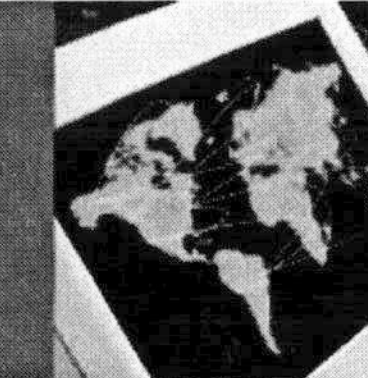

You have just landed a job as a trainer for an international company that makes engines for fighter planes. Your job is to train new engineers, line managers, and other employees to assemble specific engine parts. Your first training session will be carried out online, and your job is to prepare the online training materials for the session.

On Friday afternoon before the training begins the following Monday, your manager tells you that many employees taking the training are not from the United States. Participants live in Russia, Taiwan, Germany, and Japan. In addition, your boss explains that many of the trainees do not speak English.

How do you revise your training materials so international employees can understand them?

COMMUNICATION DILEMMA

Explain to students that many employees all over the world read online instructions, so this dilemma is common in the workplace. For nonnative speakers of English, instructions should be visual. However, students must keep in mind that graphics have different meanings in different cultures. For example, the color red does not mean "stop" in many countries. Likewise, the color green does not always mean "go." Some hand gestures that are not offensive in the United States are very offensive in other parts of the world. In addition, some cultures read from right to left, rather than left to right. Stress that students should find out as much as they can about an international audience and design their instructions accordingly. A good guideline is to conduct a field test with the target audience to make sure instructions are clear.

GUIDELINES FOR WRITING ONLINE INSTRUCTIONS

To write online instructions, keep in mind the strategies presented in this chapter for writing and explaining steps, using white space and graphics, and providing cautions and warnings. In addition to the guidelines for writing paper-based instructions, online instructions should:

- Limit each unit of instruction to one screen size so the user does not need to scroll down the page.
- Use consistent design—font, font sizes, colors, graphics, and headers—so the reader learns to anticipate the organization and feels comfortable nagivating.
- Provide a tree or map of the site and topics so readers can see the site at a glance.
- Insert navigational aids such as a link to the home page and to other important pages.
- Evaluate the usefulness of the instructions with a field test and revise them if necessary.

Also, if you are teaching users to perform tasks on a screen, configure instructions so they do not take up the entire screen. By configuring your instructions this way, you allow users to work on the screen while they read the instructions.

RETEACH

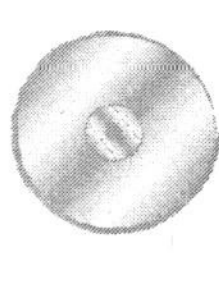

Show the Checklist for Online Instructions Transparency on the IRCD.

Stop and Think

What strategies should you keep in mind when writing online instructions?

ONGOING ASSESSMENT

Stop and Think

Limit each unit of instruction to one screen size, use consistent design, provide a tree or map of the site, and insert navigational aids.

TEACHING RESOURCES
IRCD
Chapter Activities, Ch. 7
Work Is A Zoo!, Ch. 7
PowerPoint® Slides, Ch. 7
Exam*View*® CD, Ch. 7
techwriting.swlearning.com, Ch. 7

CLOSE
Summary
Ask students to evaluate a set of online instructions using the summary points.

Chapter 7 Review

SUMMARY

1. Readers of instructions can be in a hurry, so writers must learn to compensate with carefully planned writing. Readers trust writers to be accurate and safety-conscious and to provide adequate explanation in their instructions.
2. All instructions contain itemized steps. Most instructions contain an introduction and graphics. Whether or not to include a list of materials, warnings, cautions, notes, or definitions will depend on the process and the audience.
3. Instructions are written in short chronological sentences using active voice and imperative mood. Each step must show an action. Explanations follow steps and tell what not to do, why a step is performed, what the results of a step are, and how to complete a step. Explanations should provide enough details to enable the reader to perform the step correctly and safely.
4. When writing online instructions, remember to limit each unit of instruction to one screen, use a consistent design (font, colors, and graphics), provide a tree or map of the site and topics, insert navigational aids in your home page, and configure instructions so users performing tasks on the screen can see them while working.

CLOSE
Checklist
Use the checklist during a peer review session. After students create their own instructions, either online or on paper, have each student exchange his or her instructions with another student and use the checklist for review.

Checklist

- Do I thoroughly understand the procedure I am writing about?
- Did I consider using graphics?
- Did I consider using an introduction, a list of materials, cautions, warnings, and notes?
- Have I written steps that move forward in time? Do my steps begin with a verb that commands? Have I used short sentences that include only one action per step? Are my steps truly steps, things to do? Have I kept the articles *a, an,* and *the*?
- Have I considered including explanations that tell what not to do and why? that include significant details to help the reader understand why a step is important? that tell the reader how to make a decision? that include descriptions of what will happen when the reader does something? that give enough details on how something should be done?
- Have I included enough precise details, such as distances, sizes, places, or time?
- Have I considered whether online instructions would be appropriate for my audience? Have I followed the additional guidelines for online instructions?
- Did I field-test my instructions with my target audience?

Build On What You Know

1. Examine each step below. What kind of information would make each instruction more specific?

   a. Rotate the tool several times around the wire, leaving the spring closed.

   b. Draw part of an oval for the head.

   c. If the fitting has a tub spout, make a hole in the wall.

   d. Clean your room before you leave.

   e. Beat the meringue until stiff peaks form.

   f. Place the selvages of the material together.

2. Break up each sentence below into shorter sentences that reflect one step per sentence.

   a. Remove the cover from the mike; press the transit button on your mike; and by using a small screwdriver with a plastic or wooden handle, adjust the transmitting frequency.

   b. Take the two upper sections of the handle; and using the shortest bolt with the nut provided, fasten together as shown in the illustration in Figure 1.

   c. Read the passage and locate all nouns, underlining them with a single line.

3. Rewrite these steps to begin each with a verb in active voice and imperative mood. The "you" can be understood.

   a. The cook should touch the AUTO DEFROST pad to begin the defrosting process.

   b. When you wish to play, you should press the START button.

   c. The aquarium floor requires a layer of gravel that, sloping from the back to the front, is about 6 to 8 centimeters deep at the front wall.

   d. We want you to come to the front of the room and use the available podium.

4. Label each of the following as steps, explanations, cautions, or warnings.

   a. When paddling, keep the canoe in line with the current.

   b. Make sure that the supply voltage matches the voltage specified on the rating plate.

   c. Separate dark clothes from light clothes to prevent colors from running.

   d. Do not overload your dryer. For efficient drying, clothes need to tumble freely.

   e. Designate a high number of rings (10 or more) for your modem calls.

   f. Install the stem correctly, or an accident can occur.

   g. To determine how tight the fasteners need to be, see the Torque Range chart in the back of this book.

ASSESS

Build On What You Know

1. **a.** Which tool? Where is the wire? Where is the spring? **b.** Where should I draw the oval? How big of a part should I draw? **c.** What is a tub spout? Where and how big should I make the hole? **d.** What is meant by cleaning (putting things away or vacuuming, washing walls, etc)? **e.** What do stiff peaks look like? **f.** What are selvages?
2. **a.** Remove the cover from the mike. Press the transit button on your mike. Using a small screwdriver with a plastic or wooden handle, adjust the transmitting frequency. **b.** Fasten together the two upper sections of the handle as shown in Figure 1. Use the shortest bolt and the nut provided. **c.** Read the passage. Underline all nouns once.
3. **a.** Touch the AUTO DEFROST pad to begin the defrosting process. **b.** Press the START button when you wish to play. **c.** Slope the layer of gravel from the back to the front. **d.** Use the podium at the front of the room.
4. **a.** step **b.** explanation **c.** step with explanation **d.** caution **e.** step **f.** warning **g.** step

ASSESS

Apply What You Learned

5. All—a, c, f, i, j; Online—b, d, e, g, h
6. Answers will vary, but possible help topics include how to save, how to change fonts, how to insert a graphic, how to use a table, how to insert clip art, and how to make a bulleted or numbered list.
7. Make sure students have completed the prewriting by writing the steps beforehand, analyzing their audience, and using the checklist.
8. Ask students to go through the procedure several times and take notes. Then tell them to write the instructions, following the guidelines in the chapter. Ask them to format the instructions for a help menu. More ambitious students also might provide screen shots of the instructions.

Apply What You Learned

5. Which of these guidelines for writing instructions apply to all instructions (print and online), and which apply only to online instructions?

   a. Make sure each step represents only one action, unless the actions are so closely related that they need to be expressed in the same step.

   b. Limit each unit of instruction to one screen size.

   c. Evaluate the usefulness of your instructions with a field test.

   d. Use a consistent design for each screen.

   e. Provide a tree or map of your site and topics.

   f. Do not omit *a, an,* and *the.*

   g. Eliminate your reader's need to scroll down the page.

   h. Insert navigational aids such as links to important pages.

   i. Include appropriate cautions, warnings, and notes.

   j. Use active-voice verbs in imperative mood for steps.

6. For a beginner using a word processing program such as WordPerfect® or Microsoft® Word, list help topics this person would most likely use.

7. In small groups, write instructions on any of the following processes (or other process you are familiar with). Be sure to analyze your audience, follow the guidelines for composing instructions, and provide ample explanations.

making a bed	using a calculator	changing oil/tires
setting up a tent	lifting weights	playing a video game (or any other game)
setting up an aquarium	building a model	playing a sport
brushing/flossing teeth	mowing the lawn	constructing a craft
administering first aid	taking pictures	changing a diaper
cleaning a room	creating artwork	

8. Suppose you are writing a help menu program for a word processing program that you know well. Write a list of step-by-step instructions for one of these:

   - Changing the font type for an entire document
   - Underlining a word
   - Changing the margins
   - Copying and pasting a paragraph
   - Cutting and pasting a paragraph

Work Is A Zoo!

This morning during a breakfast meeting, Anya told you that the zoo is about to hire extra help before the start of the school year. She explained that when instructors bring their students to the zoo, more employees are needed to accommodate them.

Anya asked you to write instructions for using the zoo time clock. The instructions will be used to train new employees to record the time they work on a daily basis. She explained that some of these employees do not speak English as their first language, so you must accommodate these nonnative speakers of English in your instructions.

Write the instructions for a time clock you are familiar with. (If you have not used a time clock, write the instructions for completing a weekly time sheet.)

First, decide whether your instructions should be paper-based or online.

Include the appropriate sections in your instructions:

- Introduction
- Definitions
- Preparations
- Warnings and cautions (if necessary)
- Steps and explanations
- Closing

If appropriate, include any graphics that will help the audience.

The Work Is A Zoo! worksheet for this activity is on the Data CD.

WORK IS A ZOO!

Tell students to start by mapping the steps. When they are finished, they can go back and determine any necessary definitions, preparations, and warnings/cautions.

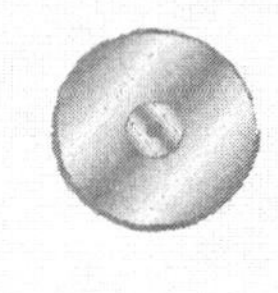

The Work Is A Zoo! worksheet for this activity is on the IRCD.

ORAL PRESENTATIONS

GOALS

LEARN to plan for your audience, your topic, and stage fright

DETERMINE how to organize and compose presentations

PREPARE note cards and graphic aids

REHEARSE for a presentation and **PRESENT** with confidence

ORGANIZE a group presentation

See the Data CD for Write-to-Learn and In The Know activity worksheets.

TEACHING RESOURCES

IRCD
- Lesson Plans, Ch. 11
- Chapter Activities, Ch. 11
- PowerPoint® Slides, Ch. 11
- Sample Documents, Ch. 11

techwriting.swlearning.com, Ch. 11

Exam*View*® CD, Ch. 11

CHAPTER OVERVIEW

Prepares students to make effective oral presentations. Explains the importance of presentation skills and provides the steps in developing and delivering effective oral reports.

WRITE-TO-LEARN

Recall speakers whose performance you have enjoyed. For instance, you may have an instructor who holds your attention from the moment you sit down until the end of class. Perhaps you appreciated a speaker you heard at a club meeting or special event. Consider what makes these speakers effective communicators. List the qualities and actions you think help these speakers effectively reach their audiences. Your list might include:

- Opening with a good joke.
- Using language you can understand.
- Walking through the audience.

In The Know

adrenaline a stimulant, something that excites and creates extra energy

anecdote a short narrative

auditory relating to the sense of hearing or perceived through the sense of hearing

direct approach a presentation strategy in which you state the main idea first and then explain and support that idea with details

external audience listeners outside an organization

feedback the verbal and nonverbal response to a communication process or product

indirect approach a presentation strategy in which the main idea is not presented up front; you build evidence to convince the audience of your point

internal audience listeners within an organization

preview statements an overview of the order of ideas in a presentation

rhetorical question a question designed to provoke thought; a question for which the speaker expects no answer

sans serif type faces without cross strokes on the tops and bottoms of letters, such as Arial

serif type faces with cross strokes on the tops and bottoms of letters, such as Times New Roman

stage fright anxiety or fear experienced when a person speaks to or performs for an audience

Writing@Work

Denny Kramer is a relationship manager at a large financial services company in Covington, Kentucky. In his position, he helps companies set up and administer retirement plans. He also maintains and upgrades these plans.

Denny often meets with current and prospective clients and those who may take their business elsewhere. He presents information about the products and services his company offers and the fees for these services. He answers questions about setting up, maintaining, and upgrading retirement plans.

Denny says: "Winging a presentation does not work. Inevitably you are asked a question that you should have been ready for, but were not." Preparation is the key to a productive, informative presentation. An important part of preparation is learning about your audience. In Denny's case, the president of the company may have different concerns from other members of the audience. Knowing all these concerns is helpful. Denny offers these tips: Do not go in blind; do research ahead of time; and consider any possible issues your audience might have and how they might react.

Many people find that using notes refreshes their memory when making presentations. Denny suggests including only key words or phrases so you are not tempted to read. Another suggestion that Denny offers is to videotape your presentation before you give it. "It helps," he says, "to then watch the presentation with the sound off, listen to the presentation with the video turned off, and then watch and listen to the video. This technique will help you evaluate your body language and hear any unnecessary pauses or extra words."

When you present to an audience, keep in mind several key factors. A good start is to summarize your agenda. Making eye contact with members of your audience is important. Paraphrasing questions from the audience to make sure you have understood them correctly is also a good idea. If appropriate, put humor in your presentation–the more conversational your presentation, the more likely you are to hold the audience's attention. Denny suggests checking periodically to make sure no one has any questions. "I always try to resolve issues that I am aware of up front. That way, I feel more confident that the audience will be paying attention to the rest of the presentation."

Denny has a bachelor's degree in management from Xavier University. He has been in his current position for six years. Prior to this job, Denny worked in several positions at two different banking institutions.

APPLY

Writing@Work

This profile offers suggestions for preparing and making presentations. Have students discuss other workplace examples where presentations may be given.

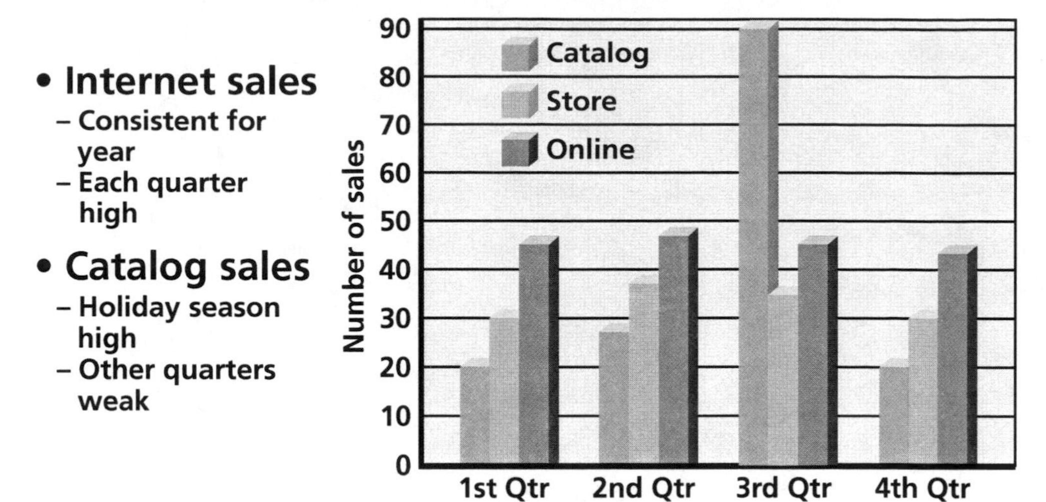

Figure 11.1 Sample Graphic Aid for Oral Presentations

PLANNING

You have many opportunities to speak before groups in business, industry, and school. The success with which you handle oral reporting may determine your success in your profession. You might have the best new product idea your company will ever see. For your idea to become a reality, however, you must effectively communicate it to the management team and convince them to try the product. This chapter tells you how to effectively plan, organize, compose, prepare, rehearse, and present oral reports.

The higher up the corporate ladder you move, the more you will give oral presentations. The audience, formality, and purpose may vary. For instance, you will give some presentations to **internal audiences,** perhaps above or below you in the organizational hierarchy—or both. You will give some presentations to **external audiences,** such as suppliers, vendors, or customers. Some oral presentations will be as informal as an impromptu gathering where you answer questions. Others will be elaborate, carefully prepared sessions.

The purpose of some oral reports will be to inform; others will be designed to persuade, such as a sales presentation; others will be designed to inform *and* persuade. During the course of your career, you may be asked to propose solutions to problems; outline the results of investigations; announce new policies or procedures; report on the progress of a project; sell an idea, a product, or a service; represent your organization at a conference or community group; or train personnel.

The planning stage is an important part of creating presentations. This is the stage in which you begin to work on audience analysis, a topic, and **stage fright.**

WARM UP

Think about your public speaking experiences. Perhaps you have given a report in class or led a club meeting. If you have not had many speaking opportunities, imagine what the experience would be like. List things you like and dislike about public speaking and share your list with the class.

FOCUS

Warm Up

Use the Warm Up to encourage students to discuss their likes and dislikes about public speaking. Most of them will have experience delivering book reviews or history reports. Point out the benefits of public presentations from their lists of "likes." Then show how they can overcome each dislike. Some concerns, such as a surge of nervous energy, can be an advantage to giving an effective presentation. Use students' concerns to demonstrate how they can become successful public speakers.

FIGURE 11.1

The notes point out information found in the slide that the speaker would like to emphasize. While a great deal of data is shown in the graphic, the text shown on the slide highlights the catalog and online sales.

The Internet offers many sites related to effective oral presentations. To start your search, check out the Powerful Presentations web site, which includes tips from dressing for a presentation to making impromptu speeches.

The Executive Speaker web site contains 117 tips for better presentations. These tips include how to control nervousness and advice from professional speakers.

You can find the URL for both sites in the web links at techwriting.swlearning.com.

SEE THE SITES
Remind students that they can find links to other similar sites on the web site.

TEACH
Tell students that one way to plan an oral presentation is to list everything they want to say to the audience.

AUDIENCE

Analyzing your audience is as important in an oral report as it is in a written report. You need to know how your audience feels about your topic. Start by referring to the audience analysis questions in Chapter 2, *Plan for Your Audience and Purpose.* For most presentations, you will probably use the direct approach. With the **direct approach,** you state the main idea first and then explain and support that idea with details. Stating the main idea first lets your listeners know what subject you will address, what points you will make, and how you will proceed.

If, on the other hand, you realize that your audience opposes the point you support or you want to be especially persuasive, you should consider an indirect presentation. With an **indirect approach,** you can build your evidence, convincing the audience of your point.

TOPIC AND MESSAGE

Sometimes speakers are able to choose their own topics. However, when asked to speak at work (and in school), you often will be assigned a topic. Frequently in business, managers ask employees to prepare a written document, such as a report on progress, a solution to a problem, or a report on an incident. After submitting the written report, the employee may be asked to make an oral presentation of the same information. For instance, Edith Frost, a machinist at Tarboro Machine Corporation, wrote a report that suggested three new safety measures for all machine operators. The report was submitted to the plant safety officer, the president and vice president, and all division heads. Frost's supervisor then asked her to present her plan orally at the next managers' meeting.

STAGE FRIGHT

You may think it odd that a textbook tells you to plan for stage fright when most people want to avoid it. Yet stage fright is not something to eliminate; it is energy you should use. Many professional speakers will tell you that you cannot eliminate nervous reactions when speaking, even if you want to. Those reactions, they say, are natural responses to stress. So instead of trying to suppress stage fright, let it work for you. To harness this energy, you should:

- Note how your body responds to anxiety.
- Expect and plan for these reactions.
- Use excess **adrenaline** and energy to give your introduction and important points extra emphasis.

ONGOING ASSESSMENT
Stop and Think
The audience would be more interested in how school policy affects students. Listeners are usually more interested in topics that affect them.

Would an audience of your classmates be more interested in how school policy affects taxpayers or how school policy affects students?

ORGANIZING AND COMPOSING

When you are presenting, listeners cannot refer to a previous page when ideas are unclear or confusing. So you should organize and compose your oral presentations for the listeners' situation and needs.

PREVIEWING ORGANIZATION

Regardless of the organizational strategy you use, give the audience a preview so they know what plan you are following. The preview is like a map that shows a driver where to turn and how far to go. Your preview explains the order of your ideas. Here are two examples of typical **preview statements:** "This recommendation contains four major parts: review, staffing, operational policy, and production." or "The standard operating procedure for student interns involves completing treatment plans, writing instruction memos, and recording patient progress."

COMPOSING THE INTRODUCTION

Listeners recall the first and last points they hear. Therefore, plan for a strong introduction and conclusion. If you are uncertain how to introduce your presentation, think as your audience might. What would get your attention? You would want to know the topic; the points the speaker will support; and how this issue affects you, the listener. Your introduction should announce your topic and the points you will make. In addition, you should give the listeners something to which they can relate, some connection. For example, an address by a young woman to her small town's board of commissioners began this way: "My friend Miguel died last month. He should not have been in the path of a car going 45 miles per

WARM UP

Think of messages you have prepared for oral delivery, such as planning to ask someone for a date or a favor. Compare oral composing with written composing. Note differences and similarities in a brief journal entry.

FOCUS

Warm Up

Ask students to complete the Warm Up to discover what they already know about oral composing techniques and how that compares with their written composing experiences.

ENRICH

As you discuss composing introductions, give students an opportunity to practice formulating introductions. Give them a presentation topic and ask them to write only an introduction.

To test the statement that listeners remember the first and last things they hear, call out 10 to 15 random words. Then ask students to write the words they remember. Results will probably prove that listeners do remember the first and last items more easily.

TEACH
Remind students to be careful with humor. A joke or humorous story can create rapport between the speaker and the audience. When exaggerated, though, listeners may perceive the topic as insignificant.

In an introduction, speakers may explain the situation that caused the need for the report or name the person who requested the information.

Tell students if they have conclusions or recommendations, they should present them in the introduction so listeners can understand data in the report body.

RETEACH
Remind students that choosing an effective organizational plan for the body is especially important since listeners depend on it and the preview to help them follow the message of the report.

TEACH
Speakers might consider these organizational strategies: spatial order, such as top to bottom or east to west or left to right; chronological order, such as 1950 to the present or the beginning of a work shift to the end of the shift; most-important-to-least-important order; least-important-to-most-important order; and problem-solution order.

Show the Tips for Composing the Body Teaching Master on the IRCD.

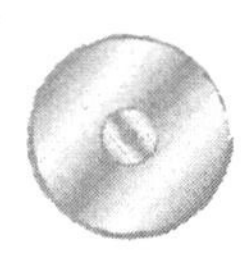

hour, nor should any of your children, grandchildren, or neighbors. Our town must protect its citizens by providing bicycle paths and enforcing the helmet laws."

Depending on your audience and purpose, try one of several introductions. Some openings include using:

- A direct quotation (usually from a well-known source).
- A **rhetorical question.**
- A startling fact or statistic (that would grab a listener's attention).
- A statement you then disprove.
- An **anecdote** or a humorous story.

For example, if you were making a class presentation on the advantages of modern medicine, you might begin this way:

> If you were born in the United States in 1990, at the time of your birth you had a life expectancy of 75.4 years. On the other hand, people born in 1970 were expected to live only 70.8 years. According to these statistics, you will outlive your mother and father by 4.6 years. (United States: National Center for Health Statistics)

The startling fact that the audience's generation is expected to live 4.6 years longer than their parents' should grab the listeners' attention, especially since these statistics relate to the audience's own mortality.

COMPOSING THE BODY

These guidelines will help you compose the body of an oral presentation:

- Address people. Remember that your audience is made up of people much like yourself. Include the words *you* and *your* early and often.
- Use words your audience will know. Define unfamiliar terms.
- Use simpler sentences than when writing. You should not have to say so many words that you cannot catch your breath.
- Give your audience the information they want or need. Explain to listeners how your information impacts them; make it relevant. Remember, it is as easy to ramble in speaking as it is in freewriting, so avoid that pitfall.
- Emphasize main points and make transitions from one point to the next. Since listeners take in only a small percent of what they hear, emphasize the essential ideas. Repeat or restate main points. Announce transitions so the audience will not miss the connection, as if you are saying to the listener, "Now we are leaving the discussion of Point A to move on to Point B. Follow me."
- Consider questions your audience is likely to ask and include those answers in your presentation.
- Plan for a time limit. Determine what your audience expects and frame your report for that time—or less.

Focus on Ethics

You live in an age when a lot of business is conducted globally. That means at some point in your career, you may have an opportunity to attend a meeting in Japan, give a presentation in Australia, or create and present a training course via videoconferencing in Brazil.

Because business is increasingly being conducted globally, knowing the proper method for presentations across cultures is extremely important. Beginning with the presentation planning stage, you must be aware of how cultural practices and expectations of your audience are different from your own. You must research the audience's culture and plan for differences to ensure a well-received presentation.

For example, while presenting to an international audience, you should be aware of gestures that are not universal. In Greece, nodding your head means "no," not "yes." In Australia, a "thumbs up" gesture is considered inappropriate.

You also should research the formality of the culture. Jokes are not appropriate for some audiences. Dressing too formally makes other audiences uncomfortable.

No matter what cultural differences you face, the most effective rule to remember is to respect those differences.

FOCUS ON ETHICS

If possible, have students interview an international businessperson who works in the United States. Students will be interested to hear what kinds of cultural differences that person had to prepare for before coming to the United States. Students should know that international business people must learn the cultural differences in the United States, just as Americans must learn cultural differences when they go to other countries.

TEACH

Speakers can appropriately say, "In conclusion ..." as they begin the conclusion. This statement is a signal for listeners to pay attention. Audiences expect key information at this point.

COMPOSING THE CONCLUSION

Conclusions are important because they are the last point or topic the audience will hear; therefore, they require as much planning as introductions. An effective conclusion should hold the audience's attention, summarize the key points, and call for action if requested.

Stop and Think

John wants to persuade his parents, who do not let him drive long distances alone, to let him drive 55 miles to the basketball tournament. Ideas he plans to share with his parents are (a) driving is the least expensive and safest way to get to the tournament, (b) John has behaved responsibly when given other opportunities, and (c) the bus does not go to this location and cab fare would be three times more than the cost of driving. Place these ideas in the most effective order for John to present to his parents.

ONGOING ASSESSMENT

Stop and Think

Assign the Stop and Think as a critical-thinking exercise. This activity also gives students an opportunity to practice organization. Solutions: The audience is opposed to the main idea, so the indirect approach should be used. Possible answer: c, b, a

WARM UP

Think about your experiences speaking with and without notes. If possible, discuss these experiences in small groups. Review the benefits of using notes and problems you have had with them.

FOCUS

Warm Up

Use the Warm Up to stress the importance of using notes or outlines for polished presentations. While answers will vary, someone will probably talk about a speech given without adequate preparation and the ensuing embarrassment or frustration. The problems might include talking too long, rambling off the topic, forgetting important points, or giving inaccurate information.

TEACH

Remind students that many of the steps in preparing for an oral presentation are familiar because they are the same steps students use to write compositions.

PREPARING

After you complete the planning process, you need to prepare notes, graphic aids, and your own image. These preparations will help you effectively deliver your presentation. Your risks are huge if you neglect preparation. Without notes, you are left with your memory, which sometimes fails, especially in stressful situations. Without graphic aids to clarify and enhance your words, listeners may wear puzzled frowns, adding to your stress level. And without personal preparation, you may become preoccupied with your clothing or hair, feeling greater frustration and losing even more ground with the audience.

OUTLINES AND NOTES

A practiced performance using an outline or notes yields an informal, conversational style. Speakers may either generate an outline using presentation graphics software, such as Microsoft® PowerPoint®, or develop an outline independently. By using an outline or notes written on index cards or sheets of paper, you will be able to talk to your audience rather than read to them.

Before you reach this point in the process, you must organize your ideas in the most effective manner. If you were writing a report, your next step would be to compose sentences, build paragraphs, and create a document. For an oral presentation, however, you should avoid extended writing. A complete paper with long sentences and dense paragraphs might encourage you to read the text, rather than interact with your audience, when you are under pressure. On the other hand, fearing you might lose your place in all of that text, you might avoid the text entirely and try to speak without any assistance.

An outline or notes should show each main point in your presentation. Under each main point, list any facts, figures, or quotations that support that point. For example, the outline below shows one section of an oral report on progress toward upgrading computers in a warehouse:

III. Shipping and Receiving

Area 1

4 installations

Problems with location of wiring, Module MJD364

Area 2

Work completed; 3 installations

Approval of supervisor

Level 3

Work incomplete; 1 installation

Relocation of shelving unit, Module SDP21

Network concern

Scheduled 9 December 20–

For precision and accuracy, do not trust your memory for such specific information, especially when your adrenaline surges in front of an audience.

For the first point of an outline or note card, write a word or a phrase that will trigger your memory for this opening point. Then go on to each idea, example, and illustration in your speech.

For each idea, prepare a point in an outline or on a note card similar to the one in Figure 11.2. This sample card reminds the speaker that this section of the talk is about tsunamis, the giant, destructive waves that sometimes strike Hawaii and Japan.

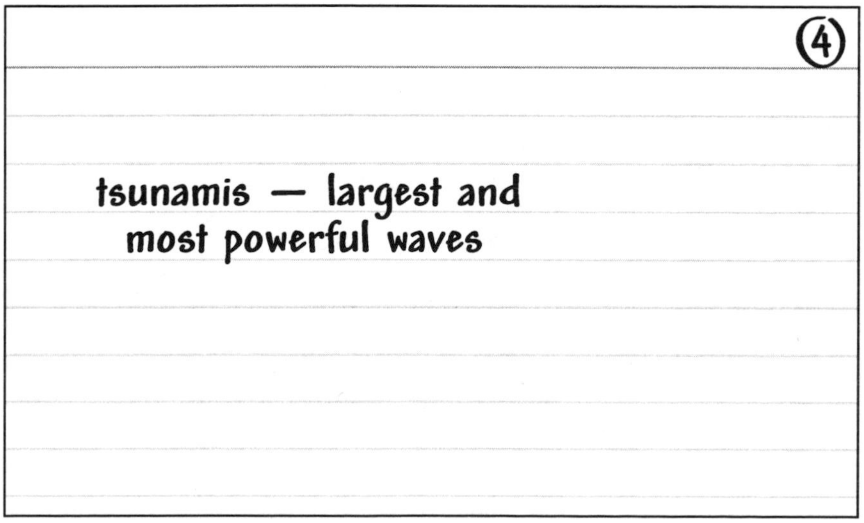

(4)

tsunamis — largest and
most powerful waves

Figure 11.2 Note Card for Oral Presentation

TEACH

Explain that notes may include pronunciation guides. For instance, if speakers were to have difficulty pronouncing *tsunamis,* they could write the word phonetically on the card.

TEACH
In addition to handouts, PowerPoint® also has a notes page layout and an outline layout. All of these features may be helpful to presenters.

If you are developing computer slides for your presentation, most software packages will allow you to add notes that reinforce the logical flow of the discussion and highlight content details, such as statistics, quotations, and important facts. For instance, PowerPoint® allows you to print handouts with two, three, four, six, or nine slides per page, most of which have space for notes.

Figure 11.3 shows such a PowerPoint® handout you can use to either write notes for yourself or pass out to the audience so they can write notes as you talk.

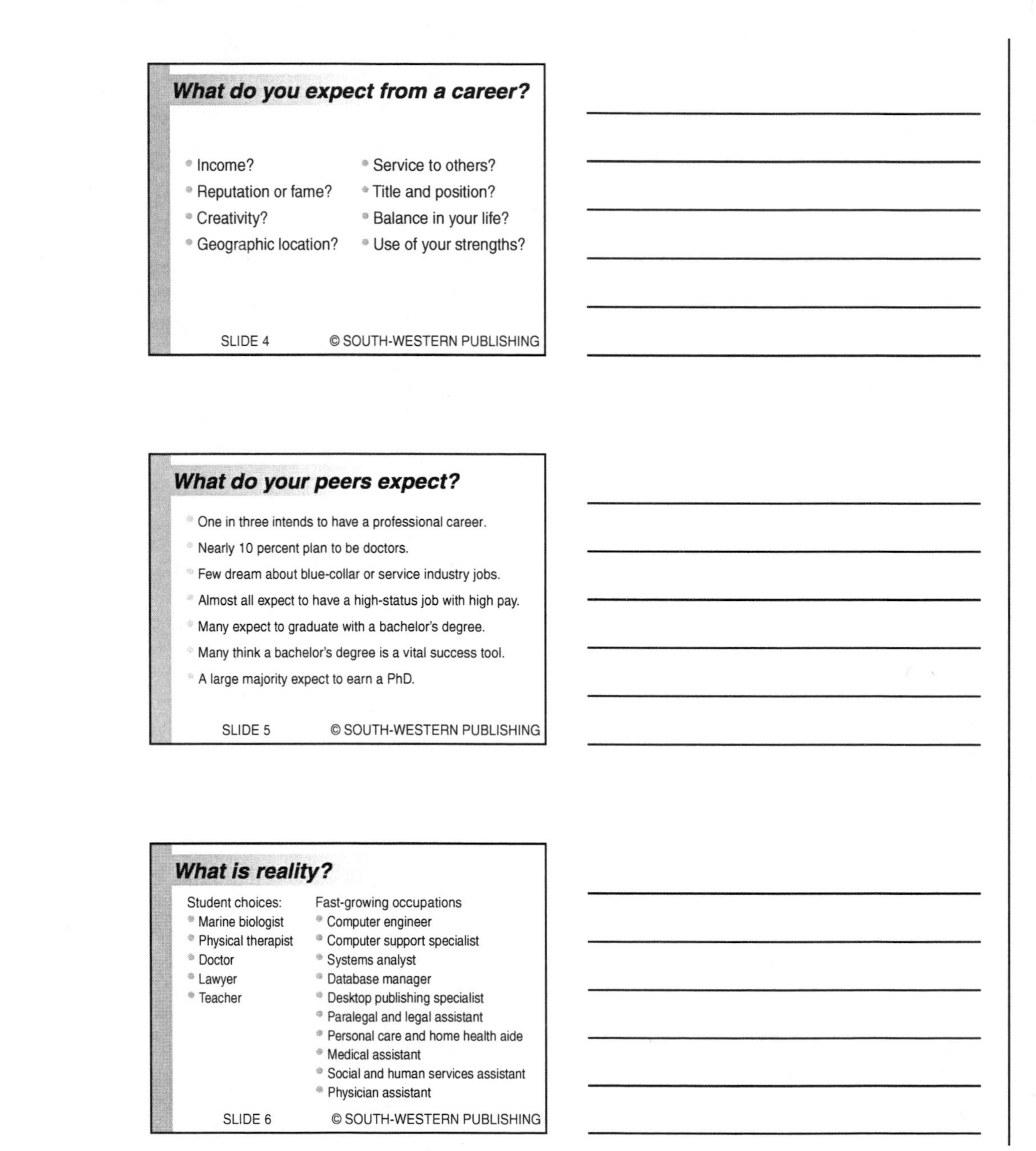

Figure 11.3 PowerPoint® Handout with Space for Notes

When preparing outlines or notes, remember these important points:

- Do not write notes as complete sentences, long phrases, or clauses. Even experienced speakers would be tempted to read if the card contained long clauses or sentences.
- Prepare neat notes that are surrounded by adequate white space so you can read them easily.
- Structure notes uniformly: numbered lists, bulleted lists, outline form.
- If you are using cards, write only one idea on each note card; if you are using printed notes or outlines, use a large, easy-to-read **serif** font. Also, print on paper that will allow you to turn pages smoothly without distracting the audience.
- Number notes or cards from beginning to end. On note cards, place the card number in the upper right corner and circle the number, as in Figure 11.2. Should your cards become disorganized, the numbers will help you sort them quickly.
- Use outlines and notes to spark your memory. Glancing at the words, you should be able to look at your audience and deliver a portion of your speech. In this way, you can truly converse (in a polished way) with your audience.

ENRICH

Invite speakers from your school's Speakers' Bureau; from business and industry; or from Toastmasters, a group that fosters the development of personal and professional speaking skills, to visit and share experiences and advice.

View films of well-known or admired speakers throughout history. Compare their styles and effectiveness. Consider John Kennedy, Martin Luther King, and Bill Cosby.

GRAPHIC AIDS

Research suggests that an audience takes in less than 25 percent of what a speaker says. So a speaker should try to increase an audience's comprehension. One way to help your audience is by using graphic aids. Graphic aids clarify ideas and highlight important information, allowing audiences to see and hear the message. The audience has two ways to comprehend your ideas.

Guidelines for choosing what to illustrate When you think of adding graphic aids, how do you know where they would be the most effective for your audience? You can ask these questions:

- What information is most important?
- What data is the most complex or difficult to understand?
- What statistics or figures are particularly important for my audience to comprehend?

Once you answer these questions, you will have selected ideas your audience needs to understand and, as a result, ideas to be illustrated. The next question is how to best illustrate a particular idea to enhance the audience's understanding.

Types of graphic aids Graphic aids can include photographs, line drawings, charts, tables, objects, multimedia, or even people. For instance, a presenter discussing environmental hazards might use a flip chart to diagram the amounts of certain chemicals found in groundwater. A student speaking

TEACH

A general guide for preparing graphic aids is to create letters 1 inch high for each 10 feet of distance between the viewers and the graphic. So if the audience member at the back of the room is 20 feet from the marker board, letters should be 2 inches or taller for easy viewing.

When preparing slides or transparencies, use 24-point or larger type.

Because about one out of every ten people cannot distinguish red and green, these colors should not be used together in graphs or charts.

Items in a bulleted list should use parallel structure.

to her class about erroneous ideas associated with cerebral palsy brought in her brother, a police detective with cerebral palsy, as a graphic aid.

The various types of graphic aids—flip charts, transparencies, slides, multimedia, dry-erase boards, handouts, physical objects, and more—range from simple and inexpensive to complex and costly. The development time and cost must be considered along with effectiveness when choosing graphic aids for your presentations. You would not want to spend a great deal of time or money to create a working prototype of a new product for an internal presentation in which no action or decision was expected. The time and expense could not be justified for a simple informational presentation. However, the investment might be reasonable if production decisions were to be made.

In addition to time and cost, the location (room or space) and audience size are factors in determining the types of graphics to use. Flip charts and posters, for instance, are appropriate for small audiences in close spaces. Objects, demonstrations, marker boards, and transparencies may work well with a medium-sized group, as long as everyone can easily see the graphic. For audiences in a large auditorium, hall, or meeting facility, multimedia presentations and films provide images that are large enough for many people to see at once.

Other factors to consider are artistic talent (your own or your company's) and equipment. If your organization has a graphic arts department that can produce quality graphs, charts, photographs, films, or electronic aids, your only challenges may be selecting the ideas you want to have illustrated and choosing from the image options the artists suggest. On the other hand, you may be required to rely on your own skills and talent. When professional graphic designers are not available, you may need to choose a simpler graphic aid because you can prepare it more effectively than a complex graphic. That is, you might create a simple slide presentation rather than planning, developing, adding sound and captions to, and editing a film.

Guidelines for creating graphic aids When you develop graphics, keep your audience's needs in mind. These guidelines will help you:

- Make the graphic large enough for everyone to see easily—even people sitting in the back of the room.
- Do not crowd numbers or images on a graphic aid.
- Remember that although attractive design counts, the message is more important. Bright colors cannot replace solid ideas. For more information on effective design principles, see Chapter 6, *Document Design and Graphics.*
- Consider handouts your audience can keep if you want listeners to think about your ideas later.

The following tips are for use specifically in presentation graphics software:

- Select landscape layout for your slides (it gives longer lines for your text, particularly if you are using columns).

- Select a font that can be read easily from a distance, such as **Times New Roman Bold** or **Arial Black.** Do not use *italic,* decorative, or **condensed** fonts.
- Because serif fonts, the fonts with feet or cross strokes on the top and bottom of each letter, improve readability, use a serif font for the text. Likewise, since **sans serif** fonts, those without the cross strokes, present a cleaner, crisper image, use a sans serif font for slide titles.
- Choose a font size that is readable and that suggests the hierarchy of elements within the slide. Use a bolder font for the slide title than for the text. Generally, these sizes are appropriate:
  a. Titles: 24–36 points
  b. Other text: 18–24 points
  c. Source notes: 14–16 points
- Use initial caps, rather than all uppercase, in slide titles. Words in uppercase are difficult to read.
- In bulleted lists, capitalize only the first word (and, of course, proper nouns and proper adjectives). Beginning each word in a list with a capital letter requires your readers to move their eyes up and down through each line, decreasing readability. Capitalizing only the beginning words helps readers scan the list and improves readability.
- Use the Notes section for inserting notes to remind you of your next point; specific facts, figures, or quotations to ensure accuracy; cues when someone else will be advancing the slide; or reminders, such as "Smile," "Make eye contact," or "Hold up the trophy for everyone to see."
- Select colors or templates with the audience in mind. Avoid colors or designs that will distract or offend.
- If you have clip art or an image that supports the text on a slide, place it in the lower right corner. The viewer's eye will be drawn from the title or heading at the top left down through the text to the image. Remember, however, to add graphics only when they enhance and support the text, not simply to brighten a slide.
- Keep slides simple and uncluttered.
- If you use transition effects between slides, make the effect meaningful. For example, choose one effect for each major section of your presentation. Or select one effect for slides that mark the beginning of a new section and another effect for all slides within sections. Since transitions may include sound, be careful not to get carried away with the bells and whistles. A presentation that boxes in one slide, fades out another, checkerboards across a third, and wipes out a fourth, complete with four different sounds, will distract viewers from the topic.
- On your speaker's notes pages, number the slides so you can easily move to a particular slide when someone asks a question.
- If available, use the spelling and style check.

TEACH

Sans means "without" in French.

Letters that are 72-point font are 1 inch tall.

Tell students to consider the effect of colors in designing graphic aids. For example, blue is a conservative color and adds formality, while yellow is brighter and less formal. Red, orange, and yellow encourage movement and anxiety, while blue and green are calming.

Tell students to think of associations their audience may have with certain colors. Since red calls to mind stop, danger, blood, or financial loss, it is not a good color choice for a pie chart showing budget projections.

Advise students that if they plan to prepare an audience handout, they should add a header or footer with the presentation title, date, speaker's name, and organization. Some speakers include telephone number, e-mail address, or postal address.

COMMUNICATION DILEMMA

This ethical dilemma is similar to the situations employees might experience. Students may use these questions: What are the organization's obligations to disclose information regarding employment? Are an employee's obligations to the company, to employees, or to both? In this case, Rouse should keep in mind that the presentation has not been delivered yet and is still being developed. The presentation may be changed drastically before delivery, if it is presented at all. Therefore, Rouse should proceed with extreme caution. Her action could cause unnecessary harm. For instance, she might give a tip to the news media, which damages the company's image and value when the story is aired. Then she learns that the company was able to reorganize so that no employees would be terminated. Yet the harm is done, perhaps so much harm that the company is forced to reduce its workforce.

ONGOING ASSESSMENT

Stop and Think

Yes, a machine part could be a graphic aid. If the audience is not familiar with the part, they would benefit from seeing it.

In certain situations, running shorts could be appropriate dress for a presentation. For a presentation about running, the presenter might wear running shorts as a graphic aid.

PERSONAL APPEARANCE

In addition to note cards and graphic aids, image has a big impact on the way listeners receive a speaker's message. You probably know how appearance can affect communication in everyday situations, such as the way some salespeople treat you when you are in your worn jeans and an old T-shirt. If you have not experienced this treatment yourself, you likely have seen others treated differently because of their clothing or grooming.

When you select clothing for a presentation, consider the audience's expectations and the situation in which you will be speaking. For instance, someone addressing your city council would probably dress as formally (business suit) as its members typically do. On the other hand, a speaker addressing children at a youth center would dress more casually. Whatever you wear, make sure the outfit feels comfortable. If you feel good about the way you look, you will speak with confidence.

If you have done everything you can to prepare for success, you are ready to move to the rehearsal phase.

Ariane Rouse, a participant in her company's executive training program, learns that 15 percent of the employees will be laid off within the next four months as part of a corporate downsizing plan when she mistakenly receives a confidential memo meant for her supervisor. However, she sees the director of informational services and public relations rehearsing a presentation for an annual company meeting in which he assures employees that all is well with the organization, that a bright future awaits. He does not mention the impending layoffs.

Rouse is disturbed by the deception she believes the director intends. She has choices to make. Should she go to upper management and protest? Should she tell her closest associates and ask their advice? Should she provide an anonymous tip to the news media?

Could a machine part be a graphic aid? Explain. Would running shorts ever be appropriate dress for a presentation? Explain.

REHEARSING

Expert presenters will tell you that you must practice in order to give a successful presentation. Practicing helps you develop a conversational style. In fact, good speeches are a conversation between speaker and audience, only slightly more polished than the conversations you have with friends. Practice provides experience, experience that soothes nerves and builds confidence, too. After several rehearsals, with adjustments each time, you will have a presentation you are pleased with. Then you believe the presentation will go well.

Using your note cards and graphic aids, practice your speech. When you first deliver the talk, you will see parts you like and dislike. Delivering the speech a second time, you may change what you do not like. When you are comfortable with your delivery, you have rehearsed enough. You have reached a conversational style.

Speakers practice speeches in different ways, including using a tape recorder, mirror, video camera, or live audience. With experience, you will decide which methods work for you.

USING A TAPE RECORDER

After recording your presentation, take a break. After you have gained some distance and perspective on the speech, listen to the tape for the following:

- Rate (how fast you talked)
- Volume (how loudly or how softly you talked)
- Pronunciation (the distinctness of your words)

WARM UP

In other skills you have developed–sports, music, art–how much practice is enough? What does this tell you about oral presentations? Respond to these questions in a brief journal entry.

FOCUS

Warm Up

Use the Warm Up to help students understand the importance of rehearsing for effective presentations. Remind students that even professional speakers who present several times every week still rehearse.

TEACH

Tell students that they do not need to own tape recorders or video cameras to use these practice techniques. Most public libraries have this type of equipment, which can be borrowed for use inside the library and, in some cases, for use in one's home. In addition, the school may allow students access to the equipment.

TEACH
Show the Oral Presentation Checklist Teaching Master on the IRCD. Students can use the teaching master for evaluating their presentation progress and success.

RETEACH
In discussing delivery, remind students of the importance of eye contact.

- Inflections (the changes in pitch or tone)
- Time (the amount of time you took to present your ideas)

USING A MIRROR

Watch yourself in a mirror as you practice your presentation. Put yourself in the role of the audience. What do you see that will enhance or detract from the message? Check for:

- Appropriate facial expressions
- Effective use of your body and hands. (Do your hand movements emphasize major points, or do they distract your listener from the topic?)

USING A VIDEO CAMERA

Do not review the tape immediately. Wait until you have greater perspective, perhaps in an hour or in the next day or two. When you do view the tape, pretend to be your audience. Look for strengths as well as weaknesses. With this **auditory** and visual **feedback,** check for the following:

1. How you sound
2. How you look
3. What message you deliver

USING A LIVE AUDIENCE

Ask a friend or family member to listen to you practice your presentation. After delivering the speech, invite comments and suggestions. Try some of these questions:

- What was my speech topic?
- What point did I try to prove?
- Did I make eye contact?
- Did I speak loudly enough?
- Did I tend to use *and uh, um,* or *like?*
- Was my conclusion effective?
- Did I correctly pronounce words?

ONGOING ASSESSMENT
Stop and Think

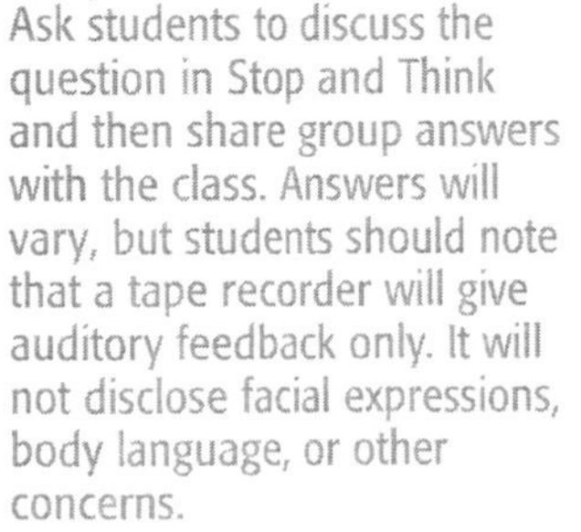

Ask students to discuss the question in Stop and Think and then share group answers with the class. Answers will vary, but students should note that a tape recorder will give auditory feedback only. It will not disclose facial expressions, body language, or other concerns.

Stop and Think

While a tape recorder gives useful feedback during rehearsal, what will it not tell you? In small groups, discuss your answers.

PRESENTING

Once you have thoroughly prepared for your presentation, you can present with confidence. Before you are ready, however, you must prepare the environment in which you will make your presentation.

© GETTY IMAGES/PHOTODISC

CHECKING THE ROOM

Arrive early for your presentation if possible. During that time, make sure listeners will be comfortable and can see and hear well. Consider seating, lighting, temperature, equipment, and graphic aids.

Seating Check how chairs are placed. Are they arranged to let you communicate effectively? For instance, if you want group discussion, the chairs should be placed so that people can see each other. Also, make sure everyone in the room will be able to see you easily.

Lighting Make certain your audience will have enough light to see. In addition, correct any glaring and overly bright spots. With an appropriately lighted room, your audience can comfortably see and concentrate on your message.

Temperature Check the temperature controls. People who are shivering from cold or sweltering from heat will not be good listeners.

Equipment and Graphic Aids Make sure all equipment is working and prepare for possible problems. Remember Murphy's Law: If something can go wrong, it will! Make sure you have an extra bulb for the projector, markers, computer disks, and anything else you might need.

WARM UP

Discuss these questions with your classmates: Can oral presenting be fun? How can you make presenting fun?

FOCUS

Warm Up

Use the Warm Up to generate discussion about the positive possibilities of public speaking.

TEACH

Explain that speakers may prepare the room 30 minutes or several days before a presentation. If it is the latter, the speaker should check the room immediately before the presentation to make sure items have not been disturbed.

Ask students to think of situations that could go wrong and how to handle those situations.

Tell students that speakers who complete their presentation despite problems (such as equipment malfunctions or dropped notes) usually earn the respect and admiration of the audience.

When using electronic slides, use the feature for blacking out or whiting out the screen when answering a question that does not relate to the current slide. Then your audience can focus on the discussion instead of reading the slide.

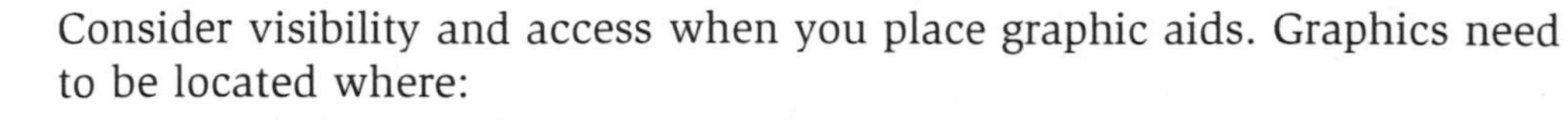

TEACH
Show the Guidelines for Delivering Oral Presentations Teaching Master on the IRCD.

Consider visibility and access when you place graphic aids. Graphics need to be located where:

- Everyone in the room can easily see them.
- You can point to the graphic as you talk.
- You can reach equipment, such as overhead projectors, to make adjustments.
- The equipment will have a power supply.

Determine before the event how you will post or display your materials.

DELIVERING THE MESSAGE

Having prepared for the presentation, you are ready to enjoy talking with your audience. Use the pointers below to help you be as effective as possible.

- Use appropriate facial expressions. For example, if you are talking about the positive outlook for jobs, an occasional smile is suitable.
- Maintain eye contact. By acknowledging your listener with eye contact, you show interest and concern for that person.
- Explain every graphic. Since each person may see or understand something differently, tell people exactly what you want them to learn from the graphic aid.
- Post or distribute handouts only when you want the audience to use or read them. Otherwise, your listeners may be flipping noisily through pages and reading what captures their attention rather than listening to you. If you do not want to disrupt your presentation but want to distribute your handouts at the appropriate time, ask someone to distribute them for you.
- Consult your notes, but do not read from them. Consult your notes only enough to follow your outline and to cue yourself to key details for your presentation. When you read directly from your note cards, you break eye contact with your audience and lose their interest and attention.
- Continue to talk even when something goes wrong. Recover the best you can, but go on with the show. Do not call attention to a mistake.
- Remember that your audience wants you to succeed. Your audience's desire for an effective presentation, along with the self-confidence you gained from being fully prepared, will ensure a positive experience.
- Give your audience an opportunity to ask questions unless the program does not allow time for questions. If you cannot answer a question, respond in a positive way: "I'm sorry that I don't have the answer to your question, but I will be happy to check my sources and get back to you later this week."

ONGOING ASSESSMENT

Stop and Think
You should display your poster before you speak only when you want the audience to refer to that graphic aid at the beginning of the presentation.

Yes, eye contact is essential.

Stop and Think

Should you display your poster before you begin to speak? Is eye contact with your audience desirable?

ORGANIZING A GROUP PRESENTATION

Presenting with others requires special consideration. Collaboration provides many opportunities to share diverse perspectives and expertise. However, group presentations require careful planning if they are to be effective. Collaborators must act as a team and plan for dividing a topic, setting time limits, moving between speakers, providing graphic aids and handouts, answering questions, and managing the presentation.

WARM UP

Imagine that three employees walk into a meeting expecting to make a sales presentation. They all expect to make the presentation alone, but when they arrive at the meeting, all three are asked to speak. How do you think the presentation will go?

FOCUS

Warm Up

Use the Warm Up to discuss the benefits and challenges of group presentations. Students may realize that the speakers, without planning or preparation, are likely to be uncertain of who will speak when, about what aspect of the topic to present, and about how long to speak. The presentation probably would not be well organized or smooth.

DIVIDING THE TOPIC

When collaborating on a presentation, speakers must plan roles and responsibilities. One important issue to discuss is who will be responsible for presenting what information. For example, three employees making a planning proposal might divide the discussion in this way: Speaker 1—introduction of speakers, their qualifications, and the problem prompting the proposal; Speaker 2—the proposed solution and the budget; and Speaker 3—the conclusion and the requested action. Topic division, therefore, may dictate the order of presenters.

In addition, sometimes a particular speaker's expertise will require that he or she deal with one aspect, such as an accountant explaining the budget. If speakers are equally qualified to present the material, the group will need to define other reasons for assigning roles.

SETTING TIME LIMITS

Just as individual speakers must plan for their presentations to fit within a time limit, group presenters have an obligation to stay within a time frame as well. After the group determines the length of the entire presentation,

Communication Update

In today's age of global communications, many presentation teams are made up of members across the globe. Therefore, presenters must have a way to keep track of presentation documents and ideas. They also must have a quick way to distribute the most current documents and keep team members up to date. That is where virtual office space comes in. This space can be over the Web or on the company's intranet. It allows the storage of shared files as well as space for discussion groups. Members also can use virtual bulletin boards to post the latest updates.

COMMUNICATION UPDATE

If you have access to computers in the classroom, create "shared folders" for students to use, much like a virtual office space. Have students form groups of two or three and use this shared folder to develop a presentation as a team. After the experience, have students write a paper about what they liked and disliked about using the shared folder.

the members should decide the total time to allot each member, keeping in mind the material each member will cover and its relative significance. The team members presenting the planning proposal, given a 30-minute slot in the day's agenda, might divide their time this way:

Speaker 1	introduction of speakers and their qualifications; problem prompting the proposal	10 minutes
Speaker 2	proposed solution and budget	15 minutes
Speaker 3	conclusion and requested action	5 minutes

Speaker 2 is allotted the most time because explaining the plan that the group is proposing and justifying its budget are critical. If the audience does not understand this information, the proposal will not be approved. Speaker 2 also receives the greatest portion of time because of the importance of proving that a significant problem exists. Speaker 3 needs less time, not because concluding is unimportant, but because conclusions should be direct and brief, giving the audience time to ask questions.

Members of groups should be even more watchful than individual speakers in preparing to stay within their time limits. If one speaker goes over his or her time limit, the time must be taken from another presenter.

TRANSITIONING BETWEEN SPEAKERS

If you have ever been in an audience when an unidentified person begins to speak, you probably remember how uncomfortable you were. People expect to be introduced to speakers. In a collaborative presentation, members may choose to be introduced or introduce themselves at the beginning of the session. Or each speaker may be introduced as he or she begins to speak.

When various speakers will be answering questions, listeners prefer to be reminded of the respondent's name. Often a moderator will name the presenter as he or she asks that a particular speaker address the question, such as "Dr. Quan, would you like to answer the question of profiling?"

PROVIDING GRAPHIC AIDS AND HANDOUTS

Group presenters should discuss the use of graphic aids and handouts when planning the presentation. Coordinating the appearance of slides, transparencies, and handouts adds to the professionalism and positive impressions of a group presentation. For example, members could agree to use one slide template; a certain color, scheme, or typeface; or the same headers and footers. Members should plan when to distribute handouts. Will all handouts be provided to listeners at one time, or will each presenter be responsible for distributing his or her own? Since some speakers do not want the audience reading handouts while they speak, those speakers may prefer to distribute all handouts at the end of the presentation. Other speakers may want listeners to have copies of their materials for taking notes during the discussion. So speakers should discuss and agree on a plan before the presentation.

Speakers also need to decide which equipment they will require. For instance, when two speakers plan to use overhead transparencies and the third wants to use an LCD projector, they should agree on where to place both pieces of equipment and know whether any equipment must be moved between presenters. Presenters using the same machine for multimedia should know their software needs and make certain the equipment is compatible with the presentation they developed.

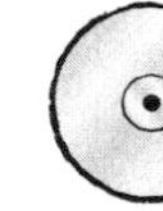

Use the Oral Report Evaluation Form worksheet on the Data CD when you practice oral presentations. This worksheet will give you the opportunity to learn from the evaluation and the advice from listeners.

TEACH

Have students use the Oral Report Evaluation Form worksheet on the IRCD when they practice oral presentations. This worksheet will give them the opportunity to learn from the evaluation and the advice from listeners.

ANSWERING QUESTIONS

Participants of group presentations should anticipate questions and plan how to answer them. In some presentations, the group may decide to allow each speaker to take questions when the speaker ends his or her portion. Other groups will answer questions only after all presenters have completed their speeches. Presenters also should know whether a moderator will assign each question to a particular presenter or whether the presenters will be responsible for assigning the questions. Speakers are smart to plan answers for questions they expect to be asked; therefore, collaborators might divide the topic areas so that each presenter could prepare for questions in a certain area.

MANAGING THE PRESENTATION

Groups may perform more effectively with leadership. For that reason, many groups have a lead presenter, a chairperson, or someone who manages the process. The lead presenter often represents the group in discussions with meeting planners and acts as liaison, then corresponds with group members to keep them informed. The lead presenter sometimes speaks first, previewing the presentation or stating objectives, or last, summarizing key points and moderating the questions. The group may choose to give the lead presenter other responsibilities as well, such as:

- Keeping speakers on schedule, calling time for those who talk too long.
- Keeping questions moving, preventing arguments and monopolization.
- Responding to requests for more information, mailing additional materials.

An effective leader will assure that all group members' talents are used and that all opinions are heard.

In a collaborative presentation, how do speakers determine who will speak when? Do groups need a lead presenter or chairperson?

ONGOING ASSESSMENT

Stop and Think

The order of speakers may be decided by the portion of the topic each speaker presents. For example, the speaker whose expertise is in the area that logically should be discussed first will be the opening presenter. If the topic does not dictate the order, the group may decide order based on how speakers feel about presenting first or last or in the middle.

While a chairperson is not necessary, groups are likely to function more effectively when someone manages the process.

Chapter 11 Review

TEACHING RESOURCES
IRCD
Chapter Activities, Ch. 11
Work Is A Zoo!, Ch. 11
PowerPoint™ Slides, Ch. 11
Exam*View*® CD, Ch. 11
techwriting.swlearning.com, Ch. 11

CLOSE
Summary
1. To present effectively, students must reduce anxiety and improve self-confidence.
2. Compose a strong introduction and conclusion and create a body that is relevant and meets the audience's needs and expectations.
3. Methods of rehearsing include using a tape recorder, a mirror, a video camera, and a stand-in audience to obtain different feedback.

Guidelines students should keep in mind as they speak are 1) use appropriate facial expressions, 2) maintain eye contact, 3) use graphics effectively, 4) consult notes but do not read from them, 5) continue with the speech if something goes wrong, 6) remember that listeners want the speaker to succeed, and 7) ask for questions. Finally, enjoy presenting after planning, preparing, and rehearsing.

CLOSE
Checklist
Have students use the checklist when planning their own presentations.

SUMMARY

1. Your ability to effectively present your ideas orally to others will affect your success in the workplace.
2. Plan for your audience, the topic and content of your presentation, and stage fright.
3. Use audience analysis to decide how to organize and preview the organizational plan to help listeners follow you.
4. Preparing involves creating an outline or notes and graphic aids and making adjustments in your image.
5. After planning and preparing, rehearse to polish your presentation using a variety of methods.
6. Check the seating, lighting, temperature, equipment, and graphics to create the best possible listening environment.
7. When presenting as part of a team, think about how the team will divide the topic among presenters; what amount of time to allot each speaker; how to move between speakers; how to handle graphics, handouts, and questions; and who will manage the presentation process.

Checklist

- Have I carefully analyzed my audience?
- Do I have a clearly defined and focused topic?
- Have I planned how I can use my response to stage fright?
- Does the beginning of my report preview the report's organization?
- Have I composed a strong and effective introduction? body? conclusion?
- Will my outline or notes allow me to deliver a conversational performance, rather than reading a speech or speaking without aid?
- What ideas will I present that need clarification or emphasis?
- What type of graphic will be most effective for enhancing the idea and for the speaking situation? Have I prepared for an appropriate and professional appearance?
- Have I rehearsed and gathered feedback for improvement?
- When presenting, have I checked the room for seating, lighting, temperature, equipment, and graphics?
- Have I effectively delivered the message using facial expressions, eye contact, graphics and handouts, notes, confidence, and questions?
- If participating in a collaborative presentation, have my team and I divided the topic among speakers, established time limits, planned transitions, coordinated graphics and handouts, planned for questions, and considered the selection of a team leader or chairperson?

Build On What You Know

1. You have been asked to speak to your nephew's fifth-grade social studies class about Mexico and your work as a volunteer for Habitat for Humanity. The social studies class lasts 50 minutes. If the teacher does not give you a time limit but tells you to talk as long as you like, what factors might you consider?
2. Mrs. Nicci, a counselor, has asked you to explain to a group of 35 first-year students how to complete their registration cards. The entire process involves using decisions the students have made previously and entering data on a preprinted form. Choose a room in your school with which you are familiar and imagine this as the location. What would be the most effective way to arrange chairs for this presentation? Consider the graphics you might use. Consider how much, if at all, you want the students consulting with each other. Another factor could be the size of the room and location of permanent features, such as built-in cabinets.
3. Using one of the topics listed below or a topic your instructor supplies, develop an idea for an effective attention-getting introduction for your peers, other students in your school. Remember to state your topic and to preview the points you will make as well as to connect with your audience.

cost of prescription drugs	teen employment	mass transit in rural or urban United States
globalization	Internet and entertainment	local pollution concerns

4. Fast-forward your life several years and imagine the time when your supervisor first says to you, "Great job on this report! Now you can present the report at the _______ (fill in the blank with managers', stockholders', team, committee, or other appropriate term) meeting." Suppose you have six weeks before the date of the presentation. Develop a timeline with the tasks you will undertake to prepare for an effective oral presentation. The plan should identify what you will do and when you will do it during the six weeks. Remember that you already have a written report, but you need to develop an oral presentation appropriate for a different audience. Also, remember that this is your first on-the-job presentation, so you will want adequate rehearsal time and constructive feedback to build your confidence level.
5. Select or create a graphic aid that you can use in a two-minute presentation to clarify or emphasize an idea. For example, you might bring a tool and demonstrate how to use it. Or you could draw a graph or chart and explain the process or statistics it illustrates. You also could show a photograph, poster, or painting and explain the idea or concept it supports.

ASSESS

Build On What You Know

1. A technical writer should consider audience first. Ask students to think of what will grab the fifth graders' attention. They may not be accustomed to 50 minutes of lecture, but they might respond enthusiastically to 15 minutes of lecture containing a five- to ten-minute slide presentation and a tortilla-making demonstration. This question should generate good critical thinking and audience consideration.
2. Since giving instructions on how to complete a form is a lecture process, the arrangement of desks in rows facing the front of the room would work well. Students also may discuss the types of graphics they could use, such as an overhead projector or a computer with an LCD projection panel.
3. The introduction to an oral report should grab the listener's attention, establish a connection, announce the topic, and preview the main points of the discussion to come.
4. Students will need to review each step in the process presented in this chapter to develop a plan for preparing for the presentation. You also can refer students to the checklist at the end of this chapter.
5. In the Preparing section, students should review the guidelines for choosing what information to illustrate; in the Presenting section, they should review the information on equipment and graphic aids.

ASSESS

Apply What You Learned

6. Encourage students to be honest about their strengths and weaknesses. They can build on their strengths while improving weak elements.
7. By recognizing factors that make other speakers effective or ineffective, students can choose those characteristics they wish to adopt for themselves.
8. Use this activity to emphasize the differences in written and oral reporting. The written report should not be read to the audience. The speaker would need to develop an outline or notes and adapt appropriate graphic aids.
9. With guidance, students will prepare for an oral presentation in small steps. The activity provides experience and builds confidence for an independent effort.
10. Use this activity to give students experience in front of an audience responding to questions and developing confidence.
11. Analyzing the audience for this activity should be easy for students; however, selecting a topic and organizing might be more challenging. Discuss graphic aids. Do speakers usually include graphics in graduation addresses? Why or why not? How does this type of presentation differ from most workplace presentations? Does the difference in purpose account for any difference in use of graphics?

Apply What You Learned

6. Review an oral report you presented recently—in school or elsewhere, formal or informal. List some changes you would make to improve your effectiveness if you were able to present again.
7. Attend the presentation of a speaker at school, in the community, or at work. If a live presentation is not possible, watch a video of a speaker, perhaps a politician, an editorial commentator, or a promoter from an infomercial. As you watch and listen to the speaker, make two lists: one for positive elements, things that make the speech work, and a second for negative elements, or things that detract from the presentation's effectiveness.
8. Choose any written report you have previously completed or find a model in a textbook. Write an essay about decisions and changes you would need to make to present the written information in an oral report.
9. Research the career you are currently considering. Look for information on employers, salaries, working conditions, educational requirements, and hiring rates. You could go to the library, talk with a counselor, visit someone working in the field, or talk with an instructor in that curriculum area. When you have as much data as you need, think of making an oral presentation to classmates who might be interested in the same career.
   a. Write a brief analysis of your audience. Refer to Chapter 2, *Plan for Your Audience and Purpose.*
   b. Decide on the focus or main idea for your presentation. Write this focus in one complete sentence.
   c. List at least two ideas for information that could be enhanced with a graphic aid.
   d. Create at least one of the graphic aids listed in item c.
   e. Prepare the outline or notes you would use for this presentation.
10. After reading an article or a speech supplied by your instructor, on a folded sheet of paper, prepare a question relating to the reading. Your instructor will collect the questions in a bag or basket. One by one you and each of your classmates then comes to the front of the room, draws a question, and answers that question. Use this activity to practice question-and-answer sessions.
11. Plan a speech that you could deliver to your own graduating class. Consider audience and purpose when planning. Will you need graphic aids for your speech? If so, what kind of graphic aids would be appropriate? Share your topic and notes with other students to gain feedback. Finally, deliver the speech to your peers and ask for additional feedback.

Work Is A Zoo!

The presentation is going to be a first for you. And since you also are hoping for the associate position, you want to do a great job.

You have completed some research, and you have prepared the agenda. Without knowing it, you have already done a lot of work.

Now is the time to think about what you are going to present and how you are going to present it. Think about why you are speaking and whom you are speaking to.

Are you and Tyrone the only speakers? Are you going to have a question-and-answer period? Will there be a relaxed feel to the meeting with opportunities for comments along the way?

Given the information you have found, write an outline for your presentation.

Include Tyrone's ideas for how the new logo can be used for promotional purposes.

Here are a few tips to help you plan:

- Start by grabbing your listeners' attention. Is there an interesting statistic you could use? or a crazy animal fact?
- Guide your listeners as you go. Do not get sidetracked.
- Give supporting evidence. Cite other zoos as backup.
- Develop a strong conclusion. Where do you intend to go? What do you want other staff members to do? How can they be involved?

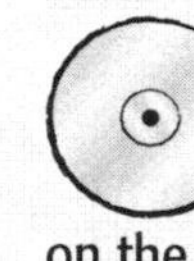

Use the Work Is A Zoo! worksheet for this chapter on the Data CD to guide you in your planning.

WORK IS A ZOO

Be sure students use the Work Is A Zoo! worksheet for

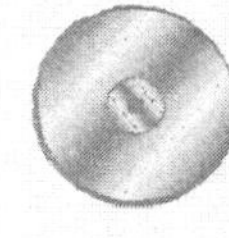

this chapter on the IRCD to guide them in their planning.

PROPOSALS

GOALS

DEFINE proposals and determine their purpose

PLAN to write proposals

COMPOSE informal proposals

COMPOSE formal proposals

See the Data CD for Write-To-Learn and In The Know activity worksheets.

TEACHING RESOURCES

IRCD
- Lesson Plans, Ch. 13
- Chapter Activities, Ch. 13
- PowerPoint® Slides, Ch. 13
- Sample Documents, Ch. 13

techwriting.swlearning.com, Ch. 13

ExamView®, Ch. 13

CHAPTER OVERVIEW

Defines formal and informal proposals and teaches students how to prepare them.

See the IRCD for Write-To-Learn and In The Know activity worksheets.

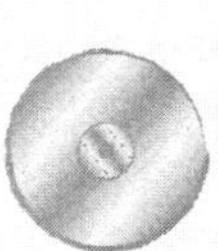

WRITE-TO-LEARN

Think of a time when you have had a successful sales experience. This experience may have been a situation in which you persuaded a person or a group of people to purchase a product or service or to agree to an idea. In a brief journal entry, write a narrative of that experience. Include ways in which you prepared to make the sale as well as a description of your audience.

In The Know

appendix usually the last element or special part of a formal report; a place to include documents, data, or graphics not necessary to the discussion in the report but perhaps helpful or interesting to the audience

executive summary a short synopsis of what a proposal is about; written to meet the needs of a busy decision maker; located at the beginning of a formal proposal

glossary an alphabetical listing of terms accompanied by their definitions, located at the end of a proposal

letter of transmittal a letter formally or officially conveying a formal report from the writers to the external audience

limitations factors or situations that prevent problem solving

memo of transmittal a memorandum formally or officially conveying a formal report from the writers to the internal audience

scope what you examine in your efforts to solve a particular problem

pagination the assignment of sequential page numbers within a document

prefatory material parts or elements of a report that come before the main text (introduction, body, and conclusion)

proposals persuasive documents that offer a solution to an identified problem or need

RFP request for proposal, an advertisement seeking proposals to solve a problem or fill a need and often listing criteria for the solution

solicited proposal a proposal that is written in response to an RFP or upon the request of a supervisor or manager

unsolicited proposal a discovery proposal, one that is written because the writer discovered a problem or need and has a solution to offer

Writing@Work

Marcia Spaeth is the CEO of a nonprofit organization called Tender Mercies, Inc. Tender Mercies owns and manages six buildings that have 150 residents who have been homeless and have a chronic mental illness. Marcia is responsible for the day-to-day operations of the organization and for budget and residential needs. Her job is to ensure that these 150 residents have permanent homes.

As a nonprofit organization, Tender Mercies depends on receiving grants from outsiders. Requesting this money is something else that Marcia is responsible for. Her philosophy in asking for donations is to be direct. "Fund-raisers cannot be afraid to ask—anybody and everybody. If you believe in what you are doing, the 'ask' should be easy." In general, Tender Mercies must raise over $500,000 each year to keep their doors open—and this is just to meet their operating budget. So obviously, Marcia has a big job to do.

When writing grant requests, Marcia says that grant guidelines must be followed to a tee. "In writing government grants, every single *i* must be dotted or you will not get funded, or you may get de-funded." Because of the strict guidelines that must be followed, clear, concise writing is essential. Marcia believes that for an organization's credibility, one proves worthy by following directions. Clear, accurate communication reflects on an organization. "Explain your program/project clearly and simply, or you risk not being funded."

Marcia stresses the importance of using money received as specified in a proposal. This is another reason why clear communication is imperative. "To prove to your donor that you are fiscally responsible, using monies received as stated is extremely important. Otherwise, you risk losing funding in the future." Tender Mercies, specifically, has each year an independent audit performed that holds them accountable for doing exactly as they say.

Marcia majored in education at Edgecliff College, and she has an honorary Doctor of Humane Letters degree from the College of Mount Saint Joseph. She initially became involved at Tender Mercies as a board member and a volunteer. As a result of her passion for the organization and her ability to talk to people about its mission, she became the CEO in 2000.

APPLY

Writing@Work
This writing assignment can be a fun one for your students. Ask them to write a few paragraphs to their parents, asking for money for something they really want. Reiterate what Marcia says: "If you believe in what you are doing, the 'ask' should be easy." If students really believe that what they are asking for is appropriate, they should have no problem with this assignment. Stress the importance of clear, persuasive writing.

PHILLIPS'
CONVENIENT MART STORES

Donovan Phillips, President
3301 Heritage Plaza/ Columbus, Ohio 43209/ 614•555•9854

MEMO TO: Donovan Phillips, Owner
FROM: Carl S. Cordova, Management Intern CSC
Convenient Mart #27, Newsome, Ohio
DATE: 10 March 20—
SUBJECT: Proposal for Improving Traffic Flow

SUMMARY

Customer complaints, accidents, congestion, and delays in service point out the need for improvements in traffic patterns through our parking and gas service areas. The addition of guide rails and painted traffic lanes throughout the lot would add order and increase the speed with which we can serve customers. Dimpoulos Paving Company, with reasonable prices and reputable work, offers the best solution to our problem. The project would take less than two weeks from the date of approval, and customers are certain to appreciate the convenience and safety added to the good value they already receive every time they shop at Convenient Mart #27.

STATEMENT OF PROBLEM

Convenient Mart #27 has wide entrances (30' and 50') from two streets, and the entire back property line is open to the Tunbridge Shopping Center parking lot. Therefore, traffic may enter our lot from all directions except the west, the Burger Barn property line. Customers walking to the store after pumping gas are in danger of being hit by a moving vehicle, and customers attempting to wedge themselves between two other vehicles to get gas have bumped into our pumps. Having drivers enter from any direction they choose and park anywhere they choose creates serious safety and efficiency problems.

SOLUTION

Dimpoulos Paving Company can remedy our problem by installing six guide rails and painting traffic lanes and parking spaces on our lot. Guide rails (metal tubes filled with concrete) at the end of each pumping station will keep vehicles in the proper lanes. Likewise, standard-size painted traffic lanes with yellow directional arrows will improve the traffic flow as well as our ability to offer speedy service. In addition, parking spaces will give in-store customers easy access to the store without impeding gas customers.

BACKGROUND

Our current situation will not improve unless we take action. Congestion and accidents will continue. Three collisions, minor yet causing costly damage—more than $750 for each incident—to the cars involved, have occurred in the last two months. Slow service is another result, according to a survey of customers conducted 20–28 February 20—. Observations over the past three weeks show that gas customers cannot get to the pumps, and other customers cannot get to the store. In addition, these problem situations harm our reputation.

Figure 13.1 Informal Proposal Model

Donovan Phillips
Page 2
10 March 20—

METHODS
Dimpoulos will install six guide rails, one at the end of each pumping station. Workers will fill these round metal tubes with concrete to make them stable and paint them yellow to make them visible. Dimpoulos' engineer said that we have room for five parking spaces around the store. Four will be painted white, and one for handicapped access will be painted blue.

The company also will paint yellow traffic lanes with directional arrows on both sides of each pumping station to create six lanes. As you can see in Figure 1 below, three lanes will enter from the north, one exiting to the east on Myrtle Street and two to the south into Tunbridge Shopping Center. One lane will enter from Myrtle and exit to the north onto Highway 102. The other two lanes will feed from the south, vehicles entering from the Tunbridge lot, and exit onto Highway 102.

Figure 1. Proposed Traffic Lanes, Guide Rails, and Parking Spaces

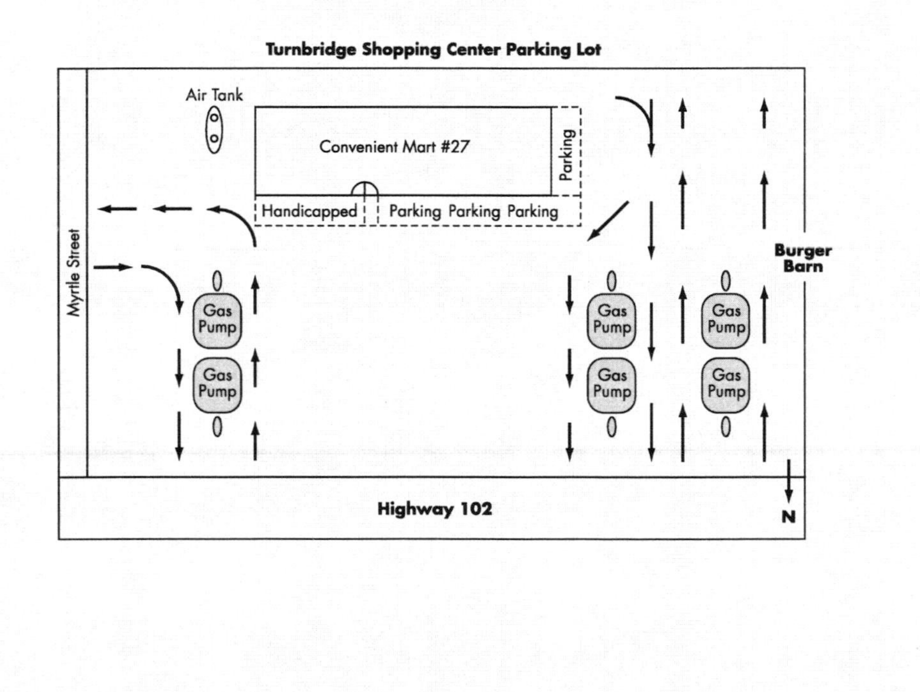

Figure 13.1 Informal Proposal Model, cont.

Donovan Phillips
Page 3
10 March 20—

SCHEDULING
The construction schedule will run as follows:

April 20	April 27	May 2
installing guide rails	painting lanes, arrows, and parking spaces	job completed

Dimpoulos' site supervisor has assured me that all work can be done at night or during our least demanding hours.

BUDGET
The following is a budget for the improvements I suggest:

Six guide rails	$1,049.00
Paint—2 gallons of white	32.86
3 gallons of yellow	48.24
1 gallon of blue	18.98
labor	2,499.00
engineering costs	945.00
	$4,593.08

CONCLUSION
Congestion, accidents, delays in service, and customer response all require that Convenient Mart #27 do something to improve traffic flow. I recommend that you authorize the placement of six guide rails and the painting of traffic lanes and parking spaces to enhance order and efficiency in the way we do business. I believe that the improvements in customer satisfaction and goodwill will more than repay the $4,593.08 cost.

Figure 13.1 Informal Proposal Model

MEMORANDUM

TO: Barkley Wolfe, Manager
Eastbrook Shopping Center

FROM: Delores O'Malley, Chief of Operations *DO*

DATE: November 23, 20—

SUBJECT: Proposal for Improving Exterior Lighting at Eastbrook

I am submitting for your review my department's proposal to upgrade the exterior lighting system at Eastbrook Shopping Center. This document responds to our October 15, 20-, tenants' meeting and subsequent discussions with you regarding safety on the property.

Of special note are the following sections addressing questions you or our tenants brought up:

Thank you for reviewing our data and suggestions. We look forward to your response. If you decide to accept our proposal, we are eager to implement the needed changes.

Figure 13.2 Formal Proposal Model

PROPOSAL FOR IMPROVED EXTERIOR LIGHTING AT EASTBROOK SHOPPING CENTER

Prepared for
Barkley Wolfe, Manager
Eastbrook Shopping Center

Prepared by
Delores O'Malley, Chief of Operations

November 23, 20—

Figure 13.2 Formal Proposal Model, cont.

TABLE OF CONTENTS

List of Illustrations

Figure 13.2 Formal Proposal Model, cont.

EXECUTIVE SUMMARY

Evidence from our security office, police records, and customer attitude survey proves that Eastbrook Shopping Center has a problem with inadequate lighting outside the building at night.

To improve the lighting so that it meets recommendations of the Illuminating Engineering Society and other experts, we need to exchange our current 150-watt bulbs for 400-watt bulbs and install five new pole lights and six new wall-mount lamps.

The recommended changes will cost less than $1,700 and will improve our security level, liability rating, and public image along with decreasing our energy costs.

Figure 13.2 Formal Proposal Model, cont.

INTRODUCTION

Problem

Inadequate illumination in Eastbrook Shopping Center's parking areas is a serious concern. As good corporate citizens, we have a responsibility to the community to maintain a safe environment. As merchants, we recognize that shoppers and employees expect and have a right to a safe environment. We risk losing customers if Eastbrook doesn't maintain a secure, peaceful image. We also must watch expenses. However, it is evident from our research that, as a result of poor lighting, safety on our grounds is not assured.

Solution

Problems with lighting can be eliminated if we upgrade our exterior lighting system to meet recommendations of local law enforcement and utilities personnel and Illuminating Engineering Society (IES)* guidelines. (Terms designated by an asterisk are defined in the glossary on page 6.) To increase illumination sufficiently in all areas outside the building, we must exchange our 150-watt mercury vapor* bulbs for HPS* bulbs as well as add six wall-mount lights and five new poles in the parking areas.

Objectives

The purpose of this proposal is to improve the quality of exterior lighting at Eastbrook Shopping Center so that customers, employees, and staff feel safe moving to and from the building and their vehicles and so that our parking area does not become the site of illegal activities.

Background

Our records for the last six months prove that we do, indeed, have a problem:

8 incidents of shoplifting (unresolved)　　3 purse snatchings

1 assault and battery　　1 kidnapping

Further, the police department rates the relative safety of Eastbrook to be low, compared to other shopping centers. (See Appendix A.)

In addition, the survey our marketing agency conducted last month showed that more than 50% of the 400 respondents feel some concern for their safety in entering or exiting our building after dark. Refer to Table 1 for the breakdown of the responses.

Figure 13.2 Formal Proposal Model, cont.

Table 1. Attitudes Regarding Eastbrook's Exterior Environment at Night
(by percentage)

Respondents By Age	Extremely Comfortable	Slightly Comfortable	Comfortable	Slightly Uncomfortable	Uncomfortable
18-20	5	31	15	42	7
21-35	15	19	39	15	12
36-50	5	14	22	23	36
over 50	1	9	13	28	49
TOTAL	26	73	89	108	104
PERCENT	7	18	22	27	26

If this unsafe image continues in the public mind, we will begin to lose valuable customers and eventually lose business occupants of our shopping center. Note particularly the high rate (49%) of persons over 50 who are uncomfortable. With the "graying of America," this group includes a large number of customers we cannot afford to lose. Businesses will move to a location where they and their customers feel safe. Moreover, we risk a lawsuit if incidents occur that we could have prevented.

Data Sources

The data used to create this proposal came from our security records, interviews with Edison Electric public safety directors at other shopping centers, a customer survey we commissioned, data and recommendations from law enforcement and the Illuminating Engineering Society*, and an experiment conducted by our staff.

Scope and Limitations

In seeking solutions, we wanted to increase safety without creating the image of an armed fortress. The solution must appeal to the public and our business occupants. In addition, any changes we make should be visually attractive and not unpleasant for our commercial and residential neighbors. We also have considered cost and energy consumption.

DISCUSSION

Methods

To determine the amount of light currently being produced, we used a footcandle meter* at the base of each pole. An Edison Electric representative recommended an average of one footcandle* per square foot (Smith). Research revealed that IES Lighting Handbook supports this recommendation, suggesting 0.9 or more footcandles (Kaufman 20-26).

Figure 13.2 Formal Proposal Model, cont.

Our results indicated that Eastbrook's lights are generally lower than the suggested illumination. The readings ranged from a high of 1.8 to a low of 0.4, as you can see in Figure 1 below.

Figure 1. Exterior Light Intensity and Proposed Fixture Additions

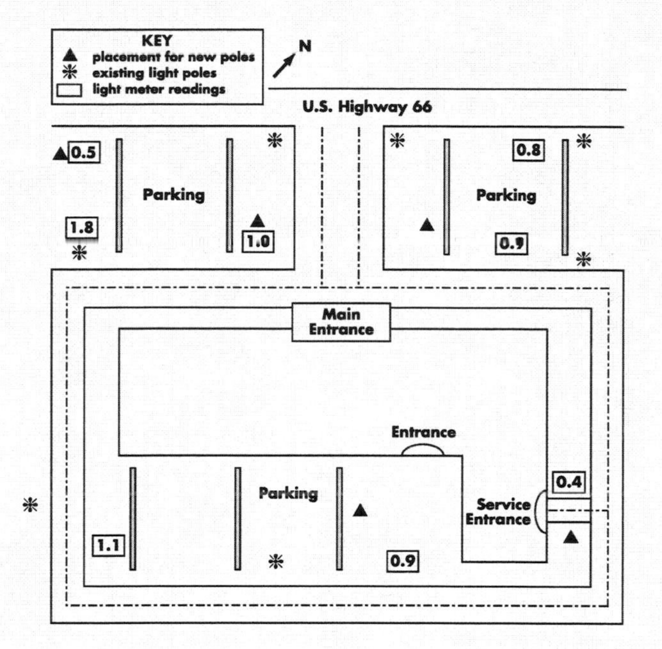

Additionally, a videotaped experiment revealed that in landscaped sections of our parking lots, a person could stand undetected beside a tree or large shrub until the observer was as close as 2 feet. Our research shows almost all parking and pedestrian walkway areas need increased lighting.

Given the videotaped experiment and the footcandle meter readings we collected, an engineer at Edison Electric recommended placement of five new poles outside our building, as indicated on the map in Figure 1 above. Along with the new pole lights, the engineer said that six wall-mount lights installed on the building should bring illumination up to the standard recommendation levels. The six lights will be mounted as follows: one on each side of the main entrance and one on each side of the back entrance, with the remaining two going on the northeast and the southwest walls (Smith).

Figure 13.2 Formal Proposal Model, cont.

Scheduling

We would like to make the suggested improvements as soon as possible. Once equipment has been ordered and received, the project should take less than two weeks, as you can see in Figure 2.

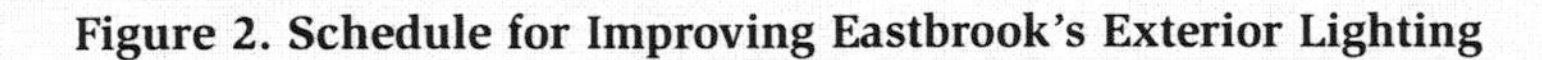

Figure 2. Schedule for Improving Eastbrook's Exterior Lighting

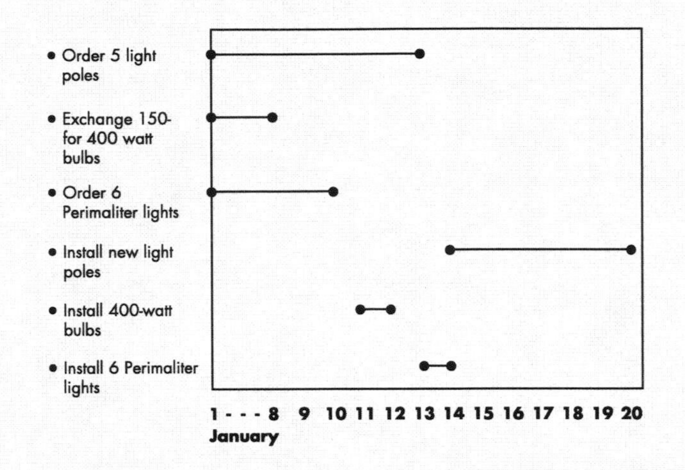

The installation of the five new poles according to IES guidelines will require an outside contractor. Edison Electric has the special equipment needed and can install the poles in one week. The utilities company also will need to replace our 150-watt bulbs with the new 400-watt bulbs since we do not have the cherry picker required to do this job. This task should take approximately one day. Three members of our own maintenance staff can install the six wall-mount lights in less than one day. The entire project should be complete and lighting improved within a month.

Materials and Equipment

We can purchase the 400-watt bulbs from our current supplier, Witherspoon Inc., for only $10 per unit more than we are paying now for the 150-watt bulbs. Moreover, Witherspoon will exchange our current stock of 150-watt bulbs for 400-watt bulbs.

Edison Electric will order the materials and erect the five new poles we need. We should contact with Edison to service the pole lights since we do not own the equipment to do so ourselves.

Figure 13.2 Formal Proposal Model, cont.

Cost

The adjustments necessary to upgrade exterior lighting and implement IES guidelines will cost $1,688.75. The following budget details the expenses for this project:

Five 40-foot metal poles	5 @ $211.95	$1,059.75
Six Perimaliter lights	6 @ $70.00	420.00
Shipping charges for exchanging bulbs		34.00
Edison Electric service fee		175.00
		$1,688.75

In addition to the one-time installation costs, service costs will affect our budget. Operating costs will decrease if this proposal is implemented. Two reasons for the decrease are the longer life and the lower energy consumption of HPS lamps. Mercury vapor lamps have an average rated life of 18,000 to 24,000 hours (Kaufman 8-102) while HPS lamps are likely to be good for 24,000 hours or more (Sorcar 57). In addition, Edison Electric experts suggest we will see an 8-10% reduction in energy use with the HPS lamps, even taking into account the increased wattage (Smith).

CONCLUSION

If Eastbrook's exterior lighting is not improved, future problems are likely to occur. We might face a decrease in the number of customers willing to shop with us in the evening hours and an increase in our insurance rates as a result of liability suits. This proposal is a corrective as well as a preventive measure that increases the safety level for everyone on the property at night. Eastbrook will benefit from a stable environment, night and day.

We recommend that $1,688.75 be allocated in this quarter's operating budget for the installation of 5 new 40-foot metal light poles and 6 new wall-mount fixtures along with the replacement of all 150-watt mercury vapor bulbs with 400-watt HPS lamps. These changes will enhance our security and our image at a reasonable cost.

Figure 13.2 Formal Proposal Model, cont.

GLOSSARY

bulb. A synthetic light source operated with electricity.

footcandle. A unit of illuminance.

footcandle meter. A meter that indicates the amount of light one candle will produce in one foot of space.

HPS. high-pressure sodium. A bulb whose light is derived mainly from sodium vapor.

IES. Illuminating Engineering Society of North America, a professional organization founded in 1906 and dedicated to the theory and practice of illuminating engineering.

lamp. A synthetic light source operated with electricity.

mercury vapor. A bulb whose "light is mainly produced by radiation from mercury vapor" (Sorcar 333).

Figure 13.2 Formal Proposal Model, cont.

WORKS CITED

Abbott, Marvin, Chief of Security, Golden Crossing Mall. Personal Interview. 5 November 19—.

———. IES Lighting Handbook: The Standard Lighting Guide. 5th ed. New York: The Illuminating Engineering Society, 1972.

Kaufman, John E., ed. IES Lighting Handbook: A Reference. New York: Waverly Press, 1984.

Smith, Jason, Chief Engineer, Edison Electric. Personal Interview. 1 November 19—.

Sorcar, Prafulla C. Energy Saving Lighting Systems. New York: Van Norstrand Reinhold, 1982.

Figure 13.2 Formal Proposal Model, cont.

APPENDIX A. Police Security Ranking for Shopping Centers and Malls

Metropolitan Police Quarterly Report
June 20— Security Ranking—Shopping Centers and Malls

1 = Most Secure Environment   5 = Least Secure Environment

Rankings are based on a formula including reported incidents, severity of crime, victims, and cost.

Monrovian Heights	1	Wrightly Way Mall	3
Riggan's Place	1	Anandana Plaza	3
Crossroads Mall	2	Caruso's Crossing	4
South Dunbury Center	2	Eastbrook Shopping Center	4
Newtown Shopping Center	2	Benton Shopping Center	5
Village Mall	2	Bargain Hunter's Way	5

Figure 13.2 Formal Proposal Model, cont.

WHAT IS A PROPOSAL?

Persuasive documents that offer a solution to an identified problem or need are **proposals.** Proposals attempt to sell an idea, a product or service, or a new concept or plan. Proposals may be brief or long. The one-page request for a room assignment change you write to your club adviser and the 2,000-page multivolume document selling a new type of amphibious tank to the Department of Defense are both proposals.

© GETTY MAGES/PHOTODISC

The term *proposal* hints at the use of this type of document. *Propose* is the base word from which *proposal* comes. Have you "proposed" a party idea to your friends recently? You might think of one person who has proposed marriage to another. If you are thinking of "to suggest" or "to make an offer," you are beginning to understand the proposal's purpose.

A proposal can be a request for support. For instance, the local Boys and Girls Club may direct a proposal to the United Way for money to resurface the club's tennis court. Another proposal might offer a customer goods and services. If a school organization carries out a fund-raising drive by selling candy, the project probably began with a proposal from the candy supplier.

The successful proposal persuades your audience to accept your offered solution and to invest in your idea, product, plan, or service. Employees can use proposals to respond to problems, rather than merely complain about them. The proposal provides a professional means of presenting the employees' ideas for change, which can be empowering.

As Figure 13.3 illustrates, proposals may be divided into several different categories relating to the audience: 1) internal or external; 2) formal or informal; 3) solicited or unsolicited; or 4) sales, research, grant, or planning.

Category	Definition of Category
A. internal	within the organization
external	outside the organization
B. formal	contains parts used in formal reports
informal	omits elements of formal reports; is often briefer
C. solicited	written in response to a request
unsolicited	written independently, without a request
D. sales	attempts to sell a product or service
research	seeks approval for a research study
grant	asks for funding for a project
planning	attempts to persuade the audience to take a certain action

Figure 13.3 Types of Proposals

WARM UP

As you think about each area of your life—school, home, work, community, and organizations—list problems or needs for which you might seek solutions.

FOCUS

Warm Up

Use the Warm Up to collect possible topics for proposals. If students have trouble thinking of problems, suggest that they think of things about which they complain, such as the lack of senior privileges at school or the policy for promotions at work.

TEACH

Review the opening models, Figures 13.1 and 13.2, with your students. Discuss the research and problem solving that was involved in creating these proposals. Use the Informal Proposal for an Internal Audience Teaching Master to point out that the

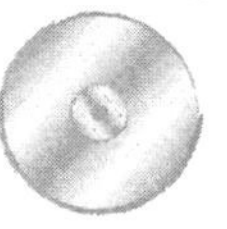

problem and solution are clearly outlined in the informal proposal model and that the solution seems to be a reasonable answer to the problem. Also, point out differences between the informal and formal model.

ENRICH

If you invite professionals to speak to your class, ask them to discuss specifically the power and effect proposals have in their work environment.

SEE THE SITES

Many proposals, especially formal proposals, have several writers who work together to contribute their ideas. Thus, writers must work effectively as teams to create a finished product. Two web sites that give you tips for working together as teams are the 3M Meeting Network web site and the MentorU web site. Both sites tell you how to practice your communication skills so you can work well with team members. You can find links to these sites at techwriting.swlearning.com.

SEE THE SITES

Have students review these sites and any other sites they might find on team building when they work on group proposals. At the MentorU site, have them take the self-evaluation for getting along with others and then form groups to discuss their results.

TEACH

Explain that internal proposals are often shorter than external proposals because internal readers are probably familiar with the problem and its background while external readers are less likely to have that understanding and background knowledge.

INTERNAL AND EXTERNAL

Readers of some proposals will be internal; that is, inside the writer's organization. Other readers will be external, or outside the writer's organization. Internal proposals usually attempt to sell an idea or a plan, such as how providing on-site day care can reduce the absentee rate at work, how merit-raise funds should be distributed, and how eliminating classes on the day before finals can ease stress and improve scores. External proposals frequently try to sell goods or services as well as ideas.

INFORMAL AND FORMAL

A proposal is called informal or formal based on the degree to which conventions of formal report writing are followed, how "dressed up" the document looks. Formal proposals contain more parts than informal proposals. Writers decide how formal a document should be based primarily on the audience and its needs.

Because they frequently address an internal audience who understands why the document was written, informal proposals are often brief, generally from one to eight pages. An informed audience eliminates the need for background information or an explanation of the problem. In addition, the report has a flexible organizational plan, uses less formal language, and is frequently presented as a letter or memo. Occasionally, however, a brief informal proposal may be written to an external audience when the subject matter and offered solution are simple and require little explanation.

A proposal going to someone close (in the ranks of the organization) to the writer is usually informal. Likewise, a problem and solution that can be explained in a simple manner are presented in an informal report. The proposal writer would not invest the often lengthy preparation time involved in a formal proposal to suggest something as simple, for example, as changing lunch schedules to allow for a company-wide meeting.

Formal proposals, on the other hand, usually address an external and often unfamiliar audience. They are organized according to standard elements of formal researched reports: cover page, letter of transmittal, title page, table of contents, list of illustrations, **executive summary,** body discussion divided by headings and subheadings, appendixes, **glossary,** and bibliography.

SOLICITED AND UNSOLICITED

A proposal is labeled solicited or unsolicited depending on the audience's role in its initiation. A **solicited proposal** is one the reader asked the writer to create. Sometimes the request comes from a manager at work who sees a problem. The manager then asks for a solution to be presented in a proposal. The request also might appear in an **RFP,** or request for proposal. The RFP states exactly what the customer seeks; proposal writers then prepare their documents to address the needs stated in the RFP. On the other hand, the **unsolicited proposal** is begun when the writer "discovers" a problem, such as an inefficient production line or a lack of water fountains for wheelchair-bound employees. The writer independently identifies a problem, explains it, and offers solutions.

SALES, RESEARCH, GRANT, AND PLANNING PROPOSALS

Based on function, or what the writer wants the audience to agree to do, proposals fall into one of four categories: sales, research, grant, and planning. The sales proposal tries to sell a product or service. The research proposal asks for approval to begin a study or an investigation. A marine biologist at a university, for instance, might request approval (and perhaps funds) for a study of the acid rain effect on a particular fish species. The grant proposal seeks money for a specified project, such as beginning a horseback riding program for children with cerebral palsy. The planning proposal attempts to persuade an audience to take a particular action, as in a plan to improve food service at a pizza restaurant's drive-through window by rearranging preparation tables for efficiency.

A single proposal may combine several categories mentioned here. As you read proposals, you may discover that as many as four categories apply to one document. For instance, the informal proposal presented at the beginning of this chapter is brief and familiar, identifies a problem, speaks to an internal audience, and attempts to persuade readers to take action. So the report is an informal, unsolicited, internal planning proposal.

ENRICH

Have students interview a professional, perhaps one in their field of interest, to determine if that professional writes or reads proposals and makes decisions based on proposals. If you wish to integrate several communication areas, ask for a letter requesting an interview appointment, a thank-you letter, and a summary of the interview.

TEACH

Use the Types of Proposals Teaching Master to cover types of proposals and their relationship to audience.

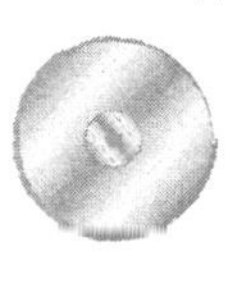

FORMATTING

The best format for a proposal is determined by the audience's needs and the function or type of proposal. If writers are submitting a formal proposal to a prospective client, they might want to prepare a bound booklike document for decision makers to read and review. The writers of an informal proposal suggesting ways to improve recycling efforts within a printing company could send their proposal to the manager as an e-mail attachment.

A company that installs electronic cable in public buildings could post a proposal to a web site for viewers' access. Some proposal writers could take advantage of images and hyperlinks to persuade the audience by sending a CD containing sound and video as well as links to useful sites.

Decision makers in many different positions in business and industry read proposals. Yet most of these proposal readers read only a portion of the document. They read the section or sections that deal with their area of interest and expertise. Thus, readers evaluate the proposal and accept or reject the suggestions based on the data presented in the section they review.

Read the models beginning on pages 320 and 323 and review the definition of *proposals* in the *In The Know* section. How do these models fulfill the definition of a proposal?

ONGOING ASSESSMENT

Stop and Think

Ask students to read the opening models and review the definition of proposals as directed in Stop and Think. Point out that the problems and solutions are clearly outlined in the model proposals and that the solutions seem to be reasonable answers to the problems.

WARM UP

Consider the impact of audience when determining the methods you use to be convincing. Do people, for example, use the same techniques to persuade a friend or sibling to go to an event as they do to convince an instructor to allow them extra time for an assignment or a boss to give them a day off work?

FOCUS

Warm Up

Students will see the differences in persuading friends or siblings and swaying instructors and supervisors since authority in the relationships is not the same. In small groups, discuss the impact audience has on developing an effective proposal and the importance of carefully analyzing the audience.

TEACH

Most students will recognize that some facet of research is a part of their everyday lives. For instance, the decision to buy new in-line skates is likely to involve secondary research–reading brochures and catalogs, –as well as primary research–surveying, and asking other users about the performance of the in-line skates; experimenting by taking the skates for a test ride; and observing others using the skates.

GETTING STARTED ON PROPOSALS

Now that you know about the different types of proposals, you are ready to plan for writing one. The proposal begins with a problem or a need. The problem may be one you have discovered yourself or one someone pointed out to you, as in an RFP or in a memo or letter from another professional.

A problem-solving strategy, such as the one listed below, can make your work as a proposal writer easier and can help you focus on the problem:

- Determine whether you have a problem.
- If you do, define the problem and your purpose.
- Conduct preliminary research.
- Determine the **scope** and **limitations** of your study.
- Identify the factors or subparts of the problem.
- Brainstorm possible solutions.
- Gather data to support the possible solutions.
- If possible, test and evaluate solutions.

Once you have gone through the problem-solving process and are ready to write your proposal, several strategies can help you appeal to your audience. Create a chart using a sheet of paper with a line drawn down the middle. On the left half of the page, write everything you think the readers need or want in the solution. For instance, if you have an RFP, the criteria, as with a job advertisement, are probably noted there. If you have no RFP, make the list based on your research and insight into the problem and audience.

On the right half of the page, list what your solution offers that the reader wants or needs. In other words, for every want or need in the left column, explain how your plan will fulfill that want or need. Thus, you will have persuasive tools ready for composing your proposal. The following example relates to a sales proposal for football helmets.

Criteria	Response
protects players	■ 1 inch of solid tempered plastic covered with fiberglass for resistance ■ ¾-inch foam padding from ear to ear ■ adjustable liner for greater protection
economical	■ $29.90 per unit, 10% less than the average ■ 10-year warranty/automatic replacement

Another technique some proposal writers use in analyzing audience is to imagine how the reader thinks and feels. Anticipating the readers' questions and concerns may help you understand the readers' point of view and anticipate their needs. Another technique you might try is to gather audience information relating to the proposal issues, as in the following examples:

Problem	■ Is the reader aware of the problem? ■ How much does the reader know about the problem? ■ What factors of the problem most concern the reader?
Solution	■ What do the criteria (perhaps in an RFP) established by the audience tell me about the audience? ■ Prioritize the decision maker's concerns: personnel, money, time, production, public image, and ethics. ■ How open-minded or how critical will your audience be?

You can add other questions to this audience analysis list as you consider the problem, solution, and benefits of the solution.

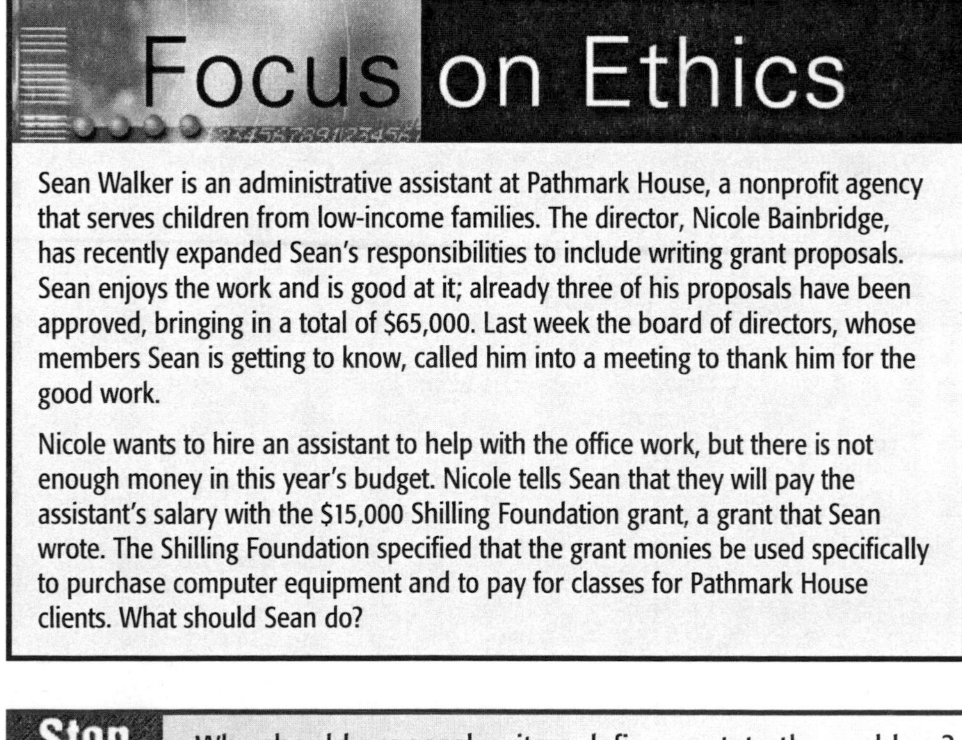

Focus on Ethics

Sean Walker is an administrative assistant at Pathmark House, a nonprofit agency that serves children from low-income families. The director, Nicole Bainbridge, has recently expanded Sean's responsibilities to include writing grant proposals. Sean enjoys the work and is good at it; already three of his proposals have been approved, bringing in a total of $65,000. Last week the board of directors, whose members Sean is getting to know, called him into a meeting to thank him for the good work.

Nicole wants to hire an assistant to help with the office work, but there is not enough money in this year's budget. Nicole tells Sean that they will pay the assistant's salary with the $15,000 Shilling Foundation grant, a grant that Sean wrote. The Shilling Foundation specified that the grant monies be used specifically to purchase computer equipment and to pay for classes for Pathmark House clients. What should Sean do?

Why should proposal writers define or state the problem?

Complete the Prewriting worksheet on the Data CD.

TEACH

Use the Prewriting Model Teaching Master to explain how

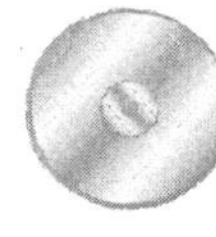

to use criteria in the RFP to generate ideas and to plan for solutions.

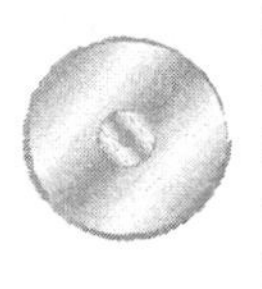

Have students complete the Prewriting worksheet on the IRCD.

FOCUS ON ETHICS

Divide the class into small groups and have them use their problem-solving skills to brainstorm creative and innovative solutions to the problem. For example, Sean could write a special grant seeking funds for an office assistant or he could organize volunteers to help in the office.

ONGOING ASSESSMENT

Stop and Think

Defining the problem is critical to writers and audience. First, many problems are created when people solve problems that were not problems at all. A worker, for instance, could view her increasing workload as a problem or as an opportunity to expand her business. Second, writers and their audience need to agree on the problem to be solved.

WARM UP

Recall several convincing people: when they talk, you listen and believe. What gives these people the persuasive edge, credibility? List any traits, characteristics, or actions that you think lend credibility to persuasive people. Be prepared to share your list with the class.

FOCUS

Warm Up

Give students class time for groups to discuss the Warm Up. In describing what traits, characteristics, or actions give persuasive people credibility, students will identify qualities they too can develop and use. Possible solutions: a personal history of integrity and reliability; a demonstrated knowledge of the subject area; and the ability to speak, write, and listen well.

TEACH

Display the Outline for Informal Proposals Teaching Master as you explain the organizational strategies for informal proposals.

COMPOSING INFORMAL PROPOSALS

The organizational strategy of the informal proposal, like that of many technical reports, is designed with the busy decision maker in mind. The proposal usually opens with the most important information the reader needs to know. So writers give information about the problem and solution at the beginning of the report. The organizational plan for the rest of the proposal is flexible to fit the many different situations writers are likely to encounter in their working environments. No matter how you organize your own proposals, you must remember your audience throughout the writing process and ask yourself if you are responding to all readers' questions and doubts.

Informal proposals begin with an Executive Summary or Abstract. Following the summary information, they contain the same parts as any written document: an Introduction, a Body, and a Conclusion. The summary or abstract is a condensed version of the proposal. The introduction presents the problem, solution, and whatever background the reader needs. The body of the proposal is the main section; it covers the facts, the specific evidence to convince the reader that the plan is worthy.

The conclusion, then, wraps up the report and spurs the reader into action.

The specific information contained, and thus the headings used (with the exception of the Executive Summary or Abstract), within each section may vary from situation to situation. Depending on the needs of the problem and solution being proposed, the writer decides which subsections to include and which to omit. Possible headings to be used in each section are listed below.

Section	Possible Headings
Introduction	Problem Addressed and Solution Objectives of Proposed Plan Background Data Sources Scope and Limitations
Body	Methods Scheduling Capabilities, Qualifications of Personnel Materials and Equipment Expected Results Plan for Evaluating Results Feasibility Budget (usually in tabular form) Justification of Budget Items, where necessary
Conclusion	Summary of Key Points Request for Action

DRAFTING THE SUMMARY

The summary or abstract is designed with the busy decision maker in mind. In a short informal proposal, this section may appear on the title page or, typically, as the first paragraph in the report. It provides a brief overview of the essential ideas presented in the proposal. The summary should include a problem statement, the proposed work objectives, the project impact, and the work plan. Cost is not usually discussed in the summary because writers want to present all their evidence to persuade readers first; then the writers hope readers will not be "turned off" by the cost but will be able to justify the expense.

DRAFTING THE INTRODUCTION

The introduction answers the "why" in the reader's mind; it explains why the proposal was written. You must identify the problem up front. Another important element of the introduction is your proposed solution to the problem. This statement should be clear but brief. Later, in the body, you will provide further details and justify your proposal.

The introduction further explains your objectives, or what you hope to accomplish, and clarifies the value of the work and why it is worth the investment you seek. This section also may require a brief historical background of the problem.

For example, a proposal recommending a change in the way student newspapers are distributed might be viewed more seriously if the writer can prove that the current distribution system encourages littering:

> Because the papers are placed in stands near doorways only one hour before students leave campus, students have papers in hand as they walk outside and away from recycling bins and waste receptacles.

Such an explanation of the background will prove to your reader that you have a grasp of the problem. In addition, the introduction may explain the need for a solution. Some readers may ask, "Why not simply leave things as they are?" In this case, note the effects of ignoring the problem.

Another element of the introduction is to discuss how you or other personnel are qualified to solve this problem. In addition, you might describe where you will seek information to help solve the problem. Data sources could be printed materials (such as books, reports, or brochures), interviews, observations, or experiments. The introduction also might define scope or the extent you will search for solutions as well as limitations or boundaries of the project, such as restrictions on time, space, equipment, money, or staff.

DRAFTING THE BODY

After the problem and solution have been described in the introduction, the body of the informal proposal becomes more specific about your plan. The specific details—the facts, figures, statistics, dates, locations, and costs—are the ammunition you use to persuade your audience. For this section, you might address the topics on the next page as needed.

TEACH

Remind students to write the summary after the proposal has been written. The summary will then be specific and accurate.

Point out that organization is not subtle in proposals, as it might be in other kinds of writing. It must be direct and clear.

Explain that proposal writers decide to write only the sections of the body for which they have collected information or only the sections that the reader needs. For example, if the proposal required no materials or equipment, the writer would not include that section.

Writers usually choose to write a feasibility section when the audience is likely to think the proposed idea is improbable, when the audience may doubt the reasonableness of the proposal.

Any items in the budget that are excessive or seem excessive should be explained in a justification section.

TEACH
Use the Informal Proposal for an External Audience Teaching Master when you discuss "Exploring the Composing Strategies with a Model."

Methods	Explain your methodology, what your approach to the problem will be, what criteria (perhaps from the RFP) you will meet, and what outcome or product you will deliver at the date you specify. Justify your plan of work and any exceptions to the RFP, as needed.
Scheduling	Present a calendar of the work planned and expected completion dates to assure your audience that you anticipate efficiency. Effectively illustrate scheduling, as appropriate. Flowcharts or timelines are excellent for visual presentation of timetables. List personnel, numbers, and qualifications of personnel. Describe facilities, both available and needed, to be used.
Capabilities	Assure your audience that you can deliver the work you propose by 1) noting the abilities of people involved and 2) describing the successful track record of your organization.
Materials and Equipment	Review materials and equipment to be used. This section is particularly important in scientific projects. Even in a proposal dealing with construction of a building or another product, the type of fabrication material is likely to be critical to the audience.
Expected Results	Explain what you think the result of your work will be.
Plan for Evaluating Results	Outline your plan for evaluating the success of the solution once it is implemented.
Feasibility	Explain how you find the conclusion reasonable to implement.
Budget	Present, typically in a chart, the costs for the work, including salaries, equipment, materials, travel, communication costs, services, and other expenses.
Justification	Clearly (and persuasively) explain the reason for any expenses your audience may question.

DRAFTING THE CONCLUSION

The conclusion should be straightforward and brief. It might include a summary of key points, such as those noted in the summary section, and it should call for the audience to take action. Make the call to action specific and clear, including dates and amounts.

EXPLORING THE COMPOSING STRATEGIES WITH A MODEL

Consider a sample problem to illustrate the composing process: Kimi Chey, a student at Martinique College, has noted that the local newspaper, *The Martinique Times,* contains little information from her school. Occasionally *The Times* carries a report of a football, soccer, or basketball game or some other sporting event, but she would like to see the newspaper cover other school news as well. You will follow Chey through the process of writing a short informal proposal in which she suggests a solution to the editor of her hometown newspaper, Gary Cedillo. Chey decides to write a summary and place it on the title page, but she will wait until later to write it. After the proposal is written, she will pull major ideas from it for her summary.

To help *The Martinique Times* editor understand the problem she has identified, Chey considers the "why" question. She writes a clear statement of the problem: **Except for sporting events, no news from Martinique College appears in *The Martinique Times*.** Beneath that statement, she lists her goals:

- Include club news.
- Note the dates of special events.
- Report on students who deserve attention for academics or other achievements.
- Highlight instructors and their contributions.
- Provide a forum for students.
- Encourage more students to read the local paper.

These goals are the things she would like to have happen as a result of her proposal.

Chey then brainstorms about how these objectives could be met. She thinks of several alternative solutions: 1) develop a student-owned, student-operated paper, 2) request that students be given space for contributions, 3) ask the newspaper to cover the school's news in a more comprehensive manner, or 4) suggest that the school administration submit articles occasionally. She also thinks about the need for the action she proposes: Is there any other way to accomplish these goals? Is anyone else concerned?

The next step Chey takes is to move from brainstorming to analysis, to become more critical in her thinking. For each of the alternate solutions she developed, Chey lists positives and negatives. For example, under solution 1, developing a student-owned newspaper, she lists the following:

Positive	**Negative**
Students would have complete control.	A great deal of money would be needed.
Students would learn by doing.	Would students have the time to do a good job?
Students would read and support their own paper.	Would work and quality be maintained with student turnover?

Chey realizes her proposal is directed to a business leader interested in the effects of her proposed action on his or her work: profits, personnel, schedule, and public image. She knows that a solid plan with accurate facts and figures is necessary to convince her reader. Having chosen the plan with the most "positives" and the least "negatives," she again brainstorms ideas to be included in the body of her proposal.

Chey decides that the best solution to the problem is to have a student-written column placed weekly in *The Martinique Times.* She then must assure the editor of a sound plan for implementing this idea. She notes who will be involved and their qualifications, who will be responsible, and how the work will be done. Using the outline for the body of the proposal, Chey explores the information she will need to convince her audience. To make the work schedule clear, Chey develops a chart that depicts each step in the development of the student-written column. The chart is labeled to identify the person responsible for each phase. She uses this chart to check for factors she might have overlooked in getting the column into the paper.

Chey prepares to write her conclusion by reviewing her strongest selling points. She knows that her closing should include a clear statement of exactly what she wants the editor to do: Does she want him to announce the beginning of the new column in the paper, call the school's president with an invitation, write to the school journalism instructor, or speak with students or a student group? To see the result of Chey's brainstorming, researching, analyzing, critical thinking, drafting, revising, and editing, read her final draft in Figure 13.4 below and continued on the next page.

Route 1, Box 704
Martinique, MI 12002
23 October 20–

Mr. Gary Cedillo, Editor
THE MARTINIQUE TIMES
113 South Main Street
Martinique, MI 12002

Dear Mr. Cedillo:

As a senior at Martinique College who is interested in pursuing a career in commercial art, I read your newspaper regularly. I have been impressed with the innovative designs and attractive page layout of your publication. However, I also have noticed one element of the TIMES that could be improved.

Problem
The problem is lack of news from Martinique College. Your reporters cover sporting events very well, yet many other events and activities supported by the student body go unmentioned. I believe that students and your other readers are interested in information about Martinique College's special events, academic and other achievements, instructors and their contributions, and club activities as well as sports.

Solution
News from all areas of interest at Martinique College could be covered and at no expense to the TIMES. If you include a weekly column devoted to Martinique College news, students can serve as reporters, gathering and writing the stories. Other students can take photographs to accompany the articles. To assure you of high-quality work, the column can be managed through the Journalism Club; Mr. Jan Justesen, English instructor and club adviser, can supervise this activity.

Objectives
Including student news could have several effects. A change in coverage probably will increase the number of students buying and reading the paper. Thus, the students will benefit by being better informed and by improving their time spent reading. Further, the paper will benefit by developing readers (customers) early in their lives. In addition, the community, by being made more aware of college events, may become more supportive of education and become avid readers of the school column. Moreover, being given a forum certainly will encourage some students to become better writers and readers, better athletes, better at whatever they do.

Figure 13.4 Informal Proposal for an External Audience

Mr. Gary Cedillo
Page 2
23 October 20–

Methods and Scheduling

If you accept this proposal and invite students to submit a weekly column, informing the student body and organizing participants should take no more than one month. During that time, we will choose a name for the column and assign specific duties. Mr. Justesen will develop a chain of command and guidelines for everyone. We currently have experienced writers in the Journalism Club, some who have previously contributed to your paper. These writers will help new staff and photographers polish their work.

Our workflow, as illustrated in Figure 1 below, is designed so that all work will be done well and on time. Once organized, we will have an editorial board; their job will be to review story ideas, select the best, assign writers and photographers, help with editing, and submit work to Mr. Justesen. Mr. Justesen will supervise the entire process and will approve all work before submission to your office.

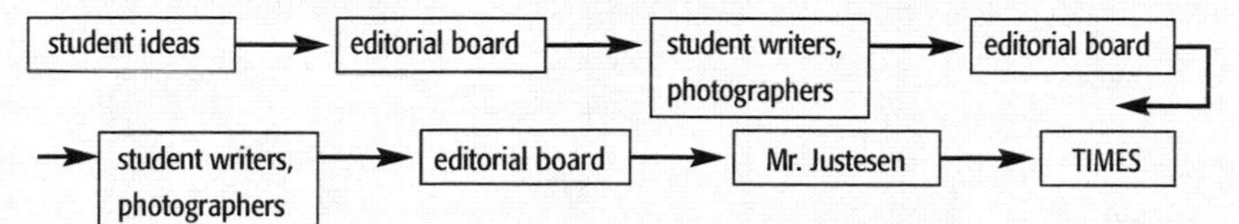

Figure 1: Workflow Process for Substituting Articles

Maintaining the Column

During summer break and school holidays, the column could be suspended. On the other hand, you could retain readers by continuing the column. Perhaps a student intern could report on Martinique College holiday activities.

Conclusion

A student-generated column in the TIMES will be beneficial in many ways. It will sell papers by creating new readers. It will keep readers informed of all areas of Martinique College. It will not cost the paper anything in time or wages. It will encourage students to be their best. It will bring us all closer together. Please help us make these things happen by allowing space for a student column in your paper. Please call Mr. Justesen at 555-0169 with an invitation now.

Sincerely,

Kimi Chey

Kimi Chey

Figure 13.4 Informal Proposal for an External Audience, cont.

In a large organization, different people are likely to read only the sections of a proposal relating to their area of expertise. Name the sections the following employees might read: CEO (chief executive officer), technical expert, and comptroller (financial officer).

ONGOING ASSESSMENT

Stop and Think

Chief executive officers are likely to read the summary first and then other sections related to the general operations of the company, such as the budget. Of all the readers, CEOs are most likely to read the entire report.

Technical experts are interested in the body sections of the proposal that contain technical descriptions and details, such as Methods, Materials and Equipment, Expected Results, and Plan for Evaluating Results.

Financial officers certainly want to review the budget and justification of the budget.

WARM UP

Select three textbooks and examine them to determine the parts that make up each book. Make a list of the elements you find. For example, how does the book begin? Is the first element you find a title page or a note to the reader?

FOCUS

Warm Up

Use the Warm Up to begin a discussion of elements of a formal proposal. Also, compare the elements students find in the textbooks with the table showing parts of a formal proposal in this section. You also could compare parts of a formal and informal proposal. Be sure students review the formal proposal model at the beginning of this chapter.

COMPOSING FORMAL PROPOSALS

In the last section of this chapter, you read about informal proposals. Informal and formal proposals are similar. They are both persuasive documents that offer the writers' answers to readers' problems or needs. In both types, writers choose from the same optional subsections in the same order under Introduction, Body, and Conclusion.

Formal proposals may differ from informal proposals in several ways:

- Tone, such as the detached, professional voice writers might use with a high-level official
- Additional report parts, such as the Glossary, Appendix, and the transmittal correspondence
- Complexity of the outcome, such as the construction of a new building or the $2 billion purchase of jet airliners

Although not used as frequently as informal reports, formal proposals are called for in many circumstances. The following examples are typical:

- A marine biologist, disturbed by the fish kills in a local estuarine system, wants to study the effect of municipal wastewater dumping on the fish. The biologist seeks funds from the State Department of Fish and Wildlife for a five-year project.
- Having received an RFP (request for proposal), a major defense contractor proposes its plan for a new amphibious tank. The potential customer is the U.S. government, and the price is over $3 billion.
- A mechanic in a ball-bearing plant is inspired to improve the precision of a robotic welding machine after studying similar machines at another facility. Having decided on the adjustments needed and the cost in work hours and materials, the mechanic requests approval from the new plant manager.

PREWRITING

Prewriting techniques should help you plan to write a formal proposal. During the prewriting phase, you collect and organize data and determine your objectives. Since a formal proposal is often longer and more involved than other technical reports, prewriting is especially important.

Planning for Persuasion Formal proposal readers need to be convinced, as a salesperson convinces a customer. If you are to be a successful proposal writer, you must address your audience effectively and prevent any skepticism. Here are some guidelines for convincing your audience:

- Collect as many facts as you can to support your proposed plan.
- Be accurate. Plan to check your data. If your reader discovers a discrepancy, an exaggeration, or a mistake, you lose credibility.
- Study your audience and the situation so that you understand the reader's point of view. Planning with an understanding of the reader allows you to write a more convincing proposal.
- Be realistic in your planning. Do not propose to do a job in two weeks to make the sale if you honestly believe the work will take a month. You may suffer the consequences later since your proposal becomes a legal document when it is accepted.

Planning for Integration Another goal of prewriting the formal proposal is planning for integration. The entire document must come together as a logical whole. The description of the problem, for example, will affect how the reader views the effectiveness of the solution. When different writers are composing different sections, a primary writer or editor must consider the entire report, not just one section, as he or she plans and edits.

RETEACH

Remind students of the value of prewriting by asking them how important planning is to their ability to present a convincing argument. They should realize that planning is crucial. Remind them that a writer might develop a marvelous solution, but if the solution does not meet the criteria set forth by the readers, it will not convince them.

A team of employees at Blue Vale Packing worked for two months on a sales proposal to a major national mail-order company. The proposal offered to supply all foam-packaging materials for the business. Since this proposal could represent a major portion of Blue Vale's business, the team worked diligently to develop and present the best plan possible. However, a serious problem arose that the team had not anticipated. Most sales proposals must be approved and signed by a person or people at the head of the organization. The team scheduled time for researching, prewriting, composing, and editing before the submission deadline. What they did not anticipate was the president of Blue Vale leaving on a four-week business trip ten days before the due date. Therefore, the president would not be available to approve or sign the proposal in time to meet the submission deadline. What could the team do? Could they salvage the situation and meet the submission deadline? How?

COMMUNICATION DILEMMA

Students should know that external proposals (as most sales proposals are) represent and commit the organization from which they are issued. Therefore, signatures from the top of the organization usually are required.

The team could consider several options for handling the deadline: finding someone who is authorized to approve and sign for the president in his or her absence, overnight shipping the document to the president for signing and shipping to the mail order company, or requesting an extension of the deadline.

TEACH

Because appendixes are attached to the end of a document, they do not interfere with the reader's concentration or the ideas being presented. At the same time, the reader can see that the supplemental information in the appendixes is available if he or she wants to investigate.

As you discuss planning for definitions, explain that having many definitions within the body of the proposal can distract the audience. Therefore, the number of terms an audience needs to have defined affects the writer's decision as to where to place definitions.

Use Parts of the Formal Proposal Teaching Master on the IRCD to show students the makeup of the entire document before you cover the formatting of individual parts.

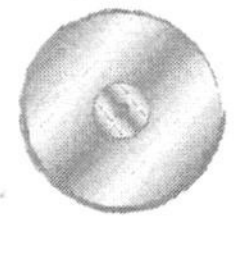

You may wish to explain *boilerplate* to your students. Tell them that many organizations, when writing proposals, develop files of materials that can be used in multiple proposals, especially materials defining the organization and its location, employees, and mission. Boilerplate files include facts and statistics readers need to evaluate a proposal and the proposing organization. These collected files mean that writers do not need to research certain information because someone has already collected it.

Planning for Graphics, Definitions, and Supplemental Materials As you gather data, consider whether a graphic could help your audience understand the information. Then decide what type of graphic aid will most clearly depict the idea. (Refer to Chapter 6, *Document Design and Graphics*, for more help with planning graphics.)

Plan for terms you will use and whether your readers will need definitions for them. If the proposal needs definitions, decide whether you better serve your audience by placing the definitions within the report or in a glossary at the end. If you need to give only a few definitions, it may be easier for you (and your reader) to include definitions within the text. However, proposals that need numerous definitions should probably include a glossary after the body of the report.

In addition to graphics and definitions, think about materials you might like your readers to have access to but do not want to include in the body of the proposal. Consider placing relevant, but not necessary, materials in an **appendix.** For example, if you have used the results of a survey in your proposal, you may wish to show interested readers exactly how you gathered data by including the survey instrument as an appendix.

PARTS OF FORMAL PROPOSALS

The format of formal proposals is designed to aid the readers. Each formal proposal follows the same basic plan so that readers and writers know what to expect and where to find information they seek. Remember, many expert readers review only one or two sections of a formal proposal.

The parts listed below make up the formal proposal. (Those parts followed by an asterisk are used in informal proposals as well.)

- Letter/Memo of Transmittal
- Title Page
- Table of Contents
- List of Illustrations
- Executive Summary (or Abstract)*
- Introduction*
- Body (or Discussion)*
- Conclusion (or Summary)*
- Glossary
- Appendixes
- Works Cited

Letter/Memo of Transmittal The **letter** or **memo of transmittal** is similar to the cover letter mailed with a resume. It is an official greeting and introduction of the document to the reader. Write a letter to accompany a proposal when addressing an external audience and a memo when addressing an internal audience. Use any accepted letter or memo format.

Since the message is usually good news for the audience, this letter or memo uses the direct strategy:

1. Begin with the purpose, the fact that you are submitting a proposal. Name the proposal topic and explain whether you are responding to an RFP, responding to a request, or initiating the proposal on your own.

2. Note any areas of special interest to the reader.
3. Thank the audience for reviewing the proposal. You may offer to provide more information or answer questions.

The letter/memo of transmittal is usually written last, after the rest of the proposal is complete.

Title Page The title page of a formal proposal, like a book cover, gives the reader important information about the document. In designing the title page, use white space to make the page attractive. Be clear, accurate, complete, and precise in composing the title page. Provide the following:

- A descriptive title of the proposal
- The company or companies involved
- The names of the writers
- The date the proposal is being submitted

Some internal proposal writers include, as part of the title page, a routing list of readers who will review the document.

Note that a precise title, such as *Proposal to Develop a Policy Governing Substitute Staffing for Absentee Technicians in the Fiber Twist Area* or *Proposal to Purchase and Install the Evermorr Secure 3120 Security System in Glynndale Condominiums* is useful because it gives readers more information than a vague title such as *Proposal to Deal with Absent Workers* or *Proposal to Improve Security in Glynndale Condominiums.*

Table of Contents The table of contents should be designed so that it is attractive, easy to read, and clear. The table of contents may appear alone on a page, or it may be combined with the list of illustrations on a page. The words *Table of Contents,* in all capital letters or initial capitals, should be centered at the top of the page. Beneath these words, the list of contents should, by indentation, visually demonstrate relationships between ideas. For example, section headings may be at the left margin while less important ideas are indented toward the right.

You may choose to double-space a short list for a table of contents, but a longer listing should be single-spaced to make reading easier. Enter headings and subheadings on the left side of the page, **pagination** on the right, and dots (periods) between the heading and its page number.

List of Illustrations Begin with the words *List of Illustrations* (in all capital letters or initial capitals) centered at the top of the page or two to four lines beneath the last table of contents entry. Two to four lines beneath the title, provide the label, number, and descriptive title of the graphic on the left and the page location on the right.

Executive Summary (or Abstract) At the top of the page, centered (in all capital letters or initial capitals), key the words *Executive Summary* or *Abstract.* The executive summary is usually written in paragraph form, two to four paragraphs, on a page by itself. It may be single- or double-spaced.

Write the executive summary after you have finished the rest of the report. Keep the reader in mind as you compose. This section, as the title Executive Summary implies, is designed with the administrator in mind. Busy

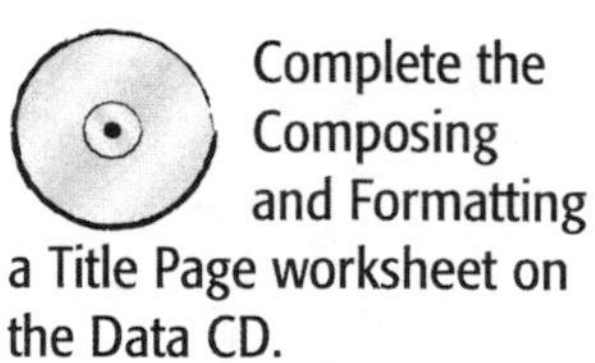
Complete the Composing and Formatting a Title Page worksheet on the Data CD.

TEACH

Use the Formal Proposal Subsection Choices Teaching Master on the IRCD. Remind students to choose outline

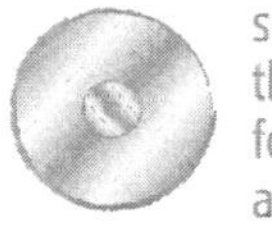
subsections that fit the data they have found and the audience needs.

Use the Title Pages for Formal

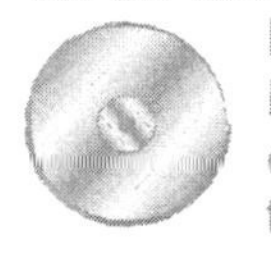
Proposals Teaching Master when you discuss composing title pages.

Have students complete the

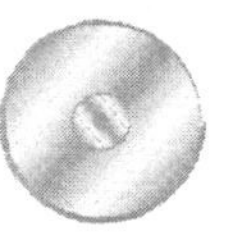
Composing and Formatting a Title Page worksheet on the IRCD.

TEACH

While teaching format for the table of contents, refer students to the table of contents in the formal proposal model at the beginning of the chapter and use the Table of Contents Using

Outlining Format Teaching Master on the IRCD.

Most word processing and graphics software allows you to create lengthy formal proposals easily. These packages have features that create a table of contents for your draft as well as styles for each section. If you are working on a group proposal, you can create a master document as the template for the rest of the proposal. In addition, drafts can be circulated throughout the team with electronic editing marks built into the draft. One click of the mouse allows you to accept or reject the editing changes.

COMMUNICATION UPDATE

Have students practice various features in Microsoft® Word that they might use when creating formal proposals. Some of the more tech-savvy students may help those who are less tech savvy.

RETEACH

Remind students that since different people will likely read different sections of the proposal, writers should be constantly aware of meeting all readers' needs.

executives want the story quickly and only the essential information: the problem, the solution, and the benefits of the solution. Because these readers are concerned with the big picture, the overall health of the organization, they may not read the specific information in the body of the proposal, only the summary. However, proposal writers should plan the summary for all readers, not just executives.

Introduction, Body of Discussion, and Conclusion In long reports (perhaps 20 pages or more), each of these major section headings may begin a new, separate part of the formal proposal. Each section starts on a new page with the heading name, such as *Introduction,* in all capital letters or initial capitals centered at the top of the page. In shorter reports, the entire body may flow from one section to another without page breaks.

The Introduction. The introduction is the framework to prepare readers for the body of the proposal. The introduction answers the questions *what* and *why.* No matter which subparts of the introduction you include in your document, clearly state for your readers the problem and a solution or alternate solutions. If you determine that the readers need background information, summarize the situation and the proposer's qualifications. Include information about your company and personnel, such as the number of years in business, staff and equipment resources, previous clients, and success with similar projects, that will enhance the credibility of your proposal. Since any proposal reviewer might read the introductory material, remember to communicate so that administrators, managers, technical experts, and financial managers can all understand.

The Body of Discussion. If the introduction sets the framework of ideas, the body of a formal proposal is the crux of the argument, the specifics of persuasion. The body is the section in which the technical data prove that your idea (solution) will work. Describe methods for carrying out the project, specific tasks, time schedules, personnel, facilities, and equipment. Include an organizational chart of people working on the project so the reader will know who is responsible for a particular area. In addition to outlining what you will do, these specific details convince the reader that your approach is the best one for the situation. The project's budget should clearly show specific costs and perhaps justify the costs. The graphics you have planned should enhance the text of your proposal, not take the place of the text.

The Conclusion. Be concise and direct when you write the conclusion for your formal proposal. You have already provided all of the information to sway your audience to your point of view. This is not the time to add to your sales pitch. Instead, summarize your most convincing points regarding the importance of the project and the benefits of the solution. Then suggest a course of action.

Glossary If you choose to include a glossary, design it so it is easy to read. In the text of the proposal, designate words appearing in the glossary by using asterisks, italics, or some other highlighting technique. Include a footnote or a parenthetical note beside the first entry, telling the readers that they can find definitions in the glossary.

At the top of the glossary page, center the title Glossary. Use all capital letters or just an initial capital *G*. Make the entry word, the word being defined, stand out by using boldface or columns. When using columns, place the entry words on the left and definitions on the right. Alphabetize all words, acronyms, and symbols, as dictionaries do.

Choose words to define and determine the extent of your definitions based on your audience's needs. Do not define words the audience already understands. At the same time, if your proposal will have several reviewers, define a term even if only one of the readers needs the definition. Write definitions using language the readers understand and consider including graphic aids if they will help the readers' understanding.

Appendixes Appendixes are materials that you want your reader to have access to but that are not a primary part of the proposal. In the body of the proposal, where the topic an appendix supports is mentioned, refer readers to the appendix, as in "See Appendix C." Each appendix must be labeled with the word *Appendix* (can be in all capitals) and given a number (or a letter of the alphabet) and a descriptive title, similar to the system for identifying graphics. Make every document an individual appendix.

Works Cited If your proposal has used ideas or words from a source you need to credit, prepare works cited or documentation pages according to the guidelines of the style manual you are using. Consult the style manual your organization or the RFP requires and follow it precisely.

Page Numbers Assigning page numbers for formal proposals works the same as pagination in books. **Prefatory material,** as in the preface or before the report begins, is numbered with lowercase Roman numerals. Prefatory material includes these:

- Letter/memo of transmittal
- Table of contents
- Title page
- List of illustrations

Since the letter or memo of transmittal is the first page, no page number is needed. In addition, a title page is not numbered. Therefore, the table of contents, the third page, would be numbered iii. Use Arabic numerals for the remainder of the proposal, except for the first page of the report itself, which usually begins with the introduction. This first page carries no page number. Place an Arabic 2 on the next page. Number all other pages of the body of the proposal, glossary, appendixes, and works cited with Arabic numerals in sequence. For pagination, follow the style manual you are using or place page numbers centered at the bottom or in the upper right corner of the page.

Who reads the Executive Summary or Abstract of a formal proposal? Where should terms be defined in this type of report?

Complete the Revising Glossary Entries worksheet on the Data CD.

TEACH

Have students complete the Revising Glossary Entries worksheet on the IRCD.

ONGOING ASSESSMENT

Stop and Think

Use the Stop and Think to review elements of a formal proposal.

Executive summaries provide essential information, an overview of the proposal, for executives who are concerned with the big picture and not the details. However, any member of the audience may choose to read this section as a preview or an orientation.

Definition of terms and their placement should be guided by the audience's needs. Definitions may be placed within the text: *Grading, or the sloping of soil for proper drainage, is necessary for site preparation. Grading, the sloping of soil for proper drainage, is necessary for site preparation. Grading (the sloping of soil for proper drainage) is necessary for site preparation.* Or terms and definitions may be placed in a glossary after the text and before the appendixes.

TEACHING RESOURCES

IRCD
Chapter Activities, Ch. 13
Work Is A Zoo!, Ch. 13
PowerPoint® Slides, Ch. 13
Exam*View*®, Ch. 13
techwriting.swlearning.com, Ch. 13

CLOSE

Summary
Use the summary to review key elements of the chapter. Also, offer students an opportunity to ask questions to clear any confusion they might have.

CLOSE

Checklist
Encourage students to use the checklist for editing and revising as well as for reviewing chapter information.

Chapter 13 Review

SUMMARY

1. Proposals are persuasive documents that suggest a solution to a problem or a change.
2. Proposals are defined and categorized according to the audience and their needs: internal or external; informal or formal; solicited or unsolicited; or sales, research, planning, or grant.
3. In prewriting, consider how your solution meets the audience's needs.
4. Proposals may be presented in memo, letter, or manuscript format, the choice being determined by the audience and complexity of the proposal. Headings and subheadings within the proposal delineate sections of the introduction, body, and conclusion.
5. The introduction identifies the problem and offers a solution, along with any background information the audience might find helpful.
6. The body uses facts, figures, statistics, graphics, and other evidence to convince the readers to accept the solution or change.
7. The conclusion restates key points and calls on the audience to take action.
8. Formal proposals include many special parts that have unique formatting guidelines. These parts may include a letter/memo of transmittal, a title page, a table of contents, a list of illustrations, an executive summary (or abstract), an introduction, a body (or discussion), a conclusion (or summary), a glossary, appendixes, and a works cited or bibliography.

Checklist

- Have I identified the problem I wish to see resolved?
- Have I carefully analyzed my audience and then listed the audience's needs?
- Have I brainstormed for alternate solutions? Have I listed positives and negatives for each solution on my list?
- Have I thought about and listed my goals?
- If my readers are unaware of the problem, have I explained the problem clearly in the introduction?
- Does the body of the proposal give my readers enough information to make a decision?
- Have I provided enough evidence, such as facts, figures, and testimony?
- Does my conclusion contain the most important ideas from the proposal? Does my conclusion also call for action from the readers?
- Have I made information easy for my readers to use by including headings and subheadings?
- If my proposal is formal, have I included all of the needed parts?

Build On What You Know

1. Interview an employee concerning a particular problem as well as the solution for which that employee was responsible. Write a description of the problem, the methods the employee used to solve the problem, the effectiveness of the solution, and the satisfaction of the employee with his or her work.
2. Use library research or interviews to learn more about a great problem solver or innovator, such as Thomas Edison, Mother Theresa, Albert Einstein, Eleanor Roosevelt, or Jonas Salk. Find out as much as you can about the methods the person used in seeking solutions. Make an oral presentation of your findings to your class.
3. Interview a proposal writer to find out how his or her company uses formal proposals, who else (within the writer's organization) writes them, and how successful the proposals have been. Ask what this writer thinks is essential in preparing an effective formal proposal.
4. Using the Internet or regional or state newspapers or professional journals in your school, public, or home library, search for requests for proposals.
   a. Copy the RFPs and bring them to class for discussion.
   b. From a careful reading of one RFP, identify the problem that needs to be solved.
   c. Identify the audience the proposal writer needs to address.
   d. Brainstorm to create a list of ideas to include in the proposal introduction.
5. Choose two problems for which you would consider proposing a solution. Write a paragraph or two describing the problem and the decision maker (audience) for each.
6. List possible solutions to a problem or need you have identified.
7. Using a problem whose solution has already been implemented, re-create the thinking proposal writers might have done by:
   a. Developing a list of positive and negative aspects of the solution.
   b. Creating a list showing how the solution meets the needs of the audience or solves the problem.
8. Write a proposal convincing your parents to take you (or to allow you to go with friends) on the perfect vacation. Identify the problem, explain the solution, convince them of the reasonableness of your plan, and justify the cost by preparing a budget.
9. Critique a proposal from business or industry. Analyze how the writers met (or did not meet) the needs of the audience. Review formatting features. Determine organizational patterns. Share the results of your critique orally or in an essay.

ASSESS

Build On What You Know

1. The process the students write about in their descriptions should help them as they learn more about proposals.
2. Students will learn about the many different ways problems can be solved.
3. Students will see how proposals are used in a work setting.
4. Responses, dependent upon the RFPs the students find, will vary. This step-by-step approach should help students see the clear connection between the RFP (the statement of the problem as perceived by the audience) and the solution the proposal suggests.

5–9. These activities will help students prepare for writing proposals on their own.

ASSESS

Apply What You Learned

10. Although responses will vary, students should be aware that **a** is the solution and **b** is the methodology or the type of information that appears in the body of a proposal. Also, this activity will help students realize the importance of audience analysis, especially since they will be working with an audience with which they are familiar.

11. Be sure students refer to the checklist in this chapter.

12. With students working as a class or in small groups, identify a problem. Ask each group of students to prepare a proposal offering the best solution(s) to the decision maker. Remind students to assign responsibilities for researching, identifying and analyzing audience, creating graphics, writing and revising, and editing. This group activity will result in a variety of experiences and learning opportunities. You can serve as group leader, or a student can be elected to manage the project.

Apply What You Learned

10. Imagine that you have asked your parents for a car. They have said, "Yes, but—." Your responsibility will be to pay for insurance, gas, and maintenance if they purchase this car for you. In an informal proposal:

a. Explain the type of car you want and why.

b. Describe how you will pay for the car's expenses if you do not have money and your parents do not want you to work more than 10 hours a week, such as would be required at a restaurant, grocery store, or department store. Identify your problem and consider alternate solutions. Be creative! Think of ways to earn money other than holding a regular job. List as many options as you can.

c. Write the solution you would propose to your parents.

11. Write an informal sales proposal to Karen Grissom, owner of Mason Office Center. You own an indoor plant service, Green Thumb Planting, and you are asking Grissom to become a new client. After visiting the office complex, you determine that the building could use 31 large and 14 medium-sized low-light plants. Your service provides plants and pots, weekly maintenance, and monthly replacement of imperfect plants. If Grissom accepts your proposal, you are ready to install the plantings within one week. For your service, Grissom will pay a $350 installation fee and a $35 maintenance fee each month thereafter. Your proposal should persuade Grissom to sign a service contract. Create and use any additional details or graphics you need to prepare an effective document.

12. With a group of classmates who share your interests, write a formal proposal to solve a specific problem. Identify a problem at school, at work, or in the community that must be dealt with by decision makers distant from you on the organizational ladder; for example, a superintendent, president, or member of the board of trustees. Your proposal should require some research. Here are examples of problems to solve:

School	Work	Community
new or improved equipment	equipment or work space	sidewalks/bike paths
access for the computer lab	wages or department budget	zoning or use of land
snack bar	improved working conditions	street/traffic signs
new club or sport	sponsorship of sports team	access for people with disabilities to neighborhood stores
needed programs	insurance/benefits	street/park lighting

Work Is A Zoo!

One weekend as you are relaxing in an Internet café surfing the Internet and drinking a glass of lemonade, you suddenly have a great idea for the zoo. You believe that older students as well as instructors would like a place where they could get a bite to eat and something to drink while they surfed the Internet to learn more about their favorite animals at the zoo. Currently the zoo does not have a café, nor does it have a place where students can learn more about animals on their own time. You become excited as you think about how much the students could learn on their own in the café. They could even form discussion groups in the café, led by zoo employees, to talk about issues at the zoo and environmental concerns. You believe that this learning café would encourage older students to spend more time at the zoo.

Even though you have this great idea in your head, you must communicate it to Anya and Tyrone so they will agree that it is a good idea. You know that the zoo just received funds from an anonymous donor, so you could explain to Anya and Tyrone that part of the money should go toward the much-needed café.

Plan and write an informal proposal to Anya and Tyrone about opening a learning café for older students at the zoo. Remember to:

- Define the problem and your purpose.
- Conduct preliminary research.
- Determine the scope and limitations of your study.
- Identify the factors or subparts of the problem.
- Brainstorm possible solutions.
- Gather data to support the possible solutions.
- Test and evaluate solutions, if possible. You also can discuss a plan for evaluating possible solutions.

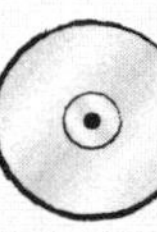

Use the brainstorming worksheet on the Data CD to think of ideas for the learning café. Be sure to follow the problem-solving steps to come up with an argument for the proposal.

WORK IS A ZOO

This case study makes a great group exercise. Have students form groups and use the

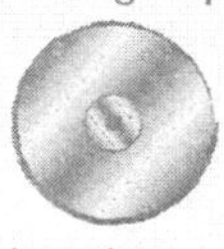

brainstorming worksheet on the IRCD to think of ideas for the learning café. Be sure they follow the problem-solving steps to come up with an argument for the proposal. You also may want students to brainstorm ideas for a learning café at your school.